पुरातत्त्व
पुरातत्त्व
PURĀTATTVA

Bulletin of the Indian Archaeological Society

No. 25 1994-95

Editor
K. N. Dikshit

Assisted by
S. Ganesh Rao, Ashwani Asthana and B.S. Hari Shankar

D.K. Printworld (P) Ltd.
New Delhi

Cataloging in Publication Data — DK
[Courtesy : D.K. Agencies (P) Ltd. <docinfo@dkagencies.com>]

Purātattva : bulletin of the Indian Archaeological Society, no. 25, 1994-95 / editor, K.N. Dikshit ; assisted by S. Ganesh Rao, Ashwani Asthana and B.S. Hari Shankar.
p. cm.
Includes bibliographical references.
ISBN 8124603006

1. Archaeology — India — Periodicals. 2. India — Antiquities — Periodicals. 3. India — Civilization — Periodicals. I. Dikshit, K.N. II. Indian Archaeological Society.

First Published in 1995
First Reprinted in 2005
ISBN 81-246-0300-6
Price for volume 25 (1994-95): Rs. 800 US $ 40

Reprint authorised by
Indian Archaeological Society
New Delhi - 110 016

The Editors are not responsible for the opinions expressed by the Contributors.

Purātattva is published annually.

Manuscripts (whether in the form of articles or notes or book reviews) offered for publication should be sent to the Editor, Purātattva, Indian Archaeological Society, B-17, Qutab Institutional Area, New Delhi - 110 016.

Published and printed by:
D.K. Printworld (P) Ltd.
'Srikunj,' F-52, Bali Nagar
New Delhi – 110015
Phone : (011) 2545 3975, 2546 6019 Fax : (011) 2546 5926
E-mail : dkprintworld@vsnl.net
www. dkprintworld.com

PURĀTATTVA

CONTENTS

OBITUARY

B. K. THAPAR
(1921-1995)

With profound grief we place on record the sad demise of Shri Bal Krishan Thapar, former Director General, Archaeological Survey of India and founder member and Secretary INTACH on the 6th September, 1995. With his passing away a luminary of post-Wheelarian era has gone behind the curtain from the Indian archaeological scene.

Born on the 24th November, 1921 at Ludhiana, Punjab, Shri Thapar graduated from Government College, Ludhiana and then went to Lahore where he obtained his M.A. degree in History in 1943 from the former Christian College, Punjab University. While he had commenced his research on Fortification system in India he felt attracted to 'archaeology' and joined the Indian School of Field Archaeology in November, 1944 and received intensive training in the discipline of archaeology under Dr. Mortimer Wheeler who had been invited by Government to head the Archaeological Survey of India. Shri Thapar joined the Survey in 1947 and worked his way up, step by step, to the post of the Director General of Archaeology in 1978. At the Directorate, he worked as Director Exploration and Expeditions abroad (1966-73), as Joint Director General (1973-77), as Additional Director General (1977-78) and finally as Director General (1978-81). During all these years in the Survey, besides participating in many excavations like Hastinapur, Sishupalgarh, Ropar and Kausambi, he conducted independent excavations at Porkalam (Kerala), 1948; Somnath (Gujrat), 1949-50; Maski (Karnataka), 1953-54. Prakash (Maharashtra); 1954-55, Kuchai (Orissa), 1961-62; Junapani (Maharashtra), 1961-62. He was also Co-director of Excavations at Kalibangan (Rajastan), 1961-68 and Purana Quiḷa (Delhi) 1971-73. His excavation reports are considered as significant contribution in understanding the archaeological past of the subcontinent. In 1975 he led an expedition to Afganistan to explore the Farrah valley and conduct preliminary reconnaissance of Begram. Early in his career, in 1959, he was awarded the Alexander Von Humboldt Fellowship for advanced studies in West-Asian Archaeology at Heidelberg University.

In the domain of archaeological discipline, Shri Thapar's contribution lies principally in the field of Neolithic Age, Harappan Culture and in the study of Chalcolithic and Megalithic cultures of the Peninsula. As an excavator he is rated as one of the best pupils of Sir Mortimer Wheeler, his reports being considered as models for young archaeologists to emulate. Shri Thapar developed a high degree of administrative acumen and this helped him in his work in the Survey and later after his retirement in the various responsibilities he shouldered as Secretary INTACH and Chairman of the Centre for Cultures Resource and Training from 1982-95. He was the General Secretary, Indian Archaeological Society and Editor, Puratattva (No. 7-9). He was elected Vice-President of the Executive Committee of ICOMOS. In 1976, he was elected member, Permanent Council Congres International des Sciences Prehistoriques at Protohistoriques and of many other national and international organizations. He was awarded Jawaharlal Nehru Fellowship in 1981 and Padmashree in 1993. He was one of the Vice-Presidents of the World Archaeological Congress held in India in 1994.

Shri Thapar, although highly respected in national and international community of archaeologists, was essentially wedded to field-archaeology and for Indian colleagues it will be difficult to bear his loss. He was always constructive in his approach, very friendly, genial and humane in all spheres of life. He believed in the doctrine: 'Work is Workship' and upto the last breath of his life he kept himself busy although for the last few years he was bedridden because of acute arthritis and injury caused by accident which needed surgical intervention.

My personal friendship with Shri Thapar which began in 1944 at Taxila and was more than half a century old and I cannot but remember the many happy moments we spent together off and on the field. However, I cannot forget his presence in the sessions of the World Archaeological Congress, his frail figure slowly moving with crutches in one hand and the other resting on the shoulder of his devoted wife, Sushila, his life-long companion in the thin and thick of life. Thapar of 1944 in Taxila was a bundle of energy and enthusiasm, but even when he was physically incapacitated and feeble, he exhibited the same devotion to duty and in fact this reverential attitude to work constitutes the message of his life.

M. N. DESHPANDE
Former Director General,
Archaeological Survey of India
D-25, Press Enclave, Saket
New Delhi 110017

PURĀTATTVA

Number 25 **1994-95**

Editorial

We are happy to present to the delegates attending the World Archaeological Congress-3 as well as to the members of the Indian Archaeological Society the 25th number of the *Purātattva* (1994-95) entitled "Special WAC–3".

We selected a few subjects for this issue and then approached authorities on them to contribute survey-papers; those who could prepare such papers deserve our heartfelt thanks. Their papers concern the decipherment of the Rigvedic Code (by Prof. Kak), Fifty Years of Epigraphical Studies in India (by Prof. Shastri) and A Survey of the Study of the Indo-Muslim Architecture (by Prof. R. Nath).

This issue also contains articles on Environmental conservation, Iron working, Copper alloys, Buddhist remains in Maldives and Rock Paintings in Bihar besides the usual columns of Notes and News as well as Book Reviews.

It is common knowledge that for all these years the Society had no building of its own; the place of work of the General Secretary was usually the office of the Society. Similarly, there was no accommodation available at Delhi for the visiting scholars. There was also no facility for the training in archaeological and historical disciplines for students and teachers in schools and colleges. The Society has now started constructing its own building at B-17, Qutab Institutional Area, South of IIT (Mehrauli), New Delhi-110016. If everything goes well the first phase of building will be ready for occupation within a period of one year from now.

This year, the Padmasri V.S. Wakankar Award for excellence in Archaeological Fieldwork was given to Prof. B.P. Sinha of Patna.

The Indian Archaeological Society has lost its most dynamic member and a stalwart in the world of Indian Archaeology, Shri B.K. Thapar on 6th September 1995. The Society conveys its deepest condolences to the bereaved family.

We need hardly mention that all this is becoming possible due exclusively to the untiring efforts of our chairman, Dr. S.P. Gupta, for whom thc service of archaeology is a mission.

We thank Sarvashri S. Ganesh Rao, Ashwani Asthana and B.S. Hari Shankar for their help in reading the proofs and seeing the publication through the press.

K.N. Dikshit

INDIAN ARCHAEOLOGICAL SOCIETY

Padmashri V.S. Wakankar Memorial Award for Excellence in Archaeology of the year 1994

Professor B.P. Sinha

Prof. B.P. Sinha, the doyen among Indian historians, was born in Bihar Sharif in 1917. During his school days, one of history teachers so impressed him that he preferred history to mathematics in which he was an outstanding student. From this time on history became an obsession with him. The result was that he topped the History (Hons.) and M.A. Examinations of Patna University which awarded a gold medal for his remarkable performance. He crowned his academic days in almamater with a Ph.D. from London University, on the subject of the Political History of the Later Guptas, where his mentor was Dr. Barns.

Prof. B.P. Sinha has graced may academic chairs from that of the lowly lecturer's to that of the Dean of Faculty of Arts. He retired from the University of Patna in 1981. His students are spread out in most of the universities in India and carry on the torch of learning passed on to them by him.

His contributions to writing India's ancient history free of bias, with total detachment and objectivity, shall remain to shine in unabated splendour as long as students rever history. His students have recently felicitated him by bringing out a volume of learned research papers in his honour.

In addition to being an eminent historian, he is also an archaeological explorer and excavator. Though he has many archievements to his credit in this field, the well known being his discovery and excavations of the site of the famous centre of learning in ancient India — the Buddhist monastery of Vikramsila. He also excavated Sonpur, Chirand and various other sites in Bihar.

He was for more than a decade the Director of Archaeology and Museums in the Govt. of Bihar.

He has written many volumes, the most recent one being *The Twilight of the Guptas*.

He married in 1943, and his wife has stood by him in all his field activities. He is still active in the academics–constantly writing.

S.P. Gupta
(Chairman)
Indian Archaeological Society

New Delhi
Date 12.12.1994

The Astronomical Code Of The Rigveda

SUBHASH C. KAK*

The term Veda means 'knowledge'. When the Vedic Saṃhitās are taken together with the *Brāhmaṇas, Āraṇyakas, Upanishads,* and *Sūtras* as well as the *Vedāṅgas* and the *Upavedas,* the claim appears true as it encompasses a variety of sciences, psychology and cosmology. To understand any of the Vedic texts it is essential to know the Vedic system of knowledge. One common classification of knowledge was in terms of *aparā* (material) and *parā* (transcendental). The *Vedāṅgas* and the *Upavedas* deal with *aparā,* whereas the Saṃhitās and their commentaries are meant to lead to *parā* knowledge. The Saṃhitās teach through paradox which is presented in tripartite fashion through *trayī vidyā* (e.g. ŚB 5.5.5.6.). Speech and language are considered to have four forms (RV 1.164.45), of which one kind, the *parā,* is unmanifest. In other words, it is believed that language cannot express all aspects of the nature of reality. Therefore, the Saṃhitās in themselves cannot teach the transcendental or unifying knowledge, they are to be viewed as a ladder that takes the reader into the open space beyond which one can fly so that the ladder itself becomes useless.

According to Indian tradition the Vedas are eternal or *apaurusheya.* Śatapatha Brāhmaṇa 6.1.1.8 speaks of how Prajāpati created the Vedas, *sa brahmaiva prathamamasrajata trayimeva vidyām.* ŚB 11.5.8 and Aitreya Brāhmaṇa 5.32 have similar passages that speak of how three lights *(jyotis),* Agni, Vāyu and Āditya, were first produced. Agni was born from the earth, Vāyu from the atmosphere, and Āditya from the sky. Rigveda was thereafter produced from Agni, Yajurveda from Vāyu, and Sāmaveda from Āditya. From these three pure sounds were born: *bhūh* from the Ric, *bhuvaḥ* from the Yajus, and *svara* from the Sāman. From these, in turn, come the sounds *a, u,* and *m,* which when taken together form the syllable *Om.*

This non-human origin of the Vedas where the Rishis saw the hymns symbolize the belief that the Vedas express eternal laws that were seen when *tapas* sharpened the consciousness of the Rishis so that it could become selfaware. Peter Raster[1] has thus argued that the multitude of phonetic symmetries in the first hymns of the Rigveda could not have been consciously designed. Raster restates the doctrine of non-human origin as:[2]

"In this restatement of the doctrine of the impersonal origin of the Veda, the reflection of nature's intelligence in a human mind is understood in a purely formal sense. What is reflected are patterns or modes of functioning, which are common to both, human intelligence and nature's intelligence. Projected onto the surface form of language, these patterns appear as patterns of sound, not of meaning. The search for traces of these patterns in the Vedic hymns, therefore, can largely disregard the meaning which is commonly associated with the Vedic hymns and adopt a formal structural approach."

The notion of equivalence *(bandhu)* amongst the *adhidaiva* (devas or stars), *adhibhūta* (beings), and *adhyātma* (spirit) play a central role in the Vedic system of knowledge (e.g. BG 8.1-2). The Vedic altar was used to show these equivalences symbolically and this equivalence was to be seen at different levels including that of the individual himself (BG 8,4). Not only does this imply that astronomi-

*Department of Electrical & Computer Engineering, Louisiana State University Baton Rouge, LA 70803-5901, USA

cal knowledge must have been represented in the design of these altars but also that these designs must parallel some characteristics of the individual. The astronomy of the altars is not systematically spelt out but there are references in many texts, including the tenth chapter of Śatapatha Brāhmaṇa, entitled *Agnirahasya*. On the other hand, the Rigveda itself is viewed as an altar of mantras in the *Sulbasūtras*[3] (BSS 7.17, ASS 14.11).

Altars were used in relation to two basic types of Vedic ritual: *Shrauta* and *Grihya*. This ritual marked specific points in the year or during the day. Two of the important Soma rituals are *agnishṭoma* and *agnichayana*[4]. Śatapatha Brāhamaṇa describes the twelve-day *agnichayana* rite that takes place in a large trapezoidal area called the *mahāvedi* and in a smaller rectangular area to the west of it, which is called the *prāchnavaṃsa* or *prāgvaṃsa*. ŚB 10.4.3.9 reveals that *agnichayana* represents ritual as well as knowledge.

The *mahāvedi* trapezium measures 30 *prakrama* on the west, 24 *prakrama* on the east, and 36 *prakrama* lengthwise. The choice of these numbers is related to the sum of these three equalling one fourth of the year or 90 days (ŚB 10.2.3.4). The nominal year of 360 days was used to reconcile the discrepancies between the lunar and solar calendars, both of which were used. In the *mahāvedi* there is built a brick altar to represent time in the form of a falcon about to take wing, and in the *prāchīnavaṃsa* there are three fire altars in specified positions, the *gārhapatya*, *āhavanīya*, and *dakshiṇāgni*. The *dakshiṇāgni* is also called the *anvāhāryapachana* where cooking is done. The additional eight *dhishṇya* hearths are built (Figure 1).

Agnichayana altars are supposed to symbolize the universe. *Gārhapatya* represents the earth (ŚB 7.1.1.13), the *dhishṇya* hearths represent space (ŚB 7.1.2.12), and the *āhavanīya* altar represents sky (ŚB 8.2.1,2). This last altar is made in five layers. The sky is taken to represent the universe; therefore, it includes space and earth. The first layer represents the earth, the third the space, and the fifth the sky. The second layer represents the joining of the earth and space, whereas the fourth layer represents the joining of space and sky. Śatapatha Brāhmaṇa (10.4.3.9) declares that knowledge is represented through altar construction in *agnichayana*.

Time is represented by the metaphor of a bird. The months of the year were ordinarily divided into six seasons unless the metaphor of the bird for the year was used when *hemanta* and *śiśira* were lumped together. The year as a bird had the head as *vasanta*, the body as *hemanta* and *śiśira*, the two wings as *śarada* and *grīshma*, and the tail as *varshā* [TB *3.10.4.1*, ŚB 10.4.5.2].

The Vedic sacrifice is meant to capture the magic of change, of time in motion. Put differently, the altar ritual is meant to symbolize the paradoxes of separation and unity, belonging and renunciation, and permanence and death. The *yajamāna*, the patron at whose expense the ritual is performed, symbolically represents the universe[5]. The ritual culminates in his ritual rebirth, which signified the regeneration of his universe. In other words, the ritual is a play dealing with paradoxes of life and death enacted for the *yajamāna's* family and friends. In this play symbolic deaths of animals and humans, including the *yajamāna* himself, may be enacted.

The recent discovery of the Rigvedic astronomical code[6] helps us see Vedic ritual in a new light. It shows the inadequacy of the earlier interpretations by scholars, philosophers, and theologians. It shows that the Rigvedic Indians were the foremost astronomers of the day. The tripartite system of knowledge and its representation in terms of the altars represents an extremely subtle approach to reality using science. The existence of this code also implies that the internal astronomical evidence in the Vedic texts first argued by Tilak and Jacobi and later by others[7] cannot be ignored. This internal evidence compels the conclusion that the prehistory of the Vedic people in India goes back to the fourth millennium and earlier. Such a conclusion is in consonance with the new archaeological discoveries that show a continuity in the Indian tradition going as far back as 6500 B.C.E. if not more.[8]

Note further that it is now believed that the Sarasvatī river dried up around 1900 B.C.E. which led to the collapse of the Harappan civilization that was principally located in the Sarasvati region. Francfort has even argued that the Drishadvatī river was already dry before 2600 B.C.E.[9] which is of course doubtful. Now the region of the Sarasvatī and the Drishadvatī rivers, called Brahmāvarta, was especially sanctified (e.g. RV 3.23.4) and Sarasvatī was one of the mightiest rivers of the Rigvedic period. With the understanding of the Sarasvatī drying up it is easy to accept that the Rigvedic era ended before 1900 B.C.E. but if one accepts Francfort's interpretation of the data on the Drishadvatī then the Rigvedic age must be anterior to 2600 B.C.E.

2. Vedic Astronomy

We turn to the Śatapatha Brāhmaṇa to provide us an overview of certain aspects of Vedic astronomy. The sixth chapter *(Kāṇḍa)* of the book provides significant clues. Speaking of creation under the aegis of the Prajāpati (reference either to a star or to abstract time) mention is made of the emergence of *Asva, Rāsabha, Aja* and *Kūrma* before the emergence of the earth. Clearly these refer to stars or constellations. Viśvanatha Vidyālaṅkāra (1985) argues that these should be identified as the sun *(Aśva)*, Gemini *(Rāsabha)*, Capricorn *(Aja)* and Casiopeia *(Kūrma)*. This identification is based on contemporaneous definitions as well as etymological considerations. RV 1.164.2 and Nirukta 4.4.27 define *Asva* as the sun. *Rāsabha* which literally means the twin asses are defined in Nighaṇṭu 1.15 as *Asvinau* which later usage suggests are Castor and Pollux in Gemini. In Western astronomy the twin asses are to be found in the next constellation of Cancer as Asellus Borealis and Asellus Australis. *Aja* (goat) is defined by Nighaṇṭu 1.15 as a sun and owing to the continuity that we see in the Vedic and later European names for constellations (as in the case of the Great Bear) it is reasonable to identify it as the constellation Capricorn *(caper* goat + *cornu* horn). *Kūrma* is a synonym of Kasyapa (tortoise) which is linguistically close to Casiopeia (from Greek *Kassiopeia)*. Etymologically, *Kāsyapīya*, slow like a tortoise, seems appropriate for Casiopeia (from Greek *Kassiopeia)* since it is near the pole. This last name may point to an epoch when this constellation was even closer to the north pole.

The Rigveda describes the universe to be infinite. It also refers to the five planets as gods and mentions Brihaspati (Jupiter) and Vena (Venus) by name (e.g. RV 4.50.4 & 10.23.1). The moon's path was divided into 27 equal parts, although the moon takes about 27 1/3 days to complete it. Each of these parts was called a *nakshatra. Nakshatras* are mentioned in the Rigveda, and Taittirīya Saṃhitā (TS 2.3.5.1-3) specifically mentions that they are linked to the moon's path. RV 10.55.3 mentions the 34 lights, which are apparently the sun, the moon, the five planets, and the 27 *nakshatras*. In later literature the list of *nakshatras* was increased to 28. Constellations other than the *nakshatras* were also known. RV 1.24.10; 10.14.11; 10.63.10 mention the Rikshas (the Bears), the two divine Dogs (Canis Major and Canis Minor), and the Boat (Argo Navis). The constellation Tishya is invoked in RV 10.64.8. But since TS 2.2.10.1-2 says Tishya is Rudra, perhaps Sirius is meant. Aitreya Brāhmaṇa (AB 3.33) speaks of *Mriga* (Orion) and *Mrigavyādha* (Sirius). TS 3.4.7 calls the moon *sūrya raśmi*, one that shines by sunlight.

The lunar or synodic months was measured from full moon to full moon or from new moon to new moon (TS 7.5.6.1). Twelve lunar months constituted a lunar year. The lunar month consisted of 30 lunations (Brihadāraṇyaka Upanishad 1.5.14). In analogy with a civil day, a lunar as reckoned by dividing the lunar year into 360 parts called *tithis* (AB 32.10). That different approximations to this notion of *tithi*[10] were used has caused confusion regarding this measure. Obviously, Vedic astronomy was not based on the use of accurate clocks, but fine time units were defined in relation to events across longer durations. To preserve correspondence between lunar and solar years, intercalary months were inserted at regular intervals (see e.g. RV 1.25.8).

3. The Context of Vedic Studies

The Vedic literature provides its own exegesis. The details of the ritual as well as the philosophical basis are to be found in the Brāhmaṇas, the Āraṇyakas, and the Upanishads. Further explanation is provided by the *Bṛhaddevatā*, the Epics, and the Purāṇas. The Brāhmaṇas, the *Nirukta*, the *Bṛhaddevatā* and other texts show how linguistic perspectives are basic to any analysis. A triadic representation is used in a recursive fashion to describe the unity of the fundamental ground substance. The deities are thus described as belonging to either Agni, or Indra, or Sūrya paralleling the division of the physical universe into the earth, the space, and the sky. But that these are linguistic devices to describe a unity made infinite by time and space is clear by assertions such as "In Indra are contained Prajanya, Rudra, Vāyu, Bṛhaspati, Varuṇa, Ka, Mṛtyu, and the god Brahmaṇaspati; Manyu, Viśvakarman, Mitra, Kṣetrapati, Yama, Tārkṣya, as well as Vāstoṣpati, ..., and Agni, Soma, ..."[11]

Yāska's *Nirukta* is one in a continuous series of commentaries that culminates in Sāyaṇa's commentary in the 14th century. The later commentators did not themselves understand the importance of the astronomical basis of the Vedic system and were thus limited. The past century has seen resurgence of interest in Vedic scholarship in India thanks to the work of Dayānanda Sarasvatī and Aurobindo. This approach is now becoming increasingly popular[12].

The analysis by academic scholars has always been informed by the prevailing philosophical attitudes which in turn have been shaped by the dominant paradigm in physics, the fundamental scientific discipline. Much of the recent scholarship related to the Vedas has been deficient because it has remained stuck in the mechanistic paradigm of analysis. Although the mechanistic model has been superseded by the relativistic and the quantum mechanical paradigms a similar shift has not occurred in the academic Vedic scholarship. On the other hand, the older Indian tradition of Vedic analysis rings true because it is based on the notion of an interpenetrating unity, which is paradoxically modern as well since the most advanced physics metaphor of quantum mechanics is in accord with it. Other aspects of the Vedic system deal with information and meaning, again in accord with newer scientific disciplines that have not yet been discovered by Vedic scholars in the Western academe.

The nineteenth century Indologists were also influenced by other attitudes that were inimical to the spirit of free inquiry. There were those who wished to fit the Vedic chronology within the straitjacket of Biblical chronology and this coloured their interpretations. There were others who thought that ideas of evolution were clearly at work in the different layers of the Vedic literature. Most dismissed the idea of an underlying unity because such an idea had not yet arrived in physics; the governing metaphor being that of a mechanistic physics. The gods had 'therefore' to have precise functions and domains just as different physical forces do. Unfortunately, these notions soon got frozen and when science itself changed, there was no corresponding revolution in the academic Vedic exegesis.

The nineteenth century academic also suffered from the attitudes popular in the post-French Revolution period where an attempt was made to classify all phenomena in a naturalistic sense. Although this attitude was fruitful in many disciplines, in Vedic studies it was used in the most speculative manner. This led to a considerable amount of description and less an attempt to find the grammar behind the Vedic civilization. Thus Rudolf Roth (1821-1895), one of the first major European Indologists, would not see anything more than old religious lyrical poetry in the Vedas. A. Kuhn (1812-1881) and Max Müller (1823-1903) sought parallels between the Vedic and other Indo-European mythologies but without a proper understanding of the Vedic system. Abel Bergaigne (1838-1888) saw the Vedic gods as anthropomorphic masks for forces of nature and this allowed him to see the identity between the cosmic, the ritual, and the moral order spelt out in the Vedas. Richard Pischel (1849-1908) and Karl Geldner (1852-1929) argued for interpretations within the framework of the Indian context. But their attempt was to see some kind of a primitive nature religion in the system. Scholars like Hermann Oldenberg (1854-1920) also followed this evolutionary approach as did A.A. Macdonell and A.B. Keith. In recent years the philologist J. Gonda[13] has perceived the need for a thorough reassessment, yet his work has remained too narrow in its vision. There were no attempts to study the architecture of the Vedic texts in this tradition.

We continue to see scholars seeking in the Rigveda a sequence of attitudes going back to the most primitive. Thus Staal[14] hearkens back to the very development of language in his theory that *mantras* are to be compared to bird-songs and that they represent the very beginning of language.

The parallels between the Vedic and the European myths have been examined in the past few decades by G. Dumézil and others. Dumézil[15] speaks of a tripartite conception of the Indo-European society into priest, warrior, and cultivator reflected in the triad of gods Agni, Indra, and Viśve Devāḥ in India or Jupiter, Mars, and Quirinus in Rome. On the other hand, religious and political sovereignty is viewed as a dual category of the jurist priest (brāhmaṇa, flamen) and magician-king (*rājā*, rex). The major limitation of such analysis is that it has not been discussed in the context of the new results from archaeology.

4. The Architecture of the Rigveda

To study the design of the Rigveda it is essential to make a distinction between its index tradition and the text itself. It is also essential to recognize that in spite of the incredible fidelity with which the Vedic text has been passed down, the same fidelity may not have been true for the index tradition.

There are many references to the larger plan of the texts. ŚB 10.4.2.23-24 describes that the Rigveda has 432,000 syllables; Yajurveda has 288,000 and Sāmaveda has 144,000 syllables. The syllable count of the canonical text of the Rigveda has only 394,221[16] syllables, however. This syllable count is for the Saṃhitāpāṭha where sometimes syllables in sequence coalesce due to rules of *sandhi*. The *Rigveda Prātiśākhya* 17.14 explains: "To get the correct count for the total, resolve the coalesced combinations in the incomplete pādas." Thus Raster[17] shows how the syllable count of the first hymn, which has 9 verses in the Gāyatrī meter, can be restored from its actual 210 to the correct 216 which is 9×24. When the correct count for all the meters is made the syllable count increases to 3,94,317.

According to Śaunaka's *Anuvāka Anukramaṇī* the Rigveda of the Śākala recension consists of 1017 main hymns, divided into 10 maṇḍalas (books) of varying lengths, and an appendix of 11 *khila* hymns that are called the Vālakhila hymns[18]. The Bāshkala recension, according to Śaunaka, consisted of eight more hymns, but this recension has not survived. It is believed that the eight additional hymns of the Bāshkala recension consisted of 7 Vālakhilya hymns and the Samjñāna hymns. In other words, the two recensions differ only in the arrangement of the *khilas*.

The *Anukramaṇīs* ascribe books 2 to 7 to the rishis Grishtsamada, Viśvāmitra, Vāmadeva, Atri, Bharadvāja, and Vasishṭha or their families. Book 9 is a collection of hymns by several rishis to Soma Pavamāna, or Soma poured through the filter. Book 1 which consists of 191 hymns is classed into 15 groups of hymns by different seers. Book 10 also consists of 191 hymns and its first 84 hymns are classed into 25 groups based on rishis, and its remaining 107 hymns are counted singly.

The classification of the family books 2 to 7 is based on hymns to different gods and these groups are 5, 4, 11, 7, 5, 12, respectively. Book 8 hymns are grouped according to the particular seers of the Kaṇva family. Including the Vālakhilya hymns, these constitute 19 groups. The hymns of Book 9 are grouped into 7 according to the meter. These meters are *Gāyatrī, Jagatī, Triṣṭubh, Anuṣṭubh, Uṣṇiḥ, Pragtha,* and miscellaneous. These hymns are by a host of rishis, including Bhṛgu, Kaśyapa, and Kavi Uśanas. This information is summarized in Table 1.

Table 1 : Hymns and groups

Maṇḍalas	1	2	3	4	5	6	7	8	9	10
Hymns	191	43	62	58	87	75	104	92	114	191
Groups	15	5	4	11	7	5	12	18	7	132
Anuvākas	24	4	5	5	6	6	6	10	7	12

According to Śaunaka's *Anuvāka Anukramaṇī* the total number of Anuvākas is 85; the number of adhyāyas is 64, the number of vargas is 2,006. The total number of verses is declared to be $10,580\frac{1}{2}$; the number of half-verses is 21,232 and of the words 1,53,826. According to Shaḍguruśishya the 1/2 in the verse total comes from RV 10.20.1. Śaunaka also declares that the number of syllables is 4,32,000.

How is one to explain the discrepancy between the numbers of Śaunaka and that of the canonical text? One cannot assume that the canonical text is much smaller than the text available to Śaunaka because there exisists perfect agreement in the number of hymns, the meters of the various verses, and so on. The average per verse based on Śaunaka's verse numbers should be 40.83 to yeild the syllable count of 4,32,000. The actual average is, however, 37.65 because although *Trishṭup* (44 syllables) is the most common meter, the second most common meter is the *Gāyatrī* (24 syllables). The only conclusion that is open to us then is that the number 4,32,000 is the ideal number of syllables. Considering that RV 1.164.45 declares that speech is of four kinds, three of which are unmanifest, then the shortfall of 37,779 syllables must be in terms of unmanifest syllables.

5. Of Bricks, Enclosing Stones, Hymns and Meters

Altars were made of bricks unless such altars were constructed in songs. Bricks to be used in altar construction were classified into two types: ordinary (*lokampriṇā*) and special (*yajushmatī*). Each (*yajushmatī*) brick was consecrated in a specific manner and each such brick was marked in a unique way. Bricks were made in different shapes to different measurements.

ŚB 10.4.3.14-20 describes the total number of *yajushmatī* bricks to be 396. This was to be taken as 360 days of the year and 36 additional (including ones being the fillings between the bricks) as the days of the intercalary month. By layers, the first has 98, the second has 41, the third has 71, the fourth has 47, and the fifth has 138 (ŚB 10.4.3.14-18). The sum of the bricks in the fourth and the fifth layers refer to the 186 (together with the one space filling) *tithis* in the half-year. The number of bricks in the third layer equals the integer nearest to one fifth of the number of days in the lunar year. The number of bricks in the third layer equals the integer nearest to one fifth of the number of days in the lunar year. The number of bricks in the second and the third layers equals one third the number of days in a *nakshatra* year of 28 times 12 = 336 days. Once the basic number of 21 is substracted from the number of bricks in the first layer, the sum of the remainder together with the bricks in the second layer once again equals the integer nearest to one third the number of days in the lunar year.

The total number of *lokampriṇā* bricks is 10,800 which equals the number of *muhūrtas* in a year (1 day = 30 *muhūrtas*), or equivalently the number of days in 30 years. Of these 21 go into the *gārhapatya,* 78 into the eight *dhiṣṇya* hearths, and the rest go into the *āhavanīya* altar.

The fire altars are surrounded by 360 enclosing stones *(pariśrita),* of these 21 are around the *gārhapatya,* 78 around the *dhishnya,* and 261 around the *āhavanīya* (ŚB 10.4.3.13). The *āhavanīya* includes the *dhishṇya,* therefore the number of days assigned exclusively to the *āhavanīya* is 261–78 = 183 days, which is equal to the days in the *uttarāyaṇa* of a 366 day year. The choice of the 21 days for the *gārhapatya* is from the unique symbolism of this number. It is the sum of the first six integers. Once the numbers 21 and 183 are chosen the number 78 becomes the only choice for the *dhishṇya.* This number 78 is the sum of the first twelve integers.

The *dhishṇya* hearths are in one layer in a size of 18 *angulas* in either a square or circular form. The number of enclosing stones equals the number of bricks used in a *dhishṇya* hearth, and these are 8 each for five of them with the remaining three using 6, 11 and 21.

The meters

ŚB 10.3.1 describes how the altar can also be constructed symbolically by the meters. The altar is made with *Gāyatrī* (24 syllables) as the breath, *Ushṇiḥ* (28 syllables) as the eye, *Anushṭubh* (32 syllables) as the voice, *Brihatī* (36 syllables) as the mind, *Paṅki* (40 syllables) as the ear, *Trishṭubh* (44 syllables) as the generative breath, and the *Jagathi* (48 syllables) as the downward breathing. As we will see in Section 7 there is a correspondence with the size of the physical altar being seven (and a half) square units. Elsewhere the identification of the meters with the parts of the altar is different. The important correspondence is that of the meters being represented as a group of seven.

6. The Rigvedic Index Related to the Other Vedas

The Sāmaveda

The two main extant recensions of the Sāmaveda are Kauthuma (considered the vulgate) and the Jaiminīya; a third recension called the Rāṇāyanīya is very similar to Kauthuma. The Kauthuma recension consists of 1810 verses in two main books called the Pūrvārchika (585 single verses) and the Uttarāchika (1225 verses); in addition there are 54 verses in the Āraṇyaparvan which belongs to the Pūrvārchika, which in turn has an appendix of 11 *mahānāmnī* verses. The *mahānāmnī* verses may also be found in the fourth Āraṇyaka of Aitreya Āraṇyaka. Altogether, therefore, the recension has 1875 verses.

The Yajurveda

According to tradition there were 101 schools of the Yajurveda in two groups, viz., Krishṇa and Śukla. The surviving texts of the Krishṇa Yajurveda are placed into four main groups: Taittirīya, Kāṭhaka, Kapishṭhala, and Maitrāyaṇīya. The Taittirīya has the best preserved texts. The Śukla or the Vājasaneyī Yajurveda is represented by the Mādhyamdina and the Kāṇva recensions.

The Vājasaneyi Yajurveda is organized in a more regular fashion. It appears that out of its 40 chapters the first 18 form the core text; chapters 19-25 deal with *sautrāmaṇi* and *aśvamedha* sacrifices; chapters 26-35 are called *khilas* or supplementary material; chapters 36-39 are devoted to the *pravargya* ceremony and chapter 40 is the Iśa Upanishad. The total number of verses has been taken to be 1,975 or 1,984. The first 18 chapters add up to 1,026 verses.

The Atharvaveda

There are two extant recensions: the Paippalāda and the Śaunakīya. The Śaunakīya recension of 730 or 731 hymns is much better preserved; it consists of 20 books of which the first 18 appear to be the core. Book 19 has material arranged differently from the preceding books and book 20 is clearly supplementary. It has been argued earlier that the core text consisted of 5,226 verses[19]. According to Satvalekar the verse total for the entire text is 5,977; the Paippalāda recension has about 8000 verses.

We take up the question of the analysis of the number 4,32,000. ŚB 10.4.4.2 speaks of the number of stars in the sky being equal to the number of *muhūrtas* (1 day = 30 muhūrtas) in 1,000 years or 1000×360×30=10,800,000. This means that the ideal number of syllables in the Rigveda equals the number of *muhūrtas* in 40 years. The number of days in 40 years is 14,400 and if one took the identity of a day to a verse then this would be the number of verses in the Rigveda. The average number of syllables per verse is therefore 30, or the mean of *Gāyatrī* and *Brihatī*. Now we know tht sky (or heaven) is ascribed the number 261 in Vedic ritual. If we consider the equation that the verse is to the sky-day what the syllable is to the muhūrta, then the number of verses in a span of 40 years, considering 261 sky–days per year, equals 10,440. This is only two less than the actual count obtained by Macdonell[20], and it is likely that if this association is true then the canonical text must have had two verses less by reorganizing, say four shorter verses into two longer ones. As argued by Macdonell his count of 10,442 for the Rigveda verses can be reconciled with Śaunaka's figure by considering the 127 Dvipadās twice; this raises the count to 10,569 verses which is only 11 verses less than Śaunakas's figure. It is possible that the 11 hymns of the *khila* were counted as the remainder in a count across categories, evidence of which is common as in the number 17 counted as 12 months and 5 seasons in the brāhmaṇas.

One can propose another theory that the Rigveda is supposed to be ideally 10,800 verses with an average of 40 syllables per verse. The shortfall between this number and the actual of 10,440 is exactly 360 verses. Since 10,800 are the muhūrtas in one year, the shortfall amounts to the muhūrtas in 12 days.

We now come to another theory for the reconciliation of the verse count of 10,580 to the actual count that we have. We assume that the actual count of the Rigveda was 10,440 and that the *khila* verses were a total of 140, in other words, 60 more than the current number. But such a possibility is unlikely since there is no tradition that speaks of such a large number of lost verses.

We can also explain the significance of the actual count of syllables. Knowing that the earth number is 21 and the sky number is 261, it is likely that the actual syllables are 2,40/261 of the ideal number of 4,32,000. This amounts to 3,99,241 syllables. Now the count of syllables for the Rigveda and the *khila* verses is 397,265. Therefore, there must have been a modification required by some observation.

How do we explain the number 10,442 as the verse count in the Rigveda? It is possible that the knowledge that the year was actually 371.05 *tithis* (see Section 12) was translated into a representation of the sky number to 261.05. Over 40 years now we get 10,442 verses. If the other numbers are proportionately changed to 77.96 and 20.99, then the ratio

$$\frac{240.06}{261.05} \times 4{,}32{,}000 = 3{,}97{,}265$$

This is precisely the number of syllables that the Rigveda has.

One may further assume that when the Rigveda expanded from its core size of 10,440 verses, 2 more verses were added to it. Paralleling this, 2 verses were added to the 78 original *khila* verses.

One may assume that the logic of considering the muhūrtas of 40 years to represent the syllables of the Rigveda flows from the time span of 100 years to represent all the four Vedas. As explained above, Yajur and Sāmaveda taken together also get 40 years; the remaining 20 years would then be assigned to Atharvaveda. That such a logic must have been at work is suggested by the fact that the total number of hymns in the Śaunakīya recension, without considering only the Kuntāpa hymns of the Book 20 is 5,226, just six more than the number of hymns according to our theory[21].

The total number of hymns in the Śaunakīya recension when the remainder of the Book 20 is also considered is 5977 which equals 43×139.

The distribution of all the verses of the Vedas as they have come down to us is:

Table 2: Verses in the Vedic books

Rigveda	10522
Yajurveda	1984
Sāmaveda	1875
Atharvaveda	5977
Total	20,358

That this total is exactly 261×78 implies that the verses were, metaphorically, supposed to pervade the entire space of span 78 and breadth 261.

One might assume that the original structure started with 261×40 = 10,440 verses for the Rigveda corresponding to 40 years; Atharvaveda had 261×20= 5,220 verses for 20 years. The Yajurveda and the Sāmaveda were assigned 40 years, but by the space number of 78 and by its half 39. Also we claim that the Śatapatha Brāhmaṇa reference to the verses of Yajurveda and Sāmaveda being in the proportion 2:1 is only approximately true; the correct proportion being 25:15. This leads to the figure 78×25 = 1,950 verses for Yajurveda; and 39×15 = 585 verses for Sāmaveda. The figure for Yajurveda is very close to the value leaving out the Iśa Upanishad verses of chapter 40 and the Sāmaveda figure is identical to the Pūrvācika verses. Various considerations, like the ones for the Rigveda verse totals outlined earlier, led to modifications of these numbers with the constraint that the total had to be 261×78 = 20,358.

Other numerical and perhaps astronomical considerations must have played a role in the modifications that were introduced. It is possible that the Atharvaveda number was first increased to 5,226 because it is 78×67. From another perspective, we expect that the syllable count for the Sāmaveda by the Śatapatha Brāhmaṇa reference comes to 4,800 verses and that for the Yajurveda to 9,600. Now note that the 585 Pūrvāchika stanzas are in practice sung to double the number of tunes; this allows us to modify the total count as 1,225 + 2×585 + 54 + 11 = 2,395. This is just 5 short of the half of the total 4,800. Considering still another angle, note that Sāmaveda has 1810 verses plus 5 hymns in the Āraṇyaparva and the 11 *mahānāmnī* verses. If we add across categories we get a total of 1826, only one less than 261×7.

The basis behind the verse totals seems to have been forgotten quite early since there is no mention of it in the various *Anukramaṇīs*. The fact that the numbers, after the passage of millennia, still satisfy the number relationships further attests to the incredible fidelity with which the texts have been preserved.

7. Equivalence Through Area and Number

The *Śulbasūtras* clearly indicate that the *gārhapatya*, the *āhavanīya*, and the *dakshiṇāgni* are all to have an area of one square *purusha*. In the *agnichayana* ritual the original *āhavanīya* altar later takes the place of *gārhapatya* altar after the *uttara vedi* has been built. *Purusha* is both a linear and an areal measure; as a linear measure it may be taken to be approximately the height of a man with his arms stretched upwards (say 2 metres), then as areal measure it is about 4 square metres. The size of the altars is stated in ŚB 7.1.1.37 and 10.2.3.1 although there is a residual ambiguity in the text about the measure used being linear or square. The *gārhapatya* represents the womb or the earth and it is thus circular whereas the *āhavanīya* is the sky and it is represented by a square. The *dakshiṇāgni* is a semicircular figure.

The *mahāvedi* altars were generally made in five layers of bricks reaching to the height of the knee. Each layer in the falcon altar had 200 bricks leading thus to a total 1,000 bricks in the five layers. It appears that the Rigveda knew of such an altar because *Puruṣha* is described in RV 10.90 as "thousand headed, thousand eyed, thousand footed." In some cases ten or fifteen layers of bricks were prescribed. The basic falcon-shaped altar had an area of 7 1/2 square *purusha*. The body of the basic falcon-shaped altar was 2 × 2 (=4) square *puruṣhas*, the wings and the tail were one square puruṣha each. To make the shape look more like that of a bird, the wings were lengthened by one-fifth of a *purusha* and the tail was lengthened by one-tenth of a *purusha*. This defined the total area of 7 1/2 square *purushas* at the end of the first construction. On the second construction the area of the altar was increased by one square *purusha* to a total of 8 1/2 square *purushas*. Further constructions successively increased the area by one square *purusha* at each step until one came to the "one-hundred-and-one-[and-a-half]-fold" altar. In the construction of the larger altars the same shape as the basic altar is required and this requires solution of several geometric problems including that of the theorem of the diagonal. It is important to note that the total number of altars to be built in a sequence is 95.

The first step in abstraction requires a representation of a phenomenon through a number. If two phenomena have the same number assigned to them then it is reasonable to seek connections between them. Thus a circadian biological cycle is to be linked, in a starting theory, to the earth's rotation. Likewise monthly periods are to be linked to the phases of the moon. Equivalence through number is to be found in the earliest Vedic texts and one would expect that it must have preceded the philosophy of equivalence through area.

Consider Aitreya Āraṇyaka. The parallels between the planetary motions and man are thus drawn:

Of bones, marrow, and joints there are 360 (parts) on (the right) side and 360 (parts) on (the left) side. They make 720 together, and 720 are the days and nights of the year. Thus the self which consists of sight, hearing, meter, mind, and speech is like the days. [AA 3.2.1.4]

There are 360 syllables (vowels), 360 sibilants (consonants), 360 groups. What we call the syllables are the days, what we call sibilants are the nights, what we call groups are the junctions of days and nights... The syllables ... are physiologically the bones; the sibilants ... are the marrow; ... the groups are the joints. [AA 3.2.2.2-7]

8. Agni, Rudra and Prajāpati

Agni, the year, is also called Rudra (TS 2.2.10.4). Agni has three mothers (RV 7.59.12) which are earth, space, and sky. Rudra, similarly, has three mothers (ŚB 2.6.2.14). As symbols of time Agni and Rudra are couched in paradox. Thus Agni is the father of gods, although he is their son (RV 1.69.1); he is the bull who is also the cow (RV 10.5.7). ŚB 6.13.9-17 also symbolizes a year as Rudra, Sarva, Paśupati, Ugra, Aśani, Bhava, Mahādeva, and Iśāna. Śiva is sometimes represented collectively by the eight as Aṣṭamūrti. Rudra wields the thunderbolt (*vajra*) which is Indra's weapon. Agni and Indra are twin brothers (RV 6.59.2). Indra slays his father (RV 4.18.12) and likewise Rudra slays Daksha. These refer to the change in the reckoning of time brought about by a precession of the earth[22].

Indra-Rudra or Śiva are sometimes represented by the world axis, the *skambha* or pillar. This is done for Indra even in our times when he is represented by a pole erected during the celebrations for the new year[23].

The Śatapatha Brāhmaṇa speaks of the Seven Rishis creating seven persons in the beginning, who are later assimilated into one person. This is represented by the fire-altar (Agni) who is Prajāpati, where the body represents four and the wings and the tail the other three [ŚB 6.1.1.5-6]. Elsewhere (ŚB 10.6.4.1) Prajāpati is represented as a horse. This horse is also a metaphor for the sun. *Aśvamedha* sacrifice is to memorialize, to transcend, time.

Prajāpati is a metaphorical representation of time. Prajāpati is also the year (ŚB 5.1.1.1). So time was represented by the constellations in the sky or the processes of life and death in the world. The fire altar is a symbolic representation of time in relation to man. According to the Baudhāyana Śulbasūtra 7.17 the bricks can be replaced by mantras leading thus to the chandaśchit. The year was thus represented by the Vedic stanza called *brihatī*, which consists of 36 syllables forming four verses divided into two hemistichs (8, 8, 12, 8) (ŚB 6.4.2.10). Elsewhere (ŚB 1.3.5.9) it is stated that by using 15 *Gāyatrī* stanzas (of 24 syllables each) one obtains the days of the year and the year.

The fact that precession of the earth's axis caused the seasons to change slowly with time was expressed by myths such as that of the decapitation of Prajāpati by Rudra. Due to the precession of the earth, Prajāpati, the year, marked by the sun rising in Orion at the vernal equinox, had moved toward Rohiṇī, his daughter. This is metaphorically represented by the slaying of Prajāpati by Rudra. Much earlier a similar passage was represented by the myth of Vṛtra being slain by Indra. Indra and Rudra represent the same frame of time at different epochs. Another similar myth is that of the creation of a new world with its own axis by Viśvāmitra.[24] The frame of time was represented in Artharvaveda as skambha, the cosmic pillar (AV 10.7).

The identification of the year and man was carried on further than that of 360 days and 360 *asthis*. Śatapatha B. (12.3.2.5) speaks of the year having 10,800 *muhūrtas* (1 muhūrta = 48 minutes). Also note that 1 *purusha* = 120 *angulas* and, therefore, the area of 7 1/2 sq. *purusha* for the basic altar equals 108,000 square *angulas*.

The Rigveda had long spoken of *Purusha* (or Prajāpati)

having a 1,000 fold nature. The year was therefore represented in terms of 5 layers of 200 bricks each. On the other hand, ŚB 7.4.2.31 explains that the 5 layers represent the 5 seasons of the year.

But the most significant observation from the *agnichayana* ritual is that it described a 95 year cycle as represented by the altars going from the size of 7 1/2 square *purusha* to 101 1/2 square *purusha*. Since tradition ascribes the authorship of the Śatapatha Brāmaṇa to Yājñavalkya (Mahābhārata 12.11739), we have called this *Yājñavalkya cycle*. This cycle is obviously the product of 5×19.

9. The Seven Rishis and the Saptarṣi Era

The tradition of the seven *Rishis*, the stars of the Ursa Major, in India is an ancient one and it goes back to the Rigveda[25].

Of those *Rishis* born together, they say that the seventh is born by himself *[saptatham ekajam]* while six are twins, God-born Rishis *[shaḷ idyamā rishayo devajāh]* (RV 1.164.15; AV 9.9.16, 10.8.5).

While the Rishis are not named in the Rigveda, there is a mention of Viśvāmitra as being God-born (*devaja*) in RV 3.53.9. References in the Brāhmaṇas and the Upanishads suggest that the unpaired star is Atri which is ε Ursa major, the fifth in order of listing of the stars of the group.

Purusha Sūkta (RV 10.90) visualizes the cosmic giant Purusha who is the basis of the world. Later Prajāpati was viewed as a giant spanning the universe, framed by the constellations in the sky. Prajāpati was also the embodiment of the year [e.g. ŚB 6.1.2.19]. Brahadāraṇya Upanished 2.2.4 represents the seven Rishis as the lips of the cosmic person.

On the other hand, BU 2.2.4 speaks of these seven stars as representing the sense organs of the face of the cosmic person. Gautama and Bharadvāja are the ears, Viśvāmitra and Jamadagni are the eyes, Vasishṭtha and Kaśyapa are the nostrils, and Atri is the tongue. That this identification was only general is borne out by the slightly different labelling in the ŚB 8.1.1.6-2.6 where Vasishṭa is speech, Bharadvāja is the mind, Jamadagni is the eye, and Viśvāmitra is the ear. This representation maps also the cognitive centers in the head as the seven Rishis.

The later texts make a geographical identification of the Rishis which parallels their mapping in the sky. And as the Vedic Indians spread from their original region in the north-west India the geographical representation of the Rishis changed. This can be seen in the transition from the Vedic literature to the Epic literature and the Purāṇas. It is in this manner that south India is associated with another Rishi called Agastya who represents Canopus.

There is a further identification of the Rishis with the human head doubtless inspired by the identification of the primal person, *purusha*, in the sky.

Saptarṣi Era

ŚB 2.1.2.1-5 speaks of a marriage between the Rishis and the *nakshatras*; specifically it is mentioned that the Rishis were married to the Kṛttikās. In the Purāṇạs this notion of marriage is elaborated when it is clearly stated that the Rishis remain for a hundred years in each *nakshatra* (e.g. VP 2.37.413-417). It may be noted that the original core Purāṇa is to be dated to the same epoch as the Śatapatha Brāhmaṇa, but it is not clear that the elaboration in the Purāṇas was meant in the statement of ŚB 2.1.2.1-5.

The significant point here is that the Purāṇic elaboration implies a centennial reckoning system with a cycle of 2700 years. Such a system has been in use in parts of India for a long time that goes back centuries before C.E. and it is called the Saptarishi era[26]. Each cycle of 2700 years was called a chakra, or cycle. By current reckoning in Kashmir, that goes back at least to Kalhana, Saptarṣi era began in 3076 B.C.E.

Cunningham and Mitchiner argue that several conflicting traditions about the Mahābhārata war can be reconciled if it is assumed that a change in reckoning from a system of 28 *nakshatras* to that of 27 *nakshatras* took place sometime after the time of Chandragupta. They suggest that the original list of 28 *nakshatras* (AV 19.8.2) was amended in the medieval times to 27. Since the notion of 27 *nakshatras* also goes back very far as in TS 4.4.10.1-3, it is possible that the two traditions on the Mahābhārata war go back much further.

It appears that the above reconstruction needs to be modified in one crucial point. It is more likely that the original system of *nakshatras* was 27 and that it was modified to 28 later. This modification required the change of the beginning of the Kali Yuga from 2414 B.C.E. to 3102 B.C.E. Such a view is supported by textual astronomical evidence as described by Sengupta[27].

The Basis of the Saptarshi Era: It appears that the Saptarshi era was known during the Śatapatha Brāhmaṇa times. The altar is made in an area 7 1/2 times that of one *purusha* with 360 years considered one divine year[28], 2700 years equal 7 1/2 divine years. It may be that such a theory led to the popularity of the system of 27 *nakshatras*. It is also significant that the epoch of 6676 B.C.E. is exactly 3600 years earlier than the starting point of 3076 B.C.E. for the Saptarshi era as accepted now. Since it is clear that at the time of the Mauryas, the cycles of the Saptarshi era were counted back to 6676 B.C.E., it appears that the new count that goes back to 3076 B.C.E. was started later to make it as close to the start of the Kali era as possible.

10. More on Intercalation

For ready reference note the following facts from modern astronomy:

Solar (sidereal) year = 365.25636 solar days

Solar (tropical) year = 365.24219 solar days

Moon's sidereal period = 27.32166 solar days

Lunar month = 29.530588 solar days = 30 tithis

Tithis in a solar year = 371.06239

The solar year was known to be a litle more than 365 days, although it's nominal period was taken to be 360 days. TS 7.1.10.1-3 speaks of the 5 excess days over the *Sāvana* year of 360 days to complete the seasons, where 4 days are too short and 6 days are too long. TS 7.2.6.1 speaks of the extra 11 days (*ekādaśarātra)* over the 12 lunar months of 354 days required to complete the year. That the reckoning was done both by the solar and the sidereal or *nakshatra* counts is clear from the references to the year having 13 months (ŚB 7.1.1.32 or 7.2.3.9). Later books, such as the *Nidāna Sūtras*, speak clearly of the *nakshatra* year being equal to 324 days which is 27 times 12. In a system of 28 *nakshatras* the *nakshatra* year equals 336 days. That Śatapatha Brāhmaṇa knows the nakshatra year will be shown when we discuss the falcon altar again.

The eleven extra days in the solar year, when compared to the lunar year, were each assigned a separate god. A triple division of space and time is a common Rigvedic theme. Rigveda speaks of the three-fold world which then leads to a total of 33 gods. RV 7.87.5 speaks of three earths.

To get further information on the length of the solar year, one can use evidence regarding the extent of intercalation needed after the nominal year period of 360 days. Was the year taken to be 365 days or 366 days? With 366 days one would require intercalation of 12 days a year, whereas 365 days imply intercalation of 11 days. ŚB 10.5.4.5 describes the 756 bricks to be used in building the fire altar. These represent the 720 lunar days and nights followed by the 36 lunar days and nights in the intercalary month. This supports an intercalation of 18 days every 1-1/2 years. In other words, the basic year was taken to be 366 days, which would correspond to 372 *tithis*. But the *ekādaśarātra* also points to 365 days or 371 *tithis*. The only conclusion to be drawn is that the true length of the year was known to be between 365 and 366 solar days, or equivalent to 371 or 372 *tithis*. This is corroborated by RV 4.33.7 where we hear about the *ribhus*, the receptacles of time (RV 1.111.1; 4.34.9) who rest for 12 days after the year is over.

Further support for this is obtained from RV 3.9.9 which speaks of a total of 3339 gods in a year, personified as Agni. This corresponds to 371 *tithis* if one recognizes that in Vedāṅga Jyotisha each *tithi* is equated to nine *bhāṃśas*.

The period of 5 solar years was called a *yuga*. These years were named *saṃvatsara, parivatsara, idāvatsara, idvatsara,* and *vatsara* (TS 5.5.7.3; ŚB 8.1.4.8) or minor variations of these names. A five year period was convenient because it led to two intercalation months of 30 *tithis* each, which the Vedāṅga Jyotisha evidence suggests were added at intervals of 2 1/2 years. But this would lead to an excess of about 4.688 *tithis* in 5 years, necessitating further corrections in greater periods.

The Taittirīya Brāhmaṇa (TB 3.9.22) calls the year the day of the gods. This indicates how increasing larger yugas would have been conceived.

11. The 95 Year Yājñavalkya Period

ŚB 6.1.1.1-3 speaks of how the Rishis (here they are vital airs) created seven separate persons, who doubtlessly represent the seven cognitive centers. Now they made these seven persons into one person and this is represented by the seven (and a half) *purusha* altar. ŚB 10.2.3.18 now describes the process of building larger altars: "Prajāpati was created sevenfold in the beginning. He went on constructing (developing) his body, and stopped at the one hundred and one fold one." Later it is added that "the one hundred and one fold altar becomes equal to the seven fold one"[29].

BSS 5.6 speaks of how the altar at the *m* th augmentation is obtained with the new unit *x* after such augmentation satisfying $x^2 = 1 + 2m/15)$ where *m* runs from 1 to 94. The 101 1/2 square *purusha* altar is obtained when $m = 94$ and for this $x^2 = 13\ 8/15$. Now ŚB 102.3.11 describes a "ninety-eight-fold" bird as having dimensions of 14 square *purusha* and Seidenberg[30] convincingly shows that this must have referred to the 101–1/2 square *purusha* altar.

The *agnichayana* ritual leads to a cycle of 95 years, as explained. The logic behind this cycle is that this leads to exactly 35 intercalary months (with a residual small error) in 95 years if the year is counted as 360 *tithis*. In Section 12 we will show that 95 years represent a big period even when the year is taken to be a *nakshatra* year of 324 days. If each altar is taken to represent a yuga, the cycle would then become 475 years.

The use of the Yājnavalkya cycle at a later time is corroborated by the creation of the 2850 year cycle in the *Romakasiddhānta*, which is 30 times 95, or a "month" of such a cycle.

12. More on Altar Design

ŚB 10.4.4.2 speaks of the number of stars in the sky being equal to the number of *muhūrtas* (1 day = 30 *muhūrtas*) in 1,000 years or 1000×360×30 = 10,800,000. This is followed by consideration of *muhūrta* as a basic measure in the consideration of the grand year of 1,000 ordinary years. A *muhūrta* is to a day what a day is to a month. In other words the grand year consists of 10,800,000 units, which were presumably taken to correspond to years.

The important *gārhapatya* altar, that represents earth or the womb, has an area of 1 square *purusha* which equals 14,400 square *angulas*. This requires drawing a circle around a square of side 1 *vyāyāma* (1 *vyāyāma* = 4/5 *purusha*). It is constructed with 21 bricks in each layer (ŚB 7.1.1.34). With 7 1/2 square *purusha* considered equal to 360 days, the area of the *gārhapatya* altar equals 48 days.

Note also that the falcon altar symbolizes all the three years: *nakshatra*, lunar, and solar. The increase in the area in each new construction of the falcon altar is 1 square *purusha* which equals 48 days. The purpose of the increase is to make the altar become closer to the actual year. If the *nakshatra* year is now taken to be 324 *tithis*, the additional 48 tithis are needed to make it exactly equal to the nominal year of 372 *tithis*. On the other hand, it may indicate the size of a larger yuga by the following correspondence:

1 *tithi* = 9 *bhāmśas* like 1year (371 tithis) = 3339 *bhāmśas*;

48 days expands to a larger period of 48×9=432.

This multiplier of 9 may have also been used in going from 12 months to a period of 108.

The expansion of 48 *tithis* is required every year since it is clearly stated that the expanded altar is to be viewed as before as Prajāpati. Since we do know that the number of *tithis* in a year is supposed to be 371.06239, this implies an excess of 0.93761 *tithis* per year. In 95 years this excess would be almost exactly equal to 89 *tithis*. It appears that the period of 95 years was chosen because observationally the excess was taken to be 90 *tithis* or 3 lunar months. Every 95 years a major adjustment of the calendar would then have been required. This also means that the adopted solar year would be 372 - 90/95 = 371.05263 *tithis*. This corresponds to 365.24675 days. This is quite close to the tropical year of 365.24219 days and it is quite possible that such a year was meant.

13. The Astronomical Code

The Rigvedic hymn and the group totals for each book define a set of 20 numbers. Are these numbers accidental or is there a deliberate plan behind the choice? One would expect that if the Rigveda is considered akin to the five-layered altar described in the Brāhmaṇas then the first two books should correspond to the space intermediate to the earth and the sky. Now the number that represents space is 78. When used with the multiplier of 3 for the three worlds, this yields a total of 234 hymns. We find that is indeed the number of hymns in these two books. One may represent the Rigvedic books as a five-layered altar of books as shown in Table 3.

Table 3 : The altar of books

Book 10	Book 9
Book 7	Book 8
Book 5	Book 6
Book 3	Book 4
Book 2	Book 1

Table 4 : Hymns in the altar of books

191	114
104	92
87	75
62	58
43	191

The question arises whether the total hymn count of 1017 and the group count of 216 have any particular significance. Owing to the pervasive tripartite ideology of the Vedic books we choose to view the hymn number as 339×3.The tripartite ideology refers to the consideration of time in three divisions of past, present, and future and the consideration of space in the three divisions of the northern celestial hemisphere, the plane that is at right angle to the earth's axis, and the southern celestial hemisphere[31].

Let us consider whether there is any link between the two numbers 1017 and 216. I argue that another parallel with the representation of the layered altar was at work in the group total of 216. Since the Rigvedic altar of hymns was meant to symbolically take one to the sky, the abode of gods, it is proposed that the number 216 represents twice the basic distance of 108 taken to separate the earth from the sky. The Rigvedic code then expresses a fundamental connection between the numbers 339 and 108.

Consider now the cosmic model used by the ancients. The earth is at the center, and the sun and the moon orbit the earth at different distances. This model is at the basis of the earliest Indian astronomy as well. If the number 108 was taken to represent symbolically the distance between the earth and the sky, the question arises as to why it was done. The answer is apparent if one considers the actual distances of the sun and the moon. The number 108 is roughly the average distance that the sun is in terms of its own diameter from the earth; likewise, it is also the average distance that the moon is in terms of its own diameter from the earth. It is owing to this marvellous coincidence that the angular size of the sun and the moon, viewed from the earth, is about identical.

It is easy to compute this number. The angular measurement of the sun can be obtained quite during an eclipse. The angular measurement of the moon can be made on any clear full moon night. A easy check on this measurement would be to make a person hold a pole at a distance that is exactly 108 times its length and confirm that the angular measurement is the same. Nevertheless, the computation of this number would require careful observations. Furtheremore, 108 is an average and due to the ellipticity of the orbits of the earth and the moon the distances vary with the seasons. It is likely, therefore, that observations did not lead to the precise number 108, but it was chosen as the true value of the distance since it is equal to 27×4, where the mapping of the sky into 27 *nakshatras* has already been described.

The second number 339 is simply the number of disks of the sun or the moon to measure the path across the sky:

$$\pi \times 108 = 339$$

This represents an early approximation to π that takes it equal to 3.1389.

Once 108 was arrived at 339 could be easily calculated. These estimates may have been refined through mutually related measurements. For example, one could count the number of disks of the sun or the moon that would go into an arc of a specified extent. If the relationship between radius and circumference was not known then one would require very refined observation of the number of sun or moon disks.

For further circumstantial evidence supporting such an astronomical interpretation for the numbers 108, 339, and 78, consider that the year of 366 days was divided into two equal parts of 183 days, the *uttarāyaṇa* and the *dakshiṇāyaṇa*, where the *uttarāyaṇa* was taken to belong to the gods. The 339 steps of the sun were now reconciled with the 183 count of the gods by postulating a space count of 78, since 339=183+2×78. This is the same mapping seen in the altar construction of the Śatapatha Brāhmaṇa that has been mentioned earlier.

We may represent the altar arrangement of Tables 3 and 4 by the book sequence

2-1 3-4 5-6 7-8 10-9 *[Altar 1]*

in the five layers counting from bottom up and left to right. The choice of this arrangement was prompted by the considerable regularity in the hymn counts. Thus the hymn count separations diagonally across the two columns are 29 each for Book 4 to Book 5 and Book 6 to Book 7 and they are 17 each for the second column for Book 4 to Book 6 and Book 6 to Book 8. Another regularity is that the middle three layers are indexed by order from left to right whereas the bottom and the top layers are in the opposite sequence.

Furthermore, Books [4+6+8+9] = 339, and these books may be taken to represent the *spine* of the altar. The *underside* of the altar now consists of the Books [2+3+5+7] = 296, and the *feet and the head* Books [1+10] = 382. The numbers 296 and 382 are each 43 removed from the fundamental Rigvedic number of 339.

Now we investigate the other natural choices for comparison. Based on considerations of symmetry, these choices are:

1-2 3-4 5-6 7-8 9-10 *[Altar 2]*

1-2 4-3 5-6 8-7 9-10 *[Altar 3]*

Altar 2 has the books arranged in the same order across the layers, whereas Altar 3 has the books arranged in alternating order across the layers. Altars 2 and 3 yield the following set of numbers for the *underside*, the *spine*, and the *feet* and the *head:*

268 367 382 *[Altar 2]*

284 351 382 *[Altar 3]*

These numbers have no apparent order which leads one to conclude that Altars 2 and 3 were not the actual designs.

We return to a further examination of the numbers 296, 339, and 382 in the design of Altar 1. We propose that since 339 has an obvious significance as the number of sun-steps during the average day or the equinox, the other numbers are likely to have a similar significance. We suggest that 296 is the number of sun-steps during the winter solstice and 382 is the number of sun-steps during the summer solstice. The background to the determination of the solstices in the Vedic times is given by Sengupta[32].

Let us evaluate this proposal. Since the number of sun-steps represent the length of the day, we have a ratio for the longest to the shortest day which is equal to 382/296 = 1.29. We know that the hymns of the Rigveda were composed in the region of the Drishadvatī and the Sarasvatī rivers which flowed in the latitudes of 30° to 22°. If we accept the tradition that Krishṇa Dvaipāyana Vyāsa arranged the hymns into the current form, then again we must accept the same region for his work. Now the question arises whether these facts square up with our interpreatations of the numbers 296 and 382.

The length of the day varies with the latitude. If θ is the latitude of the place of observation and ϕ is the inclination of the earth's axis to its orbit, then the Ratio R, the duration of the longest day divided by the duration of the shortest day, for a spherical earth on a circular orbit and without an atmosphere is given by:

$$R = \frac{\cos(\theta - \phi)}{\cos(\theta + \phi)} \qquad (1)$$

This figure needs correction because of the flattening of the earth and since refraction causes the sun to rise earlier and set later than it would if the earth had no atmosphere. This refraction causes the duration of daylight to be extended by about 6 or 7 minutes at the expense of the duration of darkness. This necessitates a correction of about 2°'s from the value obtained by Eqn (1).

Now consider ϕ, the obliquity of the ecliptic. Although its current value is about 23.5°, it is believed to vary slowly between about 24° and 22°. According to one estimate it changes about 47 seconds in a century. Considering that the settlements on the Sarasvatī were in their golden age in the third millennium B.C.E., a further error of about 1° could have been caused by changing ϕ.

Considering refraction effects one obtains a value of R = 1.2929 for the latitude of 22°. With a further correction for ϕ and noting that it might have been smaller than the current value, this value can be revised to about 23°. The latitude of 23° passes through Gujarat close to where Sarasvatī would have emptied into the sea.

Note that Lagadha in the Vedāṅga Jyotisha speaks of the ratio of the longest to the shortest day being 1.5. After corrections are made this corresponds to a latitude of 34° which is correct for northwest India to the north of the Sarasvatī valleys. Since Vedāṅga Jyotisha was composed after the early Rigvedic age when the focus of the civilization had passed east to the Yamunā-Gaṅgā region and west to upper Indus region, the figure of 34° accords with this sequence.

If one accepts the interpretation of the Rigvedic code sketched above, two further possibilities need to be examined. Was the ratio of 382/296 a precise value reflecting the region where Sarasvatī met the sea or was the value obtained after adjustment made in consonance with a theory?

We speculate that the figure may have been arrived at indirectly in the following fashion. TS 7.2.6. speaks of how the seasons were born of the *Ekādaśarātra* rite. Now the birth of seasons implies a shortening and lengthening of days. For two such rites at the two solstices leaves us with a total of 366-22=344 days. From the winter to the summer solstice this implies a total of 172 days. Since the lengthening was a total of 86 sun-steps, a growth of half a sun-step each day must have been assumed. If this is what happened then the latitude of 23° that we arrived at could only have been a rough value and any of the general region of the Sarasvatī valleys could have been implied. Note also that a linear model of shortening and lengthening of days is assumed in Vedāṅga Jyotisha as well.

To return to the Rigvedic code, it appears that the primary number must have been the figure of 339 from which the other two numbers were derived by substracting and adding 43. The number 339 could have been found through a geometric construction once the distance that the sun is 108 sun diameters away from the earth was agreed upon. Certainly, all these numbers would have been checked through independent measurements.

Note also that the figure of 339 could be measured at day or night by determining the sun or moon-steps over a certain arc. Such a process would have required time-keeping and if water clocks were used then the temperature variation over different parts of the day and night would introduce errors. The progress of time during night could be measured by the *nakshatras* rising in the night sky but again refraction and flattening of the earth would introduce errors.

14. Planetary Periods from the Rigvedic Code

It appears that the Vedic Indians did study the planets but since this knowledge was not of significance in calendrical concerns texts like Vedāṅga Jyotisha had no need to mention this knowledge. On the other hand, in cosmological theory and speculation, as is the concern of the Rigvedic code, information about the planets should show up. With this background we take up the question of planetary astronomy. We will show that there is considerable evidence in the organization of the Rigveda that leads to the conclusion that period information on the planets were known. We will also sketch how the hymn numbers might have been chosen.

The references to the five planets in the Vedic literature are commonly expressed in the mention of the thirty-four lights (RV 10.55.3) which are the twenty-seven *nakshatras*, the sun, the moon, and the five planets. The five planets are apparently mentioned in RV 1.105.10 and *Bṛhaspati* (Jupiter) is referred in RV 4.50.4 and *Vena* (Venus) is mentioned in RV 10.123. It is possible that Venus may also have been known as *Śukra* (RV 3.32.2), as suggested by ŚB 4.2.1. The identification of Vena with Venus has been disputed but it appears to be supported by serveral independent references. The reference to the *sapta sūryāḥ* (seven suns), as in RV 1.105.5 and RV 8.72.16, seems to indicate the sun, the moon, and the five planets.

If we accept that the Rigvedic Indians had carefully observed the planets then it stands to reason that they must have determined their periods. But it is plausible that the knowledge was obtained only at the time of the arrangement of the hymns into the Rigveda. If this were true then the credit for this knowledge should go to Krisṇa Dvaipāyana Vyāsa, who was the arranger according to tradition. Furthermore, in such case references to the planets may not be found in the Rigveda hymns. On the other hand it has been suggested that the correct interpretation of the solar eclipse described in RV 5.40.5-9 is that Atri knew when the eclipse will be over. The fifth book is by Atri and his family and tradition considers him to be one of the teachers of astronomy. Tradition also considers Vyāsa as a great teacher of astronomy. It is likely that he was one in a long chain of astronomer-seers.

If the periods of the five planets were known it is quite likely that they are contained in the Rigvedic astronomical code. The sidereal and the synodic periods are given in days in Table 5.

Table 5: Sidereal and Synodic Periods in Days

Planet	Sidereal Period	Synodic Period
Mercury	87.97	115.88
Venus	224.70	583.92
Mars	686.98	779.94
Jupiter	4332.59	398.88
Saturn	10759.20	378.09

We consider the sidereal periods first. We would expect that the three sidereal periods less than 1017 will be found amongst the combinations. But there is evidence that the approximation of 87 was used for the Mercury period. One reason for it may be that Mercury is very hard to observe. It appears that the synodic period of Mercury was taken to be one third of the year and that 87 is one third of the sky number 261 which played some role in this choice. This latter reason would then stand for modifying observations to fit a theory. Although numerical considerations may have compelled the use of 87 as the period of Mercury we believe that this period was not computed to the same accuracy as others. The sidereal periods can be factored into the components given in Table 6.

Table 6: Sidereal Periods Factored

$87=87\times1$ (Mercury)
$225=58+75+92=75\times3$ (Venus)
$687=191\times3+114\approx43\times16$ (Mars)
$4332=62\times70\approx58\times75$ (Jupiter)
$10760\approx104\times104\approx92\times117$ (Saturn)

Factors from each of these equations show up in the Book hymn numbers. It may be supposed that these factors were the starting points in the construction of the code. Similarly, factors of the year were used in the choice of the number of bricks in different layers of the *agnichayana* altar. It is likely that the specific factors of the sidereal periods were chosen so that other astronomically significant numbers would be obtained. This is why the sidereal periods also show up as number of hymns in Book combinations.

Now consider the synodic periods. One may see that for Mercury, Venus, Mars, Jupiter, and Saturn 23, 5, 8, 9, and 29 synodic periods are completed in nearly 10, 8, 17, 10 and 30 years, respectively. One would expect a new cycle to begin every 2040 years. A different fit is provided by the synodic periods 3, 72, 15, 120 and 30 which would then be completed in 3, 115, 32, 130 and 31 years. The least common multiple of the synodic periods is now 1080. The emphasis on the number 108 that we saw in the altar construction of *agnichayana* indicates that the second fit may have been the one used. This also indicates that the period of Mercury was not represented with the same accuracy as that of the other planets. References of *yugas* of large periods are to be encountered in the earliest Brāhmaṇas.

Table 7: Synodic Periods in Days by Books

Books [3+4] = 120 (Mercury)
Books [1+5+9+10] = 583 (Venus)
Books [1+5+7+8+9+10] = 779 (Mars)
Books [2+3+5+8+9]=398 (Jupiter)
Books [2+4+5+6+9]=377 (Saturn)

Apart from these numbers we also obtain 118, 780 and 379 that provide even better approximations.

Might the fame of the Rigvedic book arrangement have spread by the fact that it also gives the synodic periods in *tithis* especially since the use of the *tithi* (the lunar year divided into 360 parts) seems to have been commonly used in altar ritual ? But how can we be certain that the usage of *tithi* during the Rigvedic phase was similar to its later usage? The Vedāṅga Jyotisha takes a *yuga* of five years to be equal to 1,830 sidereal days or 62 synodic months or 1,860 *tithis*. Much later Varāhamihira takes the *yuga* to contain 1,830 civil days rather than sidereal days. It is clear that the measure of *tithi* could not have been determined by precise measurement but that it was used in relation with the year or several years to check the sun and the moon against the stars. It is because of this reason that it might have been used in more than one sense. Our usage is based on that of a lunar year divided into 360 parts so that a solar day is approximately 1.0159 tithis. This appears to be the earliest and the most commonly used definition of *tithi*. Indirect support for this definition comes from the fact that 1,000 bricks were assigned to the 1.017 sūktas of the Rigveda. If each brick also symbolized a solar day, this corresponds almost exactly with the definition of the *tithi*.

To consider the parallel with the representation of the tropical year by 371 or 372 *tithis* although the correct value is close to 371.05 *tithis* one would expect that the *tithis* for each synodic period would be rounded to the next higher number if the fractional part is significant. The synodic periods in *tithis* are 117.72, 593.20, 792.34, 405.22, and 384.10, respectively. For Saturn one would expect both 384 and 385 to be used. In other words, the periods would be taken to be 118, 594, 793, 406 for Mercury, Venus, Mars, and Jupiter and 384 for Saturn. All of these numbers also show up in the combinations.

15. Probabilistic Validation

To summarize, there are several independent arguments that suggest that the planet period information went into the definition of the code. These include the fact that the hymn totals of the books are the factors of the sidereal periods of the planets and that the sums of these numbers yield the sidereal periods. Although the combinations are very many, it is important to note that the combinations of very few terms yield astronomically significant numbers. One would expect that the Rigvedic astronomers did not attempt all the combinations but checked if the numbers of significance did show up. The fact that this happened was proof to these astronomers that the code expressed significant relationships (*bandhu*) between diverse phenomena.

Support for this argument is obtained by considering all the combinations of the numbers of hymns in the *Ashṭaka* division of the Rigveda. The number of unique combinations generated equals 179. These do not include any of the sidereal periods and only two of the five synodic periods in *tithis*, and the significant sun-step number of 339 is also not generated. In other words, these combinations contain very few of the astronomically significant numbers that the combinations of the Book hymn numbers have yielded.

From a probabilistic point of view it is to be expected that the 179 *Ashṭaka* numbers out of 1017 would give two fits out of randomly chosen ten numbers which is what we obtain. On the other hand, the 451 Book (*Maṇḍala*) numbers should give correct choices only in half the cases. But we get the hymn numbers that are factors of the sidereal periods, and we get combinations for the three sidereal periods, five synodic periods in days as well as the five synodic periods in *tithis*..

Let the probability of picking a correct number be p. Considering a random model of choice, in a sample of n expected number of correct picks is μ=np and the variance is $\sigma^2=np(1-p)$. A sample of twenty three numbers, as in our case, implies that m=11 and σ=2.39. And that all the twentythree numbers are correct implies that we are five standard deviations away from the mean. The probability of that happening is 2.87×10^{-7}.

Now one might argue that only ten of the twentythree numbers must be considered to be primary and that the comparison should be based on the sample size being equal to ten. In this case μ=4.5 and σ=1.58 so that the probability of obtaining ten significant random numbers in a sample of ten is 2.33×10^{-4}. These probabilities are so small that the claim that the Book numbers were deliberately chosen may be taken to be confirmed.

Our analysis shows that the Rigvedic astronomers knew the planetary periods. It appears that the hymn numbers were chosen so as to reflect the periods as well as the constraints of the sun-steps during the equinox and the solstices. The fact that many other astronomical numbers were produced by the code must have contributed to the significance attached to the arrangement of the hymns made by Vyāsa.

Corroboration for the conclusion that the Vedic world knew the planetary periods may be sought in the artifacts and astronomical designs from the Harappan ruins, since that civilization is now increasingly viewed as being Vedic. It also becomes reasonable to re-examine the Vedic literature for further knowledge about the planet motions.

16. Conclusions

The Brāhmaṇas speak of ritual that parallels the passage of the year. Monthly rites like the *darśapūrṇamāsa* and seasonal rites like *chaturmāsya* required careful observation of the movements of the sun and the moon across months. Such rites necessitated the definition of the *tithi*, the division of the lunar year into 360 parts. A specific session called *gavāmayana* was for the daily observation for the movements of the sun and the disappearance of the moon. No wonder astronomy as *jyotisha* was one of the fundamental sciences of the Vedic times.

In historical times too one sees importance accorded to time measurements. Arthaśāstra of Kauṭilya describes in the twentieth chapter of the second book the duties of the *mānādhyakṣa,* or the Superientendent of Measurements, among which is the duty of timekeeping. Time was measured by the gnomon and the water-clock.

The equivalences by number were at the basis of the altar as the year. This allows us to obtain considerable knowledge about the astronomy of the Ṛigveda and the Śatapatha Brāhmaṇa. We find a 95 year cycle as a part of the *agnichayana* ritual. The areas of the fire altars correspond to the broad astronomical facts about the year. The fact that the altar increases by one unit area in each new construction indicates the intercalation that is necessary to bring the *nakshatra* year in line with the solar year. This increase goes on until the ninetyfifth year when an additional correction would have been made to remove this error. The details of the altar design represent, in code, astronomical facts; we have sketched broad aspects of this code but the details of its are yet to be deciphered.

In other words, we find that the main elements of the astronomy of Vedāṅga Jyotisha are already contained in Śatapatha Brāhmaṇa and earlier books. Specifically, we find clear references to the nominal year of 372 *tithis,* the *nakshatra* year of 324 *tithis*, and a solar year of 371 *tithis.* The choice of 371 *tithis* for the solar year corresponds to 365.1949 days. But the fact that a further correction was required in 95 years indicates that these figures were in themselves considered to be approximate. Assuming intercalation at the end of the 95 year Yajnavalkya period we conclude the duration of the year was taken to be 365.24675 days which is quite close to the tropical year. In view of the above facts the dating of second millennium for the Vedāṅga Jyotisha is not inconsistent with a conservative dating of 2nd millennium B.C.E. for Śatapatha Brāhmaṇa. Of course, Śatapatha Brāhmaṇa does not speak of any details of motions of planets, but that is not surprising considering that its main purpose is ritual.

There was a clear conception of the great *yuga* during the age of the Brāhmaṇas. The existence at the same time of the notion of the primal person being made out of 7 1/2 *purushas.* When a *purusha* is also equated with 360 years leading to a longer cycle of 2700 years, suggests that the Saptarshi era was known then. The nominal size of the Rigveda being considered to be 4,320,000 syllables also suggests a theory of a much larger *yuga* of that extent in years since the Rigveda was considered to represent the universe symbolically.

One may theorize that the planetary periods were determined at the end of the Rigvedic age and incorporated in the code. If this was the case then the credit for the discovery of these periods should be assigned to Krishṇa Dvaipāyana Vyāsa. It is possible that after the determination of these periods the knowledge became widespread and its significance in the organization of the Rigveda was forgotten.

It was suggested by van der Waerden[33] that a primitive epicycle theory was known to the Greeks by the time of Plato. He argued such a theory might have been known in the wider Indo-European world by early first millennium B.C.E. which led to the development of very different epicycle models in Greece and India.

The existence of an independent tradition of observation of planets and a theory thereof as suggested by our analysis of the Rigvedic code helps explain the puzzle why the classical Indian astronomy of the Siddhānta period uses many constants that are different from that of the Greeks. This confirms the thesis that although Siddhāntic astronomy from the time of Āryabhaṭṭa developed in full knowledge of Greek methods, the reason why it retained its characteristic form was because it was based on an independent, old tradition.

Analysis of the Siddhāntic and the practical *karaṇa* texts by Billard[34] provides still further support for this conclusion. These texts provide a set of elements from which the planetary positions for future times can be computed. The first step in these computations is the determination of the mean longitudes which are assumed to be linear functions of time. Three more functions, the vernal equinox, the lunar mode and the lunar apogee, are also defined. Billard investigated these linear functions for the five planets, two for the sun (including the vernal equinox) and three for the moon. He checked these calculations against the values derived from modern theory and he found that the texts provide very accurate values for the epochs when they were written. Since the Siddhānta and the *karaṇa* models are not accurate, beyond these epochs deviations build up. In other words, Billard refuted the theory that there was no tradition of observational astronomy in India.

Our work also implies that the belief that observational astronomy began in Babylon during the middle of the first millennium B.C. is no longer supported by facts. The fact that the earliest Vedic ritual was astronomical is attested by textual references within the Rigveda and this provides further support to our analysis of the Rigvedic hymn numbers.

It is generally accepted that the references to the Vedic gods Mitra, Varuṇa, Indra and the Nāsatyas in the Hittite-Mitanni treaty of the second millennium B.C.E. refers to the Indo-Aryan rather than the Iranians. It appears that the Indic element was intrusive into South-western Asia starting about the beginning of the second millennium. If this intrusion was triggered by the collapse of the Harappan economy caused by the desiccation of the Sarasvatī river around 1900 B.C.E. then one can see how this intrusion would have been accompanied by a transmission of the astronomy of the fire altars and the planetary period values of the Rigveda.

The continuing interaction in subsequent centuries is mirrored in certain interesting parallels between Indian and Babylonian astronomies. We have mentioned that the ratio of longest to shortest daylight changes from 1.29 to 1.5 as the focus of Vedic astronomy shifts from Sarasvatī valleys to north-west India. The latter value is to be found in Vedāṅga Jyotisha of the latter half of the second millennium. One finds the same ratio of 1.5 in the Babylonian texts of the first millennium, although the earliest Babylonian texts spoke of a ratio of 2.0. The other significant parallel that exists is that the Babylonian texts use a linear zig-zag function to determine the length of daylight in intermediate months which we have found is already present in the Rigvedic model. One might speculate that the Vedic astronomy was taken over by the Babylonians and it was built upon further during the flowering that took place there starting around 700 B.C.E. If a primitive epicycle theory was also communicated then one can see the parallels between the Greek and the Indian epicycle theories as a result of a transmission of ideas.

The recognition of the central role of astronomy in the Vedic world view has great significance for the interpretation of the Vedic literature. In particular, many Rigvedic hymns turn out to have allusions to astronomical phenomena. Also many hymns, hitherto considered paradoxical or unclear, can be understood within an astronomical framework.

Our recognition of the code is also of importance for another reason. The astronomical references in the Vedic literature cannot be brushed aside any longer. There references can be helpful in constructing a chronology of the Vedic era.

Abbreviations for Vedic and Purāṇic Texts

AA	Aitreya Āraṇyaka
AB	Aitreya Brāhmaṇa
AV	Artharvaveda
ASS	Āpastamba Śulbasūtra
BSS	Baudhāyana Śulbasūtra
BU	Bṛhadāraṇyaka Upanishad
MP	Matsya Purāṇa
RV	Rigveda
ŚB	Śatapatha Brāhmaṇa
TB	Taittirīya Brāhmaṇa
TS	Taittirīya Saṃhitā
VJ	Vedāṅga Jyotisha
VP	Vāyu Purāṇa

REFERENCES

1. Raster, P. 1992. *Phonetic Symmetries in the First Hymn of the Rigveda.* Innsbruck : Innsbrucker Beiträge Zur Sprachwissenschaft.
2. *Ibid,* p. 9.
3. Baudhāyana Śulbasūtra, 7.17; Āpastamaba Śulbasūtra, 14. 11.
4. Dandekar, R.N. (ed.) 1958. *Śrautakośa,* Vaidika Saṁśodhana Maṇḍala, Poona.
5. Heesterman, J.C. 1957. *The Ancient Indian Royal Consecration.* Mouton, Ś. Gravenhage.
6. Kak, S.C. 1992b. Astronomy of the Vedic altars and the Ṛgveda. *Mankind Quarterly,* 33, pp. 43-55.

   1993a. Astronomy in the Śatapatha Brāhmaṇa. *Indian Journal of History of Science,* 28, pp. 15.34.

   1993b. Astronomy of the Vedic Altars. *Vistas in Astronomy,* 36, pp. 117-140.

   1993c. Planetary Periods from the Rigvedic code. *Mankind Quarterly,* 33, pp. 396-407.

   1993d. The Structure of the Ṛgveda. *Indian Journal of History of Science,* 28, pp. 71-79.

   1993e. The Verse Structure of the Vedas. *LSU Report,* June 8.
7. Roy, S.B. 1975. *Ancient India: A Chronological Study.* Delhi; Sengupta, P.C. 1938b. *Solstice days in Vedic literature. Jr. Royal Society of Bengal Letters,* 4. pp. 415-434; Shamasastry, R. 1938. *Drapsa: The Vedic Cycle of Eclipses.* Mysore; Tilak, B.G. 1893. *Orion on Researches in the Antiquity of the Vedas,* Poona; rep. Pune, 1989.
8. Kak, S.C. 1992a. The Indus Tradition and the Indo-Aryans. *Mankind Quarterly,* 32, pp. 195-213.
9. Frankfort, H.P. 1992. Evidence for Harappan Irrigation System in Haryana and Rajasthan. *Eastern Anthropologist,* 45, pp. 87-103.
10. Kak, S.C. 1993e. The Verse Structure of the Vedas. *LSU Report,* June 8.
11. Bṛhad devatā 1. 122-131.
12. Frawley, D. 1991. *Gods, Sages and Kings.* Passage Press, Salt Lake City.
13. Gonda, J. 1975. *Vedic Literature.* Otto Harrassowitz Wiesbaden.

    1984. *Prajāpati and the Year.* North-Holland. Amsterdam.
14. Staal, F. 1989. *Rules Without Meaning.* Peter Lang, New York.
15. Dumézil, G. 1973. *The Destiny of a King.* The University of Chicago Press, Chicago.

    — 1988. *Mitra-Varuṇa.* Zone Books, New York.
16. Sarasvati, S.P. and Vidyalankar, S. 1987. *Ṛgveda Saṁhitā.* New Delhi: Veda Pratishthana.
17. Raster, P. 1992. *op. cit.*
18. Macdonell, A.A. 1886. *Kātyāyana's Sarvānukramaṇī of the Rigveda.* Oxford : Clarendon Press.
19. Kak, S.C. 1992bb/. *op. cit.*
20. Macdonell, A.A. 1886. *op. cit.*
21. Kak, S.C. 1992b. *op. cit.*
22. Tilak, B.G. 1893. *op. cit.,* and Kramrisch, S. 1981. *The Presence of Śiva.* Princeton University Press.
23. Kuiper, F.B.J. 1983. *Ancient Indian Cosmogony.* Vikas Publishing House, Delhi.
24. Santillana, G. de and Dechend, H. von 1969. *Hamlet's Mill, An essay on Myth and the frame of time.* Gambbit, Boston.
25. Mitchiner, John E. 1982. *Tradition of the Seven Ṛṣis.* Motilal Banarsidas, Delhi
26. Cunningham, A. 1883. *Book of Indian Eras* , Calcutta; rep. Delhi 1971.
27. Sengupta, P.C. 1938b. Solstice days in Vedic Literature. *Jr. Royal Society Bengal, letters,* 4, pp. 415-434.
28. Matsya Puraṇa, 142-12.
29. Śatapatha Brāhmaṇa. 10.2.4.4.
30. Seidenberg, A. 1978. The Origin of Mathematics. *Archive for History of Exact Sciences,* 18, pp. 301-342.

    1983. The Geometry of the Vedic Rituals. In *Agni,* Frits Staal (ed.), Vol. 2, 95-126.
31. Santillana, G. de and Dechend, H. von, 1969. *Hamlet's Mill, An essay on Myth and the Fame of Time.* Gambit, Boston.
32. Sengupta, P.C. 1938b. *op. cit.*
33. Waerden, B.L. van der 1974. The Earliest Form of the Epicycle Theory. *Jr. for* the History of *Astronomy,* 5, pp. 175-185.
34. Billard, R. 1971. *L'astronomie Indienne.* Paris.

Fifty Years of Epigraphical Studies in India: A Brief Survey

AJAY MITRA SHASTRI*

By the close of 2nd World War substantial progress had already been recorded in various branches of Indian epigraphy. The two most important ancient Indian scripts, viz. Brāhmī and Kharoshṭhī (or better Kharoshṭī), had already been deciphered long back. Literally thousands of inscriptions written in various languages and scripts engraved on a variety of objects and hailing from different parts of the Indian subcontinent had been published or noticed, and their unimpeachable value for historical reconstruction, especially in respect of the ancient period, was well-recognised and their invaluable evidence was already being exploited in a big way in historical writings, primarily on dynastic history. Attempts had already been made to identify the eras, named or unnamed, employed in epigraphs with a view to determine dates and their origins discussed thoroughly. The decipherment of the so-called Indus script was also attempted though without any proven success. Epigraphical studies, mainly publication of inscriptions, were primarily conducted in the Epigraphy Branch of the Archaeological Survey of India with semi-official organisations like the Asiatic Society, supplementing the official efforts. The usefulness of properly edited collections of inscriptions arranged dynastically or on some other considerations which linked them was realised and the well-known series called *Corpus Inscriptionum Indicarum* had been initiated long back, and a few, three to be exact, volumes have been published.

The year 1947, however, coincided with the tragic partition of India resulting into the separation of its north-western and eastern regions which were first included in the newly carved nation of Pakistan which had the unique distinction of being the only state comprising two wings separated from each other by over a thousand kms. The eastern wing separated from it about twenty three years later, in 1971, to form what is now known as Bangladesh.

I. SCRIPTS

1. Harappan or Indus-Saraswati Script

Ever since the discovery of the Indus Valley (more appropriately Indus-Sarasvati or Harappan) Civilization in 1921 it was known that the people inhabiting the settlements of this civilization were literate with so many inscribed seals and sealings, pottery and other objects found at the sites in course of archaeological work and otherwise. And the problem of decoding their writing has been haunting the archaeologists since then. At the time of India gaining independence all the sites of this civilization in the Uttarāpatha region of undivided India found a place in Pakistan, but the Herculean efforts of Indian archaeologists resulted in the discovery of hundreds of such centres in the Indian Punjab, Haryana, western part of Uttar Pradesh, Rajasthan and Gujarat some of which have also yielded inscribed objects.[1] The attempts at the decipherment of this script have continued unabated, without much palpable success though. And the two main strands which were in evidence earlier, viz. Dravidian or proto-Dravidian and Indo-European linguistically, remained prominent and per-

*23, Vidya Vihar, Rana Pratap Nagar, Nagpur

haps the only planks during our period.[2] We may also notice that the interest in this activity was no longer confined to archaeologists and professionals and is naturally much more in evidence with a number of scholars (and even non-scholars) of all shreds participating. The limitations of space forbid even a casual allusion to all of them, and our attempt here will be confined to a few more prominent and trend-setting ones, and that too in brief. Father H. Heras (1953) tried to read the script and felt that it was logographic and in what he called proto-Dravidian language. However, his views have not been taken seriously, obviously because of apparent flaws, inconsistencies and wild assumptions and readings. But the theory of the inscriptions being composed in Dravidian or proto-Dravidian language had several supporters even though they did not agree with Heras in other respects. In 1969 and onwards a Russian team led by Y.V. Knorozov and comprising, besides him, G.V. Alekseev, I.K. Fedorova, A.M. Kondratov, M.A. Probst, V.Y. Volchok, N.V. Gurov and M.F. Albedil made, for the first time, a careful use of computer as a tool in the decipherment of this script which, as will be noticed in the sequel, became a prominent feature of several attempts in this field. They preferred to call it proto-Indian and concluded that there were some 350 basic signs and that their language was closest to the Dravidian in grammatical structure.

About the same time a Finnish team consisting of Asko Parpola, Penti Aalto, Simo Parpola and Seppo Koskenniemi employing the same technics, arrived at the conclusion that the script was logographic, viz. each sign representing a word, to be read on the principle of homophony. They worked out some 300 basic signs and took the script to be proto-Dravidian closely following their assumption that the Harappan culture was Dravidian in nature.[3] Iravatham Mahadevan for the first time laid his trap wide enough to analyse as many as 2469 Harappan inscriptions, employing computer technics for calculations in a big way and recognised some 400 signs, some of them logographic; and felt that the language may have been Dravidian though not proven.[4] His well-propounded views appear to have found favour with Kamil V. Zvelebil who dismissed all the other views as unscientific.[5] Walter A. Fairservis Jr., who excavated the Harappan site of Allahdino, some 25 miles northeast of Karāchi (Sind, Pakistan) for several seasons, though without much linguistic background and equipment, also dabbled with the Harappan script and favoured the Dravidian language hypothesis with some 419 ideographic signs of which about 200 were more in general use. He also ventured the suggestion that the direction of writing in this script was from left to right[6] as against the almost universally held view that it was written generally from right to left and the next line was sometimes written from left to right in boustrophedon style.[7] His views have not been taken seriously for obvious reasons. Mathematical and computer technics were employed by some scholars for segmenting unusually long Harappan records. These scholars are Gift Siromoney and Abdul Haq of the Madras Christian College.[8]

Another school of scholars led by the indefatiguable S.R. Rao is inclined to hold that the Harappan script is linguistically connected with the so-called Indo-European or Indo-Aryan. After carefully examining about 2500 inscriptions Rao concluded that the (Mature) Harappan script had forty linear signs, including twenty-one homomorphs for as many sounds. They were reduced gradually to twenty two basic signs in the Late Harappan script. He used the stratigragphic evidence of the Rangpur and Lothal excavations[9] to trace the gradual development of the Harappan script. He concluded that the early Harappan script employed most pictures syllabically and a few logographically along with linear signs with a single-sound value. There are a few instances of the use of vowel-less consonantal signs also though generally the vowel-values were indicated. Gradually, pictures and syllabic formation of linear signs were dropped retaining, however, the conjunct consonants so that the writing could be alphabetic using only linear signs even for difficult expressions like *tra* and *sva* which were earlier indicated by syllabic pictures. There were signs for numerals too. Linguistically, the script represented the pre-Old Indo-Aryan. The Semitic people appear to have borrowed these linear signs from the Harappan which apparently provided a model for them.[10] J.E. Mitchiner in 1978 lent support to Rao's theory that the language belonged to the Indo-Aryan family and that the script was phonetic, the differences in some matters of detail naturalistic notwithstanding[11].

It would be obvious to anyone from the foregoing account of the attempts of and varying results arrived at by different scholars who have assigned different values to the same signs that the script still continues to remain a mystery and that the efforts have to continue. We may, however, point out that some important finds have added new dimensions to the problem. The discovery of an inscribed votive jar in Late Harappan levels in course of marine operations at Bet Dvārakā in Gujarat constitutes an epoch-making event in as much as of the seven letters of the inscription the first three appears to resemble or are identical with the Brāhmī letters *ma, ja* and *gha* when read from the right,[12] thereby furnishing an hitherto missing link between the two scripts. Another such recent most find is an inscription consisting of nine letters from the western chamber of the northern gate at Dholavīrā in Kutch. Each letter is about 37 cm in height and 25 to 27 cm in width and composed of carefully cut pieces of a crystalline material, may be rock, mineral or paste, and made of several pieces. According to R.S. Bisht, who conducted the excavation and recovered this inscription, the faint traces seen on the upper side of the letters tend to suggest that they were engraved on a wooden board which was probably positioned over the head of the supremo. As said by V.N. Misra, it was indeed the discovery of the decade in so far as the Harappan script is concerned.[13]

Of late, several scholars have identified visual representations of some Ṛigvedic rituals, pantheons and mythology in the scenes depicted on the seals and sealings found at several Indus-Sarasvati or Harappan sites.[14] This would most probably indicate the Vedic affiliation of the Harappan civilization and script. And, as we have seen above, the Indus-Sarasvati script may not have been entirely unrelated to the later Brāhmī script though it has yet to be proven.

2. Brāhmī Script

Even though David Diringer[15] and Ahmad Hasan Dani[16] reiterated the view of some of the occidental scholars that Brāhmī was based on, if not actually derived from, the North Semitic script, it is now generally agreed that it was an invention of the Indian genius.[17] However, as regards the date and the manner of invention, there exists a wide divergence of opinion. Gift Siromoney and Michael Lockwood proposed in 1977 to credit the Maurya emperor Asoka with the invention of Brāhmī from certain geometric signs to meet the necessities of his time[18], closely followed by S.R Goyal who held that the antiquity of Brāhmī[19] does not go prior to the early Maurya period, in fact earlier than the reign of Asoka.[20] This view is shared by, *inter alia*, R. Nagaswamy and S.P. Gupta[21]. All of them feel that Asoka realised the urgent need of the script for propagating his Dhamma and Buddhism and met this necessity by inventing Brāhmī. However, we are strongly opposed to this theory as it goes against all the evidence and point out in our support that had the script been brought into existence by Asoka he would have used this alone in all his edicts and no other scripts like the Aramaic, Greek and Kharoshṭhī (or Kharoshṭī) and in that case it would not have been christened Brāhmī.[22] Moreover, if Asoka just wanted to have a script and not to invent it himself, he would have adopted any script already existing and used by him in the north-western part of his empire as that would have served his purpose well. The fact actually was that Asoka got his edicts engraved in whatever scripts were already current in the different parts of his dominions and did not invent any; moreover, had he inaugurated a new script, he would have mentioned it explicity in at least some of his numerous records, as he has claimed in so many other cases. Our line of argument has found favour with M.C. Joshi.[23] Added to it, the recent find of an inscribed votive jar at the Harappan site of Bet Dvārakā, as pointed out above, perhaps marks the relationship between the Harappan and Brāhmī scripts, and the evolution (or invention) of Brāhmī over a millennium before Asoka the great.

In the period in question the works of Diringer, Dani and R.B. Pandey[24] dwelt upon the origin of Brāhmī in a general manner along with other epigraphical problems. In addition to these general books some specialised treatises on different phases of the script have been published. These include C.S. Upasak's *History and Palaeography of the Mauryan Brāhmī Script*[25] and T.P. Verma's *Palaeography of Brāhmī Script in North India*.[26] Several scholars including S.R. Goyal, K.V. Soundararajan, K.G. Krishnan, Lallanji Gopal, R. Nagaswamy, S. Sankaranarayanan, myself, T.P. Verma, M.C. Joshi, K.S. Ramachandran and S.P. Gupta contributed to what may be called the postal seminar on the *Origin of Brāhmī Script* organised by S.P. Gupta and K.S. Ramachandran. In addition there are numerous interesting papers on various aspects of this script scattered in a number of occasional publications.

3. Kharoshṭhī (or Kharoshṭī)

Kharoshṭhī or Kharoshṭī, which was, generally speaking, in use almost exclusively in undivided north-west

India and Indian Punjab and Haryana with spill over in the adjoining region of Mathurā, is almost unanimously regarded as derived from the Aramaic script of Iran adjusted to Indian requirements.[27] It has received but scant attention in India, and the only Indian scholar who has contributed utmost is B.N. Mukherjee. He has pointed out that the correct spelling of the name of the script as found in the *Mahāvastu* is Kharoshṭī, not Kharoshṭhī as the name is commonly spelt[28] and brought to light the evidence of the employment of long vowel sign in a Kharoshṭī inscription found in Gandhāra and assignable to about 1st-2nd century AD.[29] He has prepared a descriptive catalogue of Central Asian inscriptions in the National Museum, New Delhi, which is still awaiting publication and is busy doing a volume on Kharoshṭī inscriptions for the *Corpus Inscriptionum Indicarum* series. Of greatest importance is the discovery of numerous Kharoshṭī graffiti referring, among others, to Śaka and Kushāṇa rulers from Chilas, Hunza and Alam Bridge in Pak-occupied Kashmir and their publication by A.H. Dani.[30] The reason for the utter lack of interest in Kharoshṭī inscriptions among majority of Indian epigraphists is the lack of opportunity to handle them. Among foreign scholars who have been active in the field of Kharoshṭī epigraphy we may refer to A.H. Dani, E.W. Bailey, G. Fussman and G.V. Mitterwalner. The sole work on the Kharoshṭī palaeography published during the period is *The Development of Kharoshṭhī* by C.C. Das Gupta,[31] while others like Raj Bali Pandey and A.H. Dani have dealt with the subject in their general palaeographical works referred to above. After carefully considering the structure and formation of the alphabets of Brāhmī and Kharoshṭī the present author in his Presidential Address of the 14th Annual Conference of the Epigraphical Society of India held at Guwahati on 8–10th Dec., 1987, suggested that reforms in the Brāhmī-based modern scripts can derive inspiration from these two scripts and by eliminating letters for aspirated sounds (*kh, gh, chh, jh, ṭh, ḍh, th, dh, ph* and *bh*) and by indicating the aspiration by one common mark and dropping the separate letters for the vowels *i, u,* and *e* and using instead, the letter *a* with the respective medial (*mātrā*) signs attached to it the number of letter-signs of these scripts can be reduced at least by thirteen, thereby making the learning process much easier and also resulting in the reduction of letter-keys in the typewriters and printing machines.[32] Though about seven years have since elapsed and the suggestion being tradition-based would certainly be better than the arbitrary ones, no attention has yet been paid to it.

4. Mixed Script

A very important, in fact epoch making, discovery of recent years has been the find of a number of rather short inscriptions in Kharoshṭī and in a mixture of this script with Brāhmī (Kharoshṭī–Brāhmī) in areas not known to have employed Kharoshṭī. Such mixed inscriptions have been found in a fairly large number from eastern Indian states of Bihar and Bengal, Bangladesh and in south-east Asian countries which had close contacts with India.These inscriptions throw a flood of light on various aspects of the life of the people in these areas and on the commercial, agricultural and craft activities of a section of the people who were originally residing in the north-west but in later times migrated to other areas in search of bread and butter carrying with them the traditions of their original home including Kharoshṭī which they used in their newly adopted homes and also used it along side Brāhmī, which was the script of these areas, giving rise to what may be called Brāhmī–Kharoshṭī or Kharoshṭī–Brāhmī depending upon the desired stress. B.N. Mukherjee, who has pioneered this branch of study, believes that this is the *Vimisrita-lipi* mentioned in the list of scripts in the Buddhist work *Lalitavistara* (Chapter I).[33]

5. Tamil-Brāhmī

In the southern part of Tamilnadu have been found numerous inscriptions in a script that was found to be enigmatic by earlier scholars. In recent years quite a lot of work has been done in this field, and Iravatham Mahadevan, who has done pioneering research in this discipline, feels that around third-second century B.C. some Jaina monks immigrated to these places from Madhyadesa and brought with them the Brāhmī script which they adapted for writing Tamil by introducing a few signs to express typical Tamil sounds. He has also brought together all the then (1966) known inscriptions in what he named as Tamil-Brāhmī script in a *Corpus of Tamil-Brāhmī Inscriptions*[34] and proposed to date them to post-Asoka period. Some scholars, including K.V. Ramesh, however, differ from this view and are inclined to date at least a few of these records to a pre-Asokan date.[35] M.D. Sampath prefers to call this script Tamil Cave Brāhmī.[36] The ancient name of this script might have been probably Draviḍa–lipi or Dakshiṇa-*lipi* which are two of the sixty four scripts listed in the Buddhist work *Lalita-vistara* which refers to them as studied by Gautama Buddha.[37] Much work about this script is in evidence in Tamilnadu these days, and let us hope the mystery about its origin and evolution will be unravelled shortly.

6. Shell-Script (Śaṅkha-lipi)

The script is so-called because its letters bear a close resemblance in shape to a conch shell or *śaṅkha.* But such a script is not mentioned in the *Lalita-vistara* of the early centuries AD though it gives a list of as many as sixty four scripts which include all possible varieties and sub-varieties and it would be surprising if this script, which had come into existence then, were not to be included in it. On the other hand we have a script called Chakralipi at no. 34 in this list which, to us, appears to refer to the so-called Śaṅkha-lipi.[38] The shapes of the letters in this script look like whorls which could easily be described as *chakra.* The inscriptions in this script or style of writing, i.e., calligraphy, have been known for over a century and a half now, but the decipherment has been baffling scholars, and no serious effort seems to have been made. The first serious attempt in this direction was that of Richard Saloman in the seventies of this century (1976-77) and the results of this work were published in a book form in 1980[39] preceded and followed by a few papers.[40] But not much success was achieved. It was B.N. Mukherjee, under whose supervision Saloman had worked and who was in consequence familiar with general problems of the script, who ultimately succeeded in unravelling the mystery hitherto shrouding it. As luck made it, in 1983 he was able to decipher an inscription in this script engraved on the long known stone horse preserved in the State Museum, Lucknow, as *Śrī–Mahendrāditya*[41] followed by the decipherment of a number of other records in this script which gave him a key to its understanding. The script, which represents an highly ornamented and mysticised form of Brāhmī and is employed for writing only short, perhaps esoteric, records, was, generally speaking, in vogue during the first millennium A.D. There has been in evidence a lot of activity regarding this script in recent years, and a seminar was held at Rani Durgavati Vishvavidyalaya, Jabalpur, in March 1988[41a]. The Archaeological Survey of India agreed a few years back to take up the documentation of inscriptions in Shell characters. Let us hope it takes off.

7. Rājarājeśvarī– or Bānswārā–lipi

Mahārāwal Lakshmanasingh of Bānswārā in Rajasthan (A.D. 1843-1905) minted coins sometime around AD 1870 in gold, silver and copper known respectively as Lakshmaṇasāh *muhr, rupiā* and *paisā,* which bore an identical marginal legend on both sides in a script which had baffled well-known scholars, including Gaurishankar Hirachand Ojha and Karunashankar in their efforts at its decipherment. S.K. Bhatt and Narendra Kothari brought to light a bilingual inscription which enabled Chandrashekar Gupta to finally decipher it.[42] His promised monograph on this script is eagerly awaited.

Before we conclude our account of important strides taken in the decipherment of and understanding the above scripts, we may, *en passim,* mention a few important works published during the period on these and other scripts. These include, *inter alia,* C. Sivaramamurti's *Indian Epigraphy and South Indian Scripts,*[43] T.V. Mahalingam's *Early South Indian Palaeography,*[44] Shobhana Gokhale's *Indian Numerals,*[45] O.P.L. Srivastava's Hindi work on Brāhmī and Nāgarī numerals and A.K. Singh's *Development of Nāgarī Script.*[46]

II. ERAS

The eras are of inestimable value in fixing chronology and even exact dates in a state of total uncertainty as in early India. As we have already stated, most of the eras used in inscriptions had already been noticed and their epochs fixed. However, we have got enlightened more about a few of the eras. Let us take note of the latest position in respect of these eras.

1. Vikrama Era

Though it was ascertained that its epoch lay in 57 BC, there was a difference of opinion as to the event commemorated by it. Most of the scholars were of the view that the reckoning was started by or began from the accession of the Śaka-Pahlava king Azes or Vonones. In recent years the case of Vonones has been supported by D.C. Sircar[47] and Azes has found a strong advocate in B.N. Mukherjee.[48] The position that the era was of indigenous origin which was supported on vague grounds by some other earlier scholars[49], has been almost established by the present author recently.[50]

2. Śaka Era

Commencing in AD 78, the era is commonly believed by several western and most of the Indian historians to commemorate the accession of the Kushāṇa emperor Kanishka even though most of the occidental and a few Indian scholars are inclined to date this event sometime in the second century AD.[51] They explain the phenomenon of the era being called Śaka on the assumption of its long use by the Śaka Kshatrapas of Western India who are supposed to have been Kushāṇa vassals. However, we have demonstrated that there is absolutely nothing to support this assumption and that the era was really counted from or was established by Chashṭana to mark his accession.[52] There is no denying the existence of an earlier era commencing about 170 BC which has been called by some 'Older Śaka Era'.[53]

3. Kalachūri–Chedi Era

After a careful consideration of all the known dates of this era in inscriptions V.V. Mirashi concluded that the era actually commenced originally on the first day of the bright half of Kārttika, corresponding to 25th September in AD 249, though later the Kalachuris erroneously took it to be the expired year and consequently the beginning of the era came to be antedated by one year, viz. on the first day (*tithi*) of the bright half (6th October) of the month of Kārttika according to the *pūrṇimānta* system in AD 248.[54] That this conclusion has not yet been challenged by any authority by itself is a clear evidence of its finality.

4. Gaṅga Era

There was a long drawn controversy regarding the epoch of the Gaṅga or Gāṅgeya era which is found employed in a large number of inscriptions of the Imperial Gaṅgas and their vassals in the Ganjām district of Orissa and the Vishākhapatṇam and Śrīkākulam districts of Andhra Pradesh with historians proposing various dates or periods for its beginning basing on the data available to them. Subsequently, taking all the data into account Mirashi concluded that its correct epoch was the first day of the bright fortnight of Chaitra in the expired Śaka year 420, corresponding to 14th March, 498.[55] It is, however, difficult to agree with his conjecture which links the foundation of the Gaṅga dynasty and era with the conquest of Kaliṅga by Harisheṇa, the last known king of the Vatsagulma branch of the Vākāṭakas, about the close of the fifth century AD,[56] for there is nothing to support it except the hyperbolic description of his *digvijaya* in a record of his minister Varāhadeva of Ajantā (Cave 16) which just includes Kaliṅga in the list of the territories conquered by him.[57]

5. Bhauma–Kara Era

The inscriptions of the Bhauma-Karas of Orissa employ for dating an era which is commonly referred to as Bhauma–Kara era. However, about its epoch there has been some debate. D.C. Sircar proposed, basing on his reconstruction of the historical framework of the Karas vis-a-vis their Somavaṁśin neighbours as well as some astronomical details found in the Dāspallā grant of the Bhañja chief Śatrubhañja *alias* Tribhuvanakalaśa, AD 831 as the year when this era began. But S.N. Rajaguru has shown that the details of the date in the Dāspalla grant support its beginning in AD 736 as well which has the added advantage of being in conformity with what we now know of the Somavaṁśin and Kara history. We are in general agreement with Rajaguru, for, as we have shown elsewhere, his view of its epoch agrees with all the dates of the Somavaṁśins.[58]

III. SOME SIGNIFICANT EPIGRAPHICAL DISCOVERIES

During the last half a century under review literally several thousands of inscriptions have been reported or published, and all the records are important one way or other. But it is just impossible to take even a brief notice of all these epigraphs in such a short space as provided by the present survey. What we therefore propose to attempt in these pages is to very briefly highlight only a few highly significant records and their historical significance.

We may begin this section with a brief notice of Aśokan records which form the earliest precisely datable and decipherable post-Harappan epigraphs in the subcontinent. And fortunately this period has proved to be quite prolific in this respect, as a number of this monarch's inscriptions in various scripts and languages have been located in various places not only in the subcontinent but also in adjoining Afghanistan. A complete set of fourteen Rock Edicts of the emperor along with versions of Minor Rock Edicts I and II has been reported from Errāgudi in the Kurnool District of Andhra Pradesh.[59] A fragment of his

Rock Edict IX was found at Sopārā in the Thāṇe District of Maharashtra,[60] which would show that all the fourteen Rock Edicts were inscribed at the site, which was a very important centre culturally, as generally we get the entire set together. Recently at Sannati in the Gulbargā District of Karnataka have been found Rock Edicts XII and XIV and Special Sannati Edicts I and II[61] on the pattern of Special Kalinga Edicts, and several scholars have given their versions.[62] Versions of Minor Rock Edicts have also been located at several important centres. At Gujarrā in the Datia District of Madhya Pradesh was found Minor Rock Edict I which mentions the emperor as Aśoka rāja[63] and in this respct it resembles the well-known Maskī edict. The emperor finds mention under this name also in the recently discovered versions of Minor Rock Edict at Niṭṭūr and Udegolam, both in the Siriguppa taluk of Bellāry District in Karnataka.[64] At these places in Karnataka we have versions of Minor Rock Edicts I and II.[65] A version, fragmentary of course, of the Minor Pillar Edict IV has been reported from the famous Buddhist site of Amarāvatī in the Guntur District of Andhra Pradesh,[66] showing that the Great Chaitya at the place was built originally during Aśoka's time. At Aharaurā in the Mirzāpur District of Uttar Pradesh a version of the Minor Rock Edict I was found and has been published and discussed by several scholars including A.K. Narain,[67] V.V. Mirashi[68] and D.C. Sircar[69] in view of the difficulties involved in its interpretation and its fragmentary condition. However, there is no doubt regarding the great value of this version as it happens to be the only one to point out that he had undertaken the pilgrimage (on which he was for at least 256 days) immediately after the installation of the relics of the Buddha on a platform (or, may be, a *stūpa*) for worship, thereby solving the mystery of the event from which the period of pilgrimage was counted. Another version of this edict was reported from Delhi, though it was actually discovered at the village of Bahāpur to the south east of the city.[70] Its version reported from the stūpa-village of Pāngurāriā in the Budhnī Tahsil of the Sehore District of Madhya Pradesh in course of explorations by the Prehistory Branch of the Archaeological Survey of India is of great importance. It is addressed to Kumāra (prince, perhaps Aśoka's son) named Saṁva and was issued from the emperor's station in course of his pilgrimage at the Upunitha-or Opunitha-vihāra in the Māṇema-deśa which appears to have been the ancient name of the country around the provenance, and Kumāra Saṁva appears to have been placed in charge of the Māṇema-deśa.[71] Recently, there was a persistent news of the discovery of an Aśokan edict in the forest near the town of Ghuggus in the Chandrapur District of Maharashtra, but its whereabouts are presently untraceable, perhaps it might have been smuggled out. If the xerox of the impression available to us is dependable, it would appear to be a version of the emperor's Bairāṭ Stone-Slab Inscription referring to the Buddhist *tri-ratna* in the traditional order and some Buddhist texts.[72]

So far regarding Aśoka's edicts in Brāhmī. Greek and Aramaic inscriptions have also been reported from Afghanistan and were apparently meant for his subjects in that region who found it difficult (or impossible) to understand the Brāhmī script and Prakrit language. One such Greek inscription was spotted engraved on a stone lying in the ruins of Old Kandahār in front of a small Muslim mosque. It is actually a Greek rendering of the major portion of Rock Edict XII and the beginning of XIII. But it is not just a Greek translation but a free and, in some cases, an abridged adaptation from one of the Indian texts, faithful to the spirit and general meaning of the king's doctrine and is composed in very correct and fluent Greek devoid of any provincialism, with the vocabulary stemming from the best literary tradition and including several technical terms drawn from contemporary Greek philosophical and political language.[73] Obviously, there must have been at the site a complete set of the Greek version of the Fourteen Rock Edicts. Another, this time bilingual and biscriptual inscription of this sort from Kandahār has also been reported. This set of inscription represents in a general way Rock Edicts I to IV.[74] It may be presumed that these are just four of the fourteen edicts in Graeco-Aramaic version which also must have been put up there.[75] Two of his Aramaic edicts, which represent quite a different genre by themselves, have been reported from Laghman in Afghanistan.[75a] So far about Aśoka's own records.

But before we leave Aśoka, let us see a couple of records, even considerably beyond his time, as they shed welcome light about him and on points connected with his edicts. One of them is a short six-word Tamil-Brāhmī inscription from a cave-shelter at Hambai in the Thirukkoilur Taluk in the South Arcot District of Tamilnadu. Students of Aśokan edicts are aware of the reference in the emperor's Second Rock Edict to Satiyaputa and Keralaputa following the Choḍas and Pāḍas (Pāṇḍyas) among the southern rulers on the borders of his empire.[76] The identification of the Satiyaputa has been baffling scholars ever since this reference came to notice. But the inscription under review first mentions (or rather begins with) the name Satiyaputa followed by the mention of the king named Atiyaṇetumān Añchi who gave away the cave. Thus the record tells us that the Satiyaputa king named Atiyan Neṭumān Añchi ruled over the region covered by or included in the present South Arcot District of Tamilnadu.[77] This information, it will be appreciated, is of inestimable value to those interested in Aśokan studies. A Sanskrit inscription datable on palaeographical grounds to about the fifth century AD on the wall of a rock-shelter on the outskirts of Narasinghgarh in the Rājgarh District of Madhya Pradesh belonging to the Maukhari chief Aparājitavardhana records the grant of lands to the Buddhist *vihāra*, which is apparently the same as the inscribed rock-shelter. What is most interesting, however, is the information that traditionally this as well as the adjoining rock-shelter complex was regarded as established by Aśoka *(Aśoka-prahālikay-anuśruta prāktana-śūnya-vihāreshu)*.[78] This is the second post-Aśoka epigraphical reference to this great monarch, the other and earlier one being that in the Jūnāgadh inscription of the Śaka Mahākshtrapa Rudradāman I.[79]

Passing on to the subsequent period, we may refer to a few of the Sātavāhana inscriptions. One of them from Vanavāsī, the well-known Kadamba cpaital, is a memorial inscription engraved on a stone-slab commemorating (*chhāyā-patharo*) the chief queen (*mahādevī*) of the Sātavāhana king Vāsishṭhīputra Śivaśrī Puḷumāvi, the brother and a successor of Vāsishṭhīputra Puḷumāvi.[80] Its value lies in the fact that this is the only as yet known epigraph of this monarch whose very independence existence is doubted by some but which has been indisputably established by the recent find of his two silver portrait coins showing his identity as distinct from that of his uterine brother and a predecessor on the throne, viz. Vāsishṭhīputra Puḷumāvi.[81] The other is the Vāsana (locally known as Haḷe-Vāsana, Nargund Taluk, Dhārwād District, Karnataka) stone inscription of the last imperial Sātavāhana king Puḷumāvi who, too, as we learn from this record, had the metronymic Vāsishṭhīputra.[82] He was apparently a younger uterine brother and successor of Chaṇḍa Sātakarṇi who, too, is styled Vāsisṭhīputra in his Koḍavali inscription.[83] The Vāsana record under review proves that the relations between the two brothers were quite cordial as the Puḷumāvi erected a Śiva temple in his elder brother's memory. At Sannati in the Gulbargā District of Karnataka several Sātavāhana inscriptions have been reported recently. These include a private one recording some indeterminable charitable act by a Buddhist nun during the reign Vāsishṭhīputra Sātakarṇi[84] and another of his younger brother and successor Vāsishṭhīputra Śivaśrī Puḷumāvi which has lost several letters in the left margin with the result that its purport cannot be ascertained.[85] Yet another inscription refers to one Agniśarman as a *Mahāsātavāhana*, its exact purport being indeterminable due to its highly fragmentary nature.[86] This Agniśarman is as yet not known from any other source, but it is significant that he is styled Mahāsātavahana.[87] Another inscription from the same site would have proved to be very significant historically had it been preserved fully. It refers to a Sātavāhana king named Sātakarṇi, whose metronymic in its earlier part is lost, who is described as the lord of Benākaṭa, Vidarbha, Uparigiri, Aparānta, Asaka, Mūlaka and other regions and the destroyer of the Kshaharāta family and the winner of several battles, etc.[88] From the contents it would be seen to belong to Gautamīputra Sātakarṇi or, better, to his son and successor Vāsishṭhīputra Puḷumāvi describing the achievements of his illustrious father like his Nasik inscription of the nineteenth year of his reign.[89]

As to the Kārdamaka Kshatrapas, two records, both memorial, of the time of Chashṭana from Daulatpur and Andhau in the Kachchha District of Gujarat, dated respectively in his sixth and eleventh years[90], are of enormous historical value as they have revolutionised our notions about their history by proving that they had nothing to do with the Kushāṇas and lending support to the view that the Śaka era was counted from Chashṭana's accession.[91] Earlier we had four inscriptions from Andhau belonging to the year 52 of the joint reign of Chashṭana and his grand son Rudradāman I.[92] We now have another record, this time from nearby Khāvḍā, dated in the year 53 of their joint reign.[93] Another inscription from Pauni (Bhaṇḍārā District, Mahatrashtra) refers to a sculptured memorial pillar (*chhāyā-stambha*) of Rupiamma, prince (*kumāra*) under a Mahākshatrapa,[94] who had apparently come to the findspot in some connection and on his passing away a memorial pillar was put up.[95]

We may now refer to some inscriptions of a dynasty called Sada. At Guṇṭupalli (West Godāvarī District, Andhra Pradesh) was found an inscription in four copies which referred to the king (*mahārāja*) named Sada who was 'lord of Kaliṅga and Māhisaka' and belonged to the Mahāmeghavāhana lineage.[96] Another inscription of this king, now called Mahāsada, has been reported from the village Velpūru in the Sattenapalle Taluk of the Guṇṭur District in Andhra Pradesh.[97] He appears to have ruled in the Guṇṭur-Gōdāvarī region sometime towards the close of the first century AD. Another Sada king named Sivamaka Sada is known from an Amarāvatī (Guṇṭur District) inscription[98] which was wrongly attributed earlier to the Sātavāhanas as Sada was supposed to be an abbreviation of the name Sātakarṇi.[99] Coins of a number of Sada kings ruling in the first and first half of the second century AD in this region prior to its occupation by the Sātavāhana king Vāsishṭhīputra Puḷumāvi have been recently reported in course of explorations and excavations.[100] These inscriptions and coins are of great historical value as they have corrected our notions about the Sātavāhanas besides bringing a hitherto unknown ruling family of the Andhradesa to light.

The Sātavāhanas were succeeded by the Vākāṭakas in the Western Deccan, and the latter are claimants of a large crop of highly important epigraphical discoveries. Till recently no record of Rudrasena II himself was known and all our information about him was derived from the records of his successors. A few years ago at the important archaeological site of Mādhal a copper-plate charter issued by him in the fifth year of his reign has been found. Besides information on dynastic history and drafting pattern of the Vākāṭaka charters, the record sheds welcome light on the popularity of Bhāgavatism which was as much due to the monasteries of the Sātvata *charaṇa* hailing from Vatsagulma (modern Bāsim, Akolā District, Maharashtra) as to royal patronage.[101] That Padmapura was probably the capital after it was shifted from the ancestral capital at Kāñchanakā and prior to its transfer to Nandivardhana is rendered likely by these plates mentioning its eastern division (*mārga*) and Pravarasena II's Māsod plates of the nineteenth year referring to its western division[102] which make it imperative to locate it in Nagpur-Wardhā region. This Padmapura is evidently the same as that from which the Durg plates were intended to be issued, most probably during the reigns of Pṛithivīsheṇa I or Rudrasena II.[103] The seal-inscription of the recently discovered Miregaon charter of Prabhāvatīguptā, which alone has been published, solves a very controversial problem: it proves that her regency of yuvarāja Divākarasena lasting at least thirteen years was followed by the rule, in sequence, of his two brothers, viz. Dāmodarasena and Pravarasena (II), thereby demolishing the theory that these (Dāmodarasena and Pravarasena) were the names of one and the same person.[104]

The recently discovered Kevala Narasiṁha temple inscription commemorating the death of the Vākāṭaka queen Prabhāvatīguptā has proved to be of great historical value not only because it shows that what is now known as Kevala Narasiṁha temple was actually constructed to commemorate Prabhāvatīguptā after her demise and named Prabhāvatīsvāmin about AD 450, but also because it sheds welcome light on the history of her maternal family, viz. the Imperial Guptas. It referes to Chandragupta II as *tri-samudra-nātha* (lord of the three oceans), thereby indicating that the legacy of the southern conquests of his father Samudragupta continued during his son's reign, at least theoretically, and refers to Ghaṭotkacha Gupta as an imperial ruler, thereby establishing that he did ascend or declare himself as a sovereign monarch sometime during the time of his brother Kumāra Gupta I.[105] The Pauṇī plates of Pravarasena II establish that his reign lasted at least thirty two, if not more, years.[106] The Māṇḍdhaḷ (Nagpur District) plates (two sets) of Prithvisena II were found intact with seals and rings in course of excavations. These give the seal-inscription which was not known before.[107] These together with the Māhurjharī (Nagpur District) plates[108] of his seventeenth year leave no doubt about the correctness of the reading *dvi-magnavaṁś-oddhartṛi* (restorer of the family fortunes *twice*) in his unfinished Bālāghāṭ plates which were evidently issued sometime after his seventeenth regnal year[109] and consequently the untenability of its suggested correction to *nimagna* in so far as the first word of the compound is concerned.[110] And as regards the Vatsagulma branch of the dynasty, there have been equally epoch-making finds. Of the greatest importance is the Hisse-Borālā (Akolā District) inscription dated in the Śaka year 380 corresponding to AD 458 of the reign of Devasena, who evidently was ruling in that year.[111] This happens to be the only known definite date for any Vākāṭaka monarch and one of the earliest specific references to the Śaka era as such. Of almost equally great historical value is an iron replica of a copper-plate charter of this monarch hailing from Bīdar in Karnataka and now deposited in the Birla Archaeological and Cultural Research Institute, Hyderabad. This record indicates the expansion of the authority of the Vākāṭakas in northern Karnataka besides informing us that the name of the son and successor of Pravarasena of this branch was Sarvasena (II) given to him after its founder.[112] The only grant of the last known king of this branch, viz. Harisheṇa, has been reported from Thāḷner (ancient Sthālakanagara) in the Dhuliā District. It also gives the name of Sarvasena II, besides indicating the occupation of the Khāndesh region or the continuation of the family's hold over this region during Harisheṇa's reign.[113] The Vākāṭaka interest in the affairs of the Kadambas of Vanavāsī in Karnataka is also vouchsafed by the recently discovered Muḍigere (Terikere Taluk, Chikmaglūr District, Karnataka) of Simhavarman who is said to have been coronated by *Mahārāja* Sarvasena, evidently Sarvasena II.[114]

Of the successors of the Vākāṭakas, we have a copper-plate charter of the Muṇḍa king Ādityarāja, preceded by his grandfather Rāshṭramahārāja and father Rājakulamahārāja both of whom were rulers and one of whom had performed a horse-sacrifice indicating their sovereign status, from Malhārā (Achalpur Tahsil, Amarāwatī District) which has to be dated sometime in the sixth or early seventh century AD.[115] The Muṇḍaputra kings appear to have occupied the territory under the Nandivardhana branch of the dynasty after them. Five generations of the Kumbhakarṇa dynasty beginning with Jayarāja, styled the first king (*ādi-mahārāja*) of the dynasty, and ending up with Bhānusheṇa have been brought to light by the last-named ruler's Thāḷner plates. It may be presumed that Jayarāja rose to power in the Khandesh region after the end of the Vatsagulma branch.[116]

Of the Vishṇukuṇḍins of Andhra Pradesh, two highly important, and in fact epoch making, sets of copper-plate charters from Tummalaguḍem (Ramanapeṭa Taluk, Nalgoṇḍa District, Andhra Pradesh) have been published. One of these belonging to Govindavarman pushes back the genealogy of the Vishṇukuṇḍins by one or two generations.

The other grant of Vikramendravarman II dated in his eleventh regnal year corresponding to Śaka 488 = AD 566 has provided a sheet anchor for the chronology of the dynasty.[117] These records have also shed much welcome light on their religious leanings.

The earliest Pallava inscription belonging to Simhavarman was found at the village Mañchikallu in the Pālnād Taluk of the Guṇṭūr District in Andhra Pradesh, showing that the coastal Andhra formed the original territory of the dynasty.[118] A record attributable to Vishṇugopavarman and the only known charter of Mahendravarman are now deposited in the Central Archaeological Museum at Amaravati.[119] Another charter found at Bābbepalli (Prakāsham District, Andhra Pradesh) and now preserved in the State Department of Archaeology, Andhra Pradesh, Hyderabad, was issued by the Pallava king Kumāravishṇu (mid-first century AD) from his capital Kāñchī on the fifth day in the bright fortnight of the month Mahā-Kārttika on Thursday, this being the earliest allusions to a weekday.[120]

Now passing on to the north, we may refer here to the find of three inscriptions of the time of *Mahārājādhirāja* Rāmagupta on the pedestals of three images one each of the Jaina *tīrthaṅkaras*, Chandraprabha, Pushpadanta and Padmaprabha, recording their installation by him at the village of Durjanapur in the Vidishā District of Madhya Pradesh which clearly establish the general authenticity of the *Devīchandragupta* episode, which had been the bone of contention ever since the fragments of the drama were brought to light.[121] This is indeed an epoch making find of the half century under review. Another controversial point in the Gupta history has been the identity of King Chandra whose exploits are lauded in the Meharauli iron pillar inscription, scholars identifying him variously with rulers who had either Chandra as a part of their name or were otherwise known as Chandra even as a title. A postal seminar was organised on this theme, and the general consensus was favourable to his identification with Chandra Gupta II Vikramāditya.[122] This finds additional support from some Brāhmī inscriptions from the Hunzā valley referring to Chandra-Srī Deva Vikramāditya.[123]

A hoard of as many as twenty seven copper plates of the Mahārājas of Valkhā at Bagh in the Dhār District of Madhya Pradesh is indeed a unique event in the history of Indian epigraphy. The kings represented in the hoard are Bhuluṇḍa (years 47, 50, 51, 54, 55, 56, 57 and 59),

Svāmidāsa (years 63, 65 and 66), Rudradāsa (years 68, 69 and 70), Bhaṭṭāraka (years 102 and 127) and Nāgabhaṭa (year 134).[124] The hoard is of inestimable value not only for the political history of the dynasty but also for the socio-cultural conditions of the period in Central India.[125]

Recent epigraphical finds have shed lurid light on the activities of the Hūṇa king Toramāṇa. Three of these found at the town of Sañjelī (Zalod Taluka, Panchamahāl District, Gujarat) belong to the two vassals of *Paramabhaṭṭāraka Mahārājādhirāja* Toramāṇa named Bhūta (years 33 and 6) and the latter's son and successor Mātṛidāsa (year 19) and their evidence evaluated in conjunction with Toramāṇas. Other already known records from Kurā and Eraṇ show the stages of his occupation of the whole of north India upto Gujarat which had come under his authority by the third year of his reign.[126] As against these copper-plate grants, a large damaged stone inscription from Rishtal (Sītāmaū District, Madhya Pradesh) dated in the Mālava year 572 corresponding to AD 515-16 belonging to the Aulikara king Prakāśadharman in combination with the Eraṇ (Sāgar District, Madhya Pradesh) inscription of the Gupta emperor Bhānugupta, dated in Gupta year 191 or AD 510, perhaps indicates that the Guptas and the Aulikaras had made common cause against the Hūṇas and that they had vanquished Toramāṇa. This inscription is also of great value in as much as it, for the first time, brings to light an Aulikara king named Prakāśadharman who may have been either father or elder brother of the well-known Yaśodharman-Vishṇuvardhana (Mālava year 589 = AD 532) who had defeated Torāmaṇa's son and successor Mihirakula. The inscription gives five generations before Prakāśadharman which clearly reveals that Yaśodharman-Vishṇuvardhana need no longer be regarded as a meteor as has been done by some scholars.[127]

The later imperial Maukharis have also received some new light from a couple of inscriptions. The first member of the imperial Maukharis known to us hitherto was Harivarman who lived around the close of the fifth century AD.[128] It is possible that this Harivarman is identical with the homonymous king who as a vassal of the Gupta emperor Budha Gupta is known to have been ruling over the Baghelkhaṇḍ region of Madhya Pradesh in the Gupta year AD 168 or 487 from his Shaṅkarpur (Gopadavanasa Tahsil, Sidhi District, Madhya Pradesh) plate issued in that year.[129] His father *Mahārāja* Vijyavarman and grandfather *Mahārāja* Gītavarman are also named which may perhaps take back the family's ruling history to about early fifth century AD.

The Pāṇḍava king of Mekhalā (Maikal region of Madhya Pradesh) came to light for the first time as a result of the publication of the Bamhanī plates which were attributed to Bharatabala because of the inadvertent omission of a prose passage introducing his son and successor Śūrabala Udīrṇavaira.[130] However, the discovery of the latter king's Mallār (District Bilāspur, Madhya Pradesh) contained this prose passage, clearly indicating that both these charters were issued by him.[131] The discovery of these plates has further removed the erroneous notion that Bharatabala (or, for that matter, any Pāṇḍava king) was a vassal of Vākāṭaka king Narendrasena. This conclusion is reinforced by the discovery of the Malgā charter of *Samanta* Indraraja[132] which establishes that the Pāṇḍavas lived at least over a century after the end of the Vākāṭaka rule.[133] Closely connected with them were the Pāṇḍuvaṁsins of South Kosala about whom also we have now much new material and information. The Aḍhabhāra (Sakti Tahsil, Bilāspur District, Madhya Pradesh), for the first time, brought to light, Nannaraja II, son of Tīvaradeva.[134] The Senkapāṭ (Rāipur District) stone inscription of Śivagupta's time unravelled for the first time a Pāṇḍuvaṁsin chapter in the Vidarbha region of Maharashtra,[135] besides bringing to light a line of vassals ruling over, *inter alia*, this region.[136] Recently, a hoard of as many as nine-copper plate charters of Śivagupta from Sirpur (ancient Śrīpura, Pāṇḍuvaṁsin capital) in the Rāipur District and another from Mallār have been discovered which have brought to light links of Śaiva saints and their huge monastic establishment at Sirpur.[137]

The Somavaṁsins of Kosalā and Orissa have also received much new light as a result of some recent finds and a reappraisal of the known material in the perspective of new information. At Gopalpur (Bālāngīr District, Orissa) a set of three charters of Mahābhavagupta I Janamejaya has recently been located the first of which issued in his first regnal year sheds lurid light on a very crucial question connected with the dynasty. The identification of king Svabhāvatuṅga has been a matter of keen controversy, some identifying him with Mahābhavagupta Janamejaya and others with his son Mahāśivagupta Yayāti. The charter under reference shows that both these views are erroneous and that this was actually the name of Janamejaya's father, most probably Śivagupta mentioned at the beginning of all his records.[138] The place of Indraratha has also been finally determined, thanks to the discovery of his Bānpur (Purī District) plates.[139] There are numerous other records, published or unpublished, which shed welcome light on the dynastic history.[140]

The Pratihāra history has also been considerably enlightened by a few recent finds. A fragmentary inscription from Vidishā in Madhya Pradesh makes the earliest reference to the Pratihāra dynasty and the only one to the Pratihāra rulers of the Vidishā region in the fourth-fifth century AD. It refers to Pratihāra chief Bhūtimitra, his son (name lost), his son Driṇa and his son (name lost) who was a vassal of one of the descendants of Vijayanāga.[141] Thus we have for the first time a lithic record of the Imperial Pratihāra king Vatsarāja himself, dated Saka 717, who was earlier known from references in the records of his descendants as well as in those of his enemies. This record appears to have been found somewhere in North-western region of undivided India and contains much new interesting information about his military successes. It refers to his victories over the Gaṇḍa (Pāla), Karṇāṭa (Rāshṭrakūṭa), Lāṭa, Kīra and Mlechchha (Arab) kings. The inscription clearly indicates that during his time the struggle with the Rāshṭrakūṭa king Dhruva wss undecided with both the parties claiming success. What is most interesting is the reference to his victory over the Kashmir king Jayāpīḍa and the earliest allusion to the Tomaras (Tomara king named Vyāghra) whom also he defeated. It also refers to his enthroning Indrabhaṭa (same as Indrarāja) at Kānyakubja. In some of these conquests he was assisted by his loyal vassal Gollāka.[142] The reference to victory over Jayāpīḍa probably provides the rationale for the inscritption to be found somewhere in the north-west.

The Pāla history also has not remained untouched by the light shed by new finds. But the most important discovery, historically speaking, is the Māldā charter of Mahendrapāla's year 7. He is described as the son of Devapāla. It leaves no doubt that on the Pāla throne Devapāla was succeeded by his son Mahendrapāla, and it should remove the erroneous notion, hitherto prevalent, that the homonymous king mentioned in a few records found in Bihar and Bengal belongs to the Gurjara-Pratihāra dynasty and that they are indicative of the extension of the Pratihāra authority over these regions at the cost of the Pālas.[143]

The same is the case with the remaining of the three powers engaged in a conflict for political supremacy over India, viz. the Rāshṭrakūtas. The Bhindon (Aurangābād Tehsil and District, Maharashtra) plates of Karkarāja who is described as a son of Govindarāja of the family here, for the first time, called *Mahārāshṭrakūṭa*. Karkarāja is called Govindarāja's first son and Pratāpaśīla is given as his other name. His vassal in the region, Svāmirāja, made the grant recorded in the charter with his overlord's consent. The inscription tells us that Govindarāja had acquired the privilege of using all the *mahāśabdas* or titles of vassalage, thereby removing the common impression of the untrustworthiness of the description of the early history of the dynasty upto Govinda found in later Rāshṭrakūṭa records. The record also gives us an idea of the sphere of early activities of the Rāshṭrakūṭas[144] prior to the time of Dantidurga and even during the earlier part of his reign before the dynasty launched on an all-India career.[145]

We have discussed above about the Saka era. From the point of view of its early history as well as for the history of the later Mauryas of Koṅkaṇa the Vaḷā (or Vaḍā) inscription of Suketuvarman, dated Śaka 322, is one of utmost importance. The inscription was actually found at the place of this name in the Ṭhāṇe District of Maharashtra though wrongly attributed to Vālā in the Saurashtra region of Gujarat. It aims at registering the installation of the deity Koṭiśvara by one Siṁhadatta, son of Ānaṅkiparadatta in the Śaka year 322, and some grants to the divinity by one Īśuprakki, the V*allabha-Talavara* of the Maurya *Dharmamahārāja* Suketuvarman of the Bhojas. The inscription adds one more name to the list of the Mauryas of Koṅkaṇa[146] linking them to the Bhojas and, what is most interesting, contains the earliest epigraphical mention of the Śaka era by name and describes it as the era of the Śaka kings.[147]

One of the most spectacular, if not the spectacular, finds of recent years is represented by a large rectangular stone-slab (about 5 × 2 ft.) bearing a 20-line inscription recovered on 6th December, 1992, from the walls of the so-called Bābrī Masjid at Ayodhya. The inscription is composed in high-flown Sanskrit verses, except for a very small portion in prose, and is engraved in chaste and classical Nāgarī script of the eleventh-twelfth century AD. It is yet to be fully deciphered, but the portion that has been deciphered and read is of great historical significance. It was evidently put up on the wall of the temple the construction whereof is recorded in the text inscribed on it. Line 15 of this inscription clearly tells us that a beautiful temple of Vishṇu-Hari, built with heaps of stone (*śila-saṁhati-grahais*), beautified with a golden spire (*hiraṇya-kalaśa-śrī-sundaram*) and unparallelled by any other temple built by earlier kings (*pūrvvair-apy-akṛitaṁ kṛitaṁ nṛipatibhir*) was constructed. This wonderful temple (*aty-adbhutam*) was erected in the temple-city (*vibudh-ālavanī*) of Ayodhyā situated in the Sāketa-maṇḍala (district of Sāketa, line 17), indicating clearly that Ayodhyā and Sāketa were closely connected, Sāketa being the district of which Ayodhyā was a part. Line 19 describes god Vishṇu as destroying king Bali (apparently in his Vāmana incarnation) and the ten-headed one (Daśānana, i.e. Rāvaṇa). Line 20 contains an allusion to a serious threat from the west (*pāśchātya-bhīti*), apparently posed by Sultaṅ Ibrahim and his descendants, and its removal by the king.

The inscription was composed by the poet Āyushyachandra, son of Alhaṇa. Perhaps he was also the king as well as royal poet. He is said to have excelled even Sāhasāṅka and Śūrdraka (line 16) and is credited with the excavation of tanks and laying wells as well as stepped wells (line 17). In lines 7 and 11 we get references to a powerful king named Sallakshaṇa, who, in view of palaeographical considerations and in keeping with the extant information of the history of this period, was perhaps the Chandella king Sallakshaṇavarman who ruled at the close of the eleventh and the beginning of the twelfth century AD. It is also not impossible that there was another king of this name belonging to some other dynasty. The name of the Gahaḍavāla king Govindachandra has also been read in the inscription. The crucial point is that this record finally establishes the building of a magnificent temple of Hari-Vishṇu, the killer of Rāvaṇa and other demons, and it need hardly be stressed that the Indian tradition identifies incarnations, including Dāśarathi Rāma, with Vishṇu himself.[148] The inscription is now under the custody of the Central Government which is not making it available to epigraphists for decipherment. The sooner it opens it the better it would be for epigraphical studies and the honesty of the Govt. in matters of pure academics.

The above is perhaps a very cursory notice of what we regard as the most valuable of the inscriptions recovered during the last nearly half a century. This account, as natural and as stated above, does not and cannot claim to be exhaustive.

IV. Organisations and Publications

The biggest official organisation doing yeoman's work in the field of epigraphy, of course, is the Epigraphy Branch of the Archaeological Survey of India located earlier in the sylvan precincts of Ootacamund and now at Mysore. By survey and search followed by copying and publication of inscriptions it has been doing excellent work, and publication of a few articles in its official publication, *Epigraphia Indica*, is enough to establish one as a seasoned epigraphist. So far its forty-two volumes have been published. It has also been bringing out *Annual Reports of Indian Epigraphy* and an epigraphical series captioned *Corpus Inscriptionum Indicarum* and another series on *South Indian Inscription* of which ten volumes have already been published and occasional publication on individual inscriptions or a series of them. Under the *Corpus* series three volumes had already been published prior to Indian independence whereafter during the last about four decades (since 1955) only four more volumes have been released. Three of them, viz. *Inscriptions of the Kalachuri-Chedi Era*, *Inscriptions of the Vākāṭakas*, and *Inscriptions of the Śilāhāras*, all by the indefatiguable V.V. Mirashi, and a set of three bound parts of one volume, viz. *Inscriptions of the Paramāras and Chandellas* by the illustrious nonogenarian H.V. Trivedi, have been released. Though several other volumes have been alloted to a number of other scholars and there has been a scramble to get the allotments, no other scholar has as yet been able to complete his assignment, and some of them are even dead. The part of Vol. III on the *Inscriptions of the Imperial Guptas* revised by D.R. Bhandarkar and edited by B. Ch. Chhabra and G.S. Gai has also been published.

Some state departments of Archaeology are also engaged in epigraphical work. Of them special reference is due to Andhra Pradesh which has brought out several inscriptional publications including district wise lists. Tamilnadu has been doing excellent work, and in addition to publications it has also been organising seminars on epigraphy. In Karnataka and Kerala also good work is being done. The State Department of Archaeology in Orissa has also been very active and has published six volumes of the *Inscriptions of Orissa*, first five edited by S.N. Rajaguru and the last one by Snigdha Tripathy. Maharashtra also could have developed this branch but for the apathy of the concerned authorities. The present author had prepared a monograph at the express invitation of the Department in 1968 but had to get it published elsewhere four years later when he found the Department apathetic to it.[149] North Indian state departments of Archaeology are not known to have done much work in epigraphy despite the fact that there are some excellent records coming up from time to time as will be seen from the pages of the *Epigraphaia Indica* and the *Journal of the Epigraphical Society of India* as well other Indological journals and other occasional publications and the foregoing brief survey.

Realising the value and usefulness of epigraphical records for historical purposes and the enormous delay in the publication of the *Corpus* volumes the Indian Council of Historical Research, New Delhi, took up, in its formative period itself, an ambitious programme of the preparation and publication of a large number of volumes of inscriptions arranged dynastically, regionally and chronologically with the present author as its convenor. This programme has recorded a good progress over the years, and five volumes on the (i) *Inscriptions of the Western Gaṅgas* by K.V. Ramesh, (ii) *Inscriptions of the Maukharis, Later Guptas, Pushpabhūtis and Yaśovarman of Kanauj* by K.K. Thaplyal, (iii) *Inscriptions of the Sūryavaṁśin Gajapatis of Orissa* by R. Subrahmanyam, (iv) *Inscriptions of the Pallavas* by T.V. Mahalingam and (v) *Inscriptions of the Śarabhapurīyas, Pāṇḍuvaṁśins and Somavaṁśins* by the present author, have already been published. And a few other volumnes, viz. (vi, vii) *Inscription of Orissa* by Snigdha Tripathy, (viii, ix) *Inscriptions of Haryana, Punjab, Himachal Pradesh, Jammu and Kashmir and the Adjoining Hilly Region* by Jagannath Agrawal, *Inscriptions of the Early Kadambas by* G.S. Gai, (x) *Inscriptions of the Kākatīyas by* S.S. Ramachandra Murthy, are awaiting publication. Several volumes of the *Topographical List of the Insriptions of Tamilnadu* by T. V. Mahalingam and of *Vijayanagar Inscriptions* by S.H. Ritti and P. V. Parabrahma Sastry are also in the run for publication. Several other volumes are reported to be in various stages of preparation.

The foundation of the Epigraphical Society of India at Mysore in late 1973 and its continued existence for the last twenty years when it has been meeting annually at different places with a large number of old and young epigraphists coming together has contributed enormously to the popularisation of the epigraphical discipline with its various dimensions from editing inscriptions to the utilisation of the data furnished by them for historical purposes. It has hitherto been bringing out its journal regularly for the last nineteen years at the time of its annual conferences, and these volumes may now be taken to reflect the current trends of epigraphical research in India.

Several universities and other voluntary organisations have also been contributing their mite to the furtherance of epigraphical studies. The Tamil Unniversity at Tanjavur has a separate department of epigraphy, and[150] it has published the Tamil records of the Maratha Sarfoji rulers of Tanjāvur under the title *Maraṭhiyār Śeppoḍugal* compiled by Pulavar S. Raju. Similarly, the Mysore University's Kannada Research Institute has published eight volumes of the *Epigraphia Carnatica* as revised and updated by B. R. Gopal. The Uṭṭaṅkita Vidyaraṇya Trust of Kāñchī has also undertaken the work of compilation of Sanskrit inscriptions in handy volumes. Two of these volumes, viz, (i) *Vidyāraṇya* (Bharatiya, Vidya Bhavan, Bombay) and (ii) *Sanskrit Inscriptions* (from the early Period till Sixth Century AD) edited by K.G. Krishnan have been published alredy and work on subsequent volumes is underway. A *Concordance of Choḷa Inscriptions* in three volumes compiled by the team of the Japanese scholar Noburu Karashima, Y. Subbarayalu and B. Sitaraman has been released.

The abiding interest of the Japanese scholar Noburu Karashima in Tamil epigraphy is in sharp contrast with the decline and almost total lack of interest of European scholars who were doing great work in Indian epigraphy in pre-1947 period, a notable exception being Hans Bakker of the Netherlands who has recently critically edited Sanskrit records from Rāmṭek near Nagpur.

The epigraphical studies in India are completing almost a century and three quarters of another, and this period has witnessed brisk activities right from the decipherment of scripts to the present highly developed state when not only inscriptions are being edited but they are being utilised critically for the reconstruction of history in its various dimensions. What we call ancient Indian history today is mainly the creation of epigraphists, and this is no mean achievement.

REFERENCES

1. Kālibangan in Rajasthan, and Rangpur, Bet Dvārakā and Dholavīrā in Gujarat, *inter alia*, have yielded interesting inscribed objects.

2. We have not referred to the views of several scholars which on their very face appear to be unscientific and reveal only amateurish enthusiasm.

3. *Vide* Pentti Aalto, "Indus Script and Dravidian", *Studies in Indian Epigraphy (Journal of the Epigraphical Society: JESI)*, II, p. 16-30; and Asko Parpola, "Suggested Semantic and Phonetic Values of Selected Indus Pictograms", *ibid.*, pp. 31-35, in addition to the bibliography provided by Kamil V. Zvelebil at the end of his paper "Recent Attempts at the Decipherment of the Indus Valley Script and Language (1965-1980): A Critique", *Indus Valley to Mekong Delta: Explorations in Epigraphy*, ed. Noburu Karashima, New Era Publications, Madras, 1985, pp. 180-81.

4. *The Indus Script: Texts, Concordance and Tables*, Memoirs of the Archaeological Survey of India, No. 77, New Delhi, and entries in Kamil V. Zvelebil, *op. cit.*, pp. 178-79.

5. *op. cit*, pp. 151-87.

6. *Vide* the list of his writings on the subject appended to his paper by Kamil V. Zvelebil, *op. cit.*, p. 174.

7. This was first clearly established by B.B. Lal in 1961 and was strengthened by additional arguments later. *Vide* "Direction of Writing in the Harappan Script", *International Conference of Asian Archaeologists*, New Delhi, 1961, *Summaries of Papers*, p. 37; "The Direction of Writing in the Harappan Script", *Antiquity*, XL, 1966, pp. 52-55; "A Further Note on the Direction of Writing in the Harappan Script," *Purātattva*. I, pp. 15-16.

8. "Segmentation of Unusually Long Texts of Indus Writing: A Mathematical Approach," *JESI*, IX, pp. 68-77; "A Statistical Analysis of the Pairs of Indus Signs with Jar or Lance", *ibid.*, X, pp. 82-85.

9. These excavations were conducted by Rao himself.

10. *Decipherment of the Indus Script*, Asia Publishing House, Bombay, 1982; chs. 2 and 9; his "Presidential Address" of the VIth session of the Epigraphical Society of India, *JESI*, VIII, pp. 1-23.

11. *Studies in the Indus Valley Inscriptions*, New Delhi, 1978, referred to by S.R. Rao in *JESI*, VIII, pp. 9-10.

    For an excellent summary and survey of several attempts at the decipherment of this script from the beginning, see Devendra Handa, "Studies in the Indus Script: A Review", *Punjab University Research Bulletin* (Arts), XX (I), 1989, pp. 167-80. An excellent bibliography has been provided by Kamil. V. Zvelebil, *op. cit.*, pp. 171-85.

12. S.R. Rao, "Marine Archaeology in India", *Ajaya-Śrī: Recent Studies in Indology: Prof. Ajay Mitra Shastri Felicitation Volume*, ed. Devendra Handa, Sundeep Prakashan, Delhi, 1989, pp. 9-13, Pl. 8 For V.S. Pathak's views on this inscription, see his Presidential Address at the 12th session of the Epigraphical Society of India, *JESI*, XIII, pp. 5-6.

13. "Dholavira: New Horizons of the Indus Civilization", *Purātattva*, No. 20 (1989-90), pp. 80-81.

14. e.g. *vide* Iravatham Mahadevan, "The Cult Object on Unicorn Seals", *Indus Valley to Mekong Delta; Explorations in Epigraphy*, pp. 219-66; S.P. Singh, "Ṛgvedic Base of the Paśupati Seal of Mohenjo-daro", *Purātattva*, No. 19 (1988-89), pp. 19-26; P.V. Pathak, "The Indus Culture Seal of Three Forms and Seven Figures as Pictorial Representation of AV Hymn IV. 37", *ibid.*, No.22 (1991-92), pp. 59-64; V.S. Pathak, "Buffalo-Horned Human Figure on the Harappan Jar from Padri", *Man and Environment*, VII, pp. 87-90; K.V. Ramesh, *Indian Epigraphy*, I, Sundeep Prakashan, Delhi, 1984, pp. 151-59, etc.

15. *The Alphabet*, London, 1953.

16. *Indian Palaeography*. London, 1963.

17. This is the view of all the supporters of indigenous origin theory.

18. *The Invention of the Brāhmī Script*, Madras Christian College, Department of Statistics, Scientific Report, No. 30, 1977.

19. In fact, of literacy as such.

20. *The Origin of Brāhmī Script*, eds. S.P. Gupta and K.S. Ramachandran, D.K. Publishers, Delhi, 1979, pp. 1-53. In fact, this paper as well as comments were submitted for publication a few years earlier. *Vide* also S.R. Goyal, *Kauṭilya and Megasthenes*, Kusumanjali Prakashan, Meerut, 1985, pp. 82-100.

21. *The Origin of Brāhmī Script*, pp. 72-92 (R. Nagaswamy) and xx-xxi (S.P. Gupta).

22. *Ibid.*, pp. 92-98.

23. *Ibid.*, p. 123.

24. *Indian Palaeography*, 2nd ed., Motilal Banarasidass, Varanasi, 1957, pp. 35-51.

25. Nalanda Mahavihara, 1960.

26. Siddhartha Prakashan, Varanasi, 1971.

27. Only Raj Bali Pandey (*Indian Palaeography*, pp. 52-58) is of the opinion that the script is of Indian origin.

28. "A Note on the Name Kharoshṭhī", *Monthly Bulletin of the Asiatic Society*, Calcutta, May, 1980.

29. *Bulletin de l' Ecole Francaise de' Extreme Orient*, Paris 1978; *Chilas*, Islamabad, 1983; *Journal of Central Asia*, 1985.

31. Firma K.L. Mukhopadhyaya, Calcutta, 1958.

32. *JESI*, XV (1988), pp. 2-5. *Vide* also our paper "Some Suggestions for Tradition-backed Reforms in Brāhmī-based Scripts", *Pathways to Literature, Art and Archaeology; G.N. Bahura Felicitation Volume*, Vol. II, eds. Chandramani Singh and Neelima Vashishtha, Publication Scheme, Jaipur, 1991, pp. 128-32.

33. B.N. Mukherjee, Kharoshṭī and Kharoshṭī–Brāhmī Inscriptions in West Bengal (India), *Indian Museum Bulletin*, Calcutta, XXV (1990), and the bibliography of his writings on this script at p. 75 of this monograph. He has published a few other papers thereafter as well.

34. *Seminar on Inscriptions*, ed. R. Nagaswamy, Madras, 1966. For

general features of Tamil-Brahmi, see his "Some Aspects of Tamil-Brahmi Script," *JESI*, XII, pp. 27-28.

35. His paper entitled "Origin and Dissemination of the Brāhmī Script" presented at a symposium organised by the Tamil University, Tanjavur in 1988. See also *Indian Epigraphy*, pp. 66-68.

36. See the caption of his paper "Two Tamil Cave Brāhmī Inscriptions" in *EI*, XLII, p. 146.

37. For the list, see R.B. Pandey, *op. cit.*, p. 24, no. 12.

38. For the list, see *ibid*; pp. 24-25.

39. *Shell Inscriptions*, Calcutta, 1980.

40. For the list of these papers, *vide* Devendra Handa, "Studies in the Minor Scripts of India during the Last Decade", *Journal of Asiatic Society*, Calcutta, XXXII (I & II), 1990, p. 57-58.

41. *Decipherment of the Shell Script*, published as No. 31 (1983) of the *Bulletin of Museum and Archaeology*, State Museum, Lucknow. For his other contributions on this subject, see Devendra Handa's paper referred to in the preceding footnote, p. 54.

41a. For the proceedings, see R.K. Sharma (ed.), *Studies in Shell Script*, Agam Kala Prakashan, Delhi, 1990.

42. "Decipherment of the Banswara Script", *Ajaya-Śrī*, pp. 229-235.

43. *Bulletin of the Madras Government Museum*, Madras, 1952.

44. University of Madras, Madras, 1967.

45. Deccan College, Pune.

46. Parimal Publications, Delhi, 1991.

47. "The Vikrama Saṁvat", *Vikrama Volume, Ujjain*, 1948, pp. 557-86; *The History and Culture of the Indian People*, II: *The Age of Imperial Unity*, 2nd ed., edited by R.C. Majumdar and A.D. Pusalkar, Bharatiya Vidya Bhavan, Bombay, 1951, pp. 124-25, 163; *Indian Epigraphy*, Motilal Banarasidass, Delhi, 1965, pp. 256-57; *Ancient Malwa and the Vikramaditya Tradition*, Munshiram Manoharlal, Delhi, 1969, pp. 154 ff.

48. "The Vikrama and Śaka Eras — Observations on their Beginnings and their Early Use in Eastern India", *Indian Museum Bulletin*, XX, 1985, pp. 7-23.

49. Raj Bali Pandey, *Vikramāditya of Ujjayinī*, Varanasi, 1951, Chs. I–II; *Indian Palaeography*, I, pp. 199-204.

50. We have discussed the problem of the origin and early history of this era in our chapter under publication in the monograph on the system of dating in India to be brought out by the Indian National Science Academy, New Delhi.

51. *Vide* James Fergusson, *JRAS*, 1880, p. 259; E.J. Rapson, *BMC, AWK*, Introduction, pp. cv-cvii; *Indian Coins*, Strassburg, 1897, pp. 22, 83; *JRAS*, 1899, p. 365; *Cambridge History of India*, I, Cambridge, I, Cambridge, 1922, p. 528; A.M. Boyer, *JA*, 1897, pp. 120ff.; J.E. van Lohuizen de Leeuw, *The 'Scythian' Period – An Approach to the History, Art, Epigraphy and Palaeography of North India from the 1st Century B.C. to the 3rd Century A.D.*, Leiden, 1949, p. 65; A.L. Basham, *Studies in Indian History and Culture*, Calcutta, 1964, pp. 115-19; H.C. Raychaudhuri, *Political History of Ancient India*, 6th ed., Calcutta, 1953, pp. 469ff.; J.N. Banerjea, *A Comprehensive History of India*, II ed. K.A.N. Sastri, 2nd ed., New Delhi, 1987, pp. 235ff.; V.V. Mirashi, *IHQ*, XXVI, pp. 216 ff.; *Studies in Indology*, II, Sholapur, 1961, pp. 95ff.; IV, Varanasi, 1966, pp. 112ff.; D.C. Sircar, *The Age of Imperial Unity*, pp. 143-44; *Select Inscriptions bearing on Indian History and Civilization*, I, 2nd ed., Calcutta, 1965, pp. 136ff.; *Indian Epigraphy*, pp. 258ff.; B.N. Mukherjee, "The Vikrama and Śaka Eras – Observations on their Beginnings and Early Use in Eastern India", *Indian Museum Bulletin*, XX, 1985, pp. 13ff., etc.

52. *Vide* our chapter on the Śaka era in the publication of the Indian National Science Academy, referred to in note 50 above.

53. B.N. Mukherjee, *Central and South Asian Documents on the Old Śaka Era*, Varanasi, 1973.

54. *Inscriptions of the Kalachuri-Chedi Era, CII*, IV, Ootacamund, 1955, Introduction, pp. i-xxii. We are, however, doubtful about his view that it was counted from the accession of the Ābhīra chief Īśvarasena known from a Nāsik record, for there is absolutely no evidence that he ruled over such a vast empire as supposed by Mirashi. He was not so great as to induce other rulers to follow a reckoning counted from his coronation.

55. "Epoch of the Gaṅga Era", *EI*, XXVI, pp. 326-36: *Studies in Indology*, IV, pp. 166-204. He also discussed the dates of several records dated in this era with a view to verify his epoch in *EI* XXVII, p. 192; XXVIII, pp. 171-74; XXX, pp. 25-26.

56. *EI*, XXVI, p., 36, *Vide* also his *Inscriptions of the Vākāṭakas, CII*, V, Mysore, 1963, Introduction, p. xxxi.

57. *Ibid.*, p. 108, verse 18.

58. For a discussion of the problem and references, *vide* Ajay Mitra Shastri, *Inscriptions of the Śarabhapurīyas, Pāṇḍuvaṁśins and Somavaṁśins*, Part I, Indian Council of Historical Research and Motilal Banarsidass, Delhi, 1992, pp. 192-96.

59. D.C. Sircar, "Erraguḍi Edicts of Aśoka", *EI*, XXXI, pp. 1-28; *Aśokan Studies*, Indian Museum, Calcutta, 1979, pp. 1-41.

60. D.C. Sircar, *ibid.*, 42-44; "Sopārā Fragment of Rock Edicts IX of Aśoka", *EI*, XXXI, pp. 29-30.

61. I.K. Sarma and J. Varaprasada Rao, *Early Brāhmī Inscriptions from Sannati*, Harman Publishing House, New Delhi, 1993, pp. 1-56; K.V. Ramesh, "The Aśokan Inscriptions at Sannathi", *The Indian Historical Review*, XIC, pp. 36-42.

62. *Vide* I. K. Sarma, K.V. Ramesh (cited above) and K.R. Norman (quoted by I.K. Sarma, *op. cit.*, pp. 42-50).

63. D.C. Sircar, "Gujarrā Inscription of Aśoka", *EI*, XXXI, pp. 211-18; *Aśokan Studies*, pp. 86-93.

64. *Ibid.*, pp. 123-28 (Niṭṭūr) and 129-31 (Uḍegoḷam); S.H. Ritti, "Newly Discovered Edicts of Aśoka from Karnataka", *JESI*, VIII, pp. 101-04; P.R. Srinivasan, "Nittur Minor Rock Edicts of Aśoka", *EI*, XXXIX, pp. 111-16, "Uḍegolaṁ Minor Rock Edict of Aśoka", *ibid*, XXXIX, pp. 237-40.

65. For refences, see previous note.

66. D.C. Sircar, "Fragmentary Pillar Inscription from Amarāvatī", *ibid.*, XXXIV, pp. 40-43; *Aśokan Studies*, pp. 118-22.

67. *Bhāratī* (Bulletin of the College of Indology, Banaras Hindu University, Varanasi), V(I), 1960-61, pp. 97-105.

68. *Ibid.*, pp. 135-40.

69. "Ahraurā Inscription of Aśoka", *EI*, XXXVI, pp. 239-48; *Aśokan Studies*, pp. 72-81.

70. *Ibid.*, pp. 82-85; "New Delhi Inscription of Aśoka", *EI*, XXXVIII, pp. 1-4. Also *vide JRAS*, 1967, pp. 96-98.

71. D.C. Sircar, "Pāngurāriā Inscription of Aśoka", *EI*, XXXIX, pp. 1-8; *Aśokan Studies*, pp. 93-103.

72. *Vide* our paper under publication in the *Purātattva*.

73. D. Schlumberger and E. Benveniste, "A New Greek Inscription of Aśoka at Kandahār", *EI*, XXXVII, pp. 193-200.

74. J. Filliozat, "Graeco-Aramaic Inscription of Aśoka near Kandahār", *ibid.*, XXXIV, pp. 1-8.

75. Generally the set of all the fourteen Rock Edicts is set up together.

75a. For these edicts and references, see B.N. Mukherjee, *Aramaic edicts of Aśoka,* Indian Museum, Calcutta, 1984, pp. 9-22. This work brings together all the Aramaic edicts of the emperor.

76. D.C. Sircar, *Select Inscriptions*, I, p. 17, line 2.

77. *The Hindu*, Madras, dated 9th April, 1981. Information kindly supplied by Iravatham Mahadevan. But K.V. Ramesh is doubtful about this interpretation. *Vide* his "Recent Discoveries and Research Methods in the Field of South Asian Epigraphy", *Indus Valley to Mekong Delta*, pp. 2-4.

78. K.V. Ramesh, "Recent Discoveries and Research Methods in the Field of South Asian Epigraphy", *Indus Valley to Mekong Delta*, p. 8.

79. D.C. Sircar, *Select Inscriptions*, I, p. 171. line 8.

80. A.V. Narasimha Murthy and H.R. Raghunatha Bhat, "Banavāsī Inscription of Siva Siri Pulumāvi". *Studies in Indian Epigraphy (JESI)*, I, pp.34-39.

81. Ajay Mitra Shastri, "Vāsishthīputra Śivaśrī Puḷumāvi" *Raṅgavallī : Recent Researches in Indology: S.R. Rao Felicitation Volume*, eds. A.V. Narasimha Murthy and B.K. Swami Bhatt, Sundeep Prakashan, Delhi, 1983, pp. 151-62.

82. M.J. Sharma, "Vāsana Inscription of Vāsṭhīputra Siri Pulumavi", *EI*, XLI, pp. 154-58.

83. H. Krishna Sastri, "The Koḍavali Rock-Inscription of Chaṇḍasāti: The Second Year of Reign", *EI*, XVIII, pp. 316-17. Mirashi, however, reads the regnal year as 11. There is nothing to support the suggestion of K.V. Ramesh (*Indus Valley to Mekong Delta*, p. 6) that Chaṇḍasāti or Chaṇḍa Sātakarṇi was the father of the last Śatavāhana king Vāsishṭhīputra Puḷumāvi.

84. I.K. Sarma and J. Varaprasada Rao, *op. cit.*, p. 75.

85. *Ibid.*, p. 76.

86. *Ibid.*, p. 77.

87. Names of families beginning with the word which acts as prefix (to the names) are comparable. Another contemporary ruling family was called Mahāmeghavāhana. The two families are known to have risen to power about the same time and were connected with each other, though as enemies, which may have prompted some Śātavāhanas also to prefix this word to the dynastic name.

88. I.K. Sarma and J. Varaprasada Rao, *op. cit.*, p. 65.

89. D.C. Sircar, *Select Inscriptions*, I, pp. 203-05.

90. V.V. Mirashi, *The History and Inscriptions of the Sātavāhanas and Western Kshatrapas*, Maharashtra State Board of Literature and Culture, Bombay, 1981, pp. 153-56 (Daulatpur) and 115-16 (Andhau).

91. For discussion, see our contribution to the forthcoming publication on dating by the Indian National Science Academy, New Delhi.

92. *Ibid.*, pp. 118-19.

93. P.R. Srinivasan, "Three Western Kshatrapa Inscriptions", *EI*, XXXVII, pp. 139-42; V.V. Mirashi, *The History and Inscriptions*, etc., pp. 120-21. Both Srinivasan and Mirashi take it as an inscription of Rudradāman I alone before he became a *mahākshatrapa*. Besides, Mirashi takes the date as the year 63, not 53 as read by Srinivasan.

94. Mirashi (*EI*, XXXVII, pp. 201-03; *The History and Inscriptions*, etc. pp. 149-50) takes Rupiamma himself to be a Mahākshatrapa, whereas the wording (*mahakhattava-kumāra*) leaves absolutely no doubt that the composer intended to refer to Rupiamma as only a prince or son under/or a *mahākshatrapa*.

95. V.V. Mirashi has brought together all the records of the Sātavahanas and the Western Kshatrapas in his *The History and Inscriptions*, etc.

96. R. Subrahmanyam, *The Guntupally Brāhmī Inscription of Khāravela*, Andhra Pradesh Government Archaeological Series, No. 3, Hyderabad, 1968. As would be seen even from the title, Subrahmanyam attributed these inscriptions to Khāravela. It was D.C. Sircar ("Some Epigraphic and Manuscript Records: I, An Alleged Inscription of Khāravela", *Journal of Ancient Indian History*, Calcutta University, Parts I–II (1969-70) who corrected Subrahmanyam's reading and interpretation of the record.

97. D.C. Sircar (*EI*, XXXII, p. 86) had read the king's name doubtfully as Mānasada. The present author ("The Velpūru Pillar Inscription of Mahāsada", *JESI*, XIX, pp. 13-18) pointed out that the name is actually Mahāsada.

98. V.V. Mirashi, *The Inscriptions and History*, etc., pp. 66-67.

99. *Ibid.*

100. T.V.G. Sastry, M. Kasturi Bai and Veerender, *Vaḍḍmānu Excavations*, Birla Archaeological and Cultural Research Institute, Hyderabad. 1992. 156-73; P.R.K. Prasad, "Sada Coins in Coastal Andhra", *Studies in South Indian Coins*, III, pp. 53-64. The Sada kings represented are Mahāsada, Asakasada, Sivamakasada, etc. Several Sada coins cannot be attributed because of imperfect legends.

101. Ajay Mitra Shastri and Chandrashekhar Gupta, "Dvitya Rudrasenāchā Māṇḍhaḷa Tāmrapata" (Marathi), Saṁśodhanāchī Kshitije, ed. B.L. Bhole, Ameya Prakashan, Nagpur, 1985, pp. 223-29. Our joint and more detailed paper on this inscription is under publication in *EI*, XLIII.

102. Ajay Mitra Shastri and Chandrashekhar Gupta, "Māsoda Copper-Plate Charter of Pravarasena II", *JESI*, X, pp. 108-16; "The Date of the Māsoda Plates of Pravarasena II", *ibid.*, XI, p. 114.

103. See our paper captioned "Capitals of the Vākāṭakas "under publication in K.M. Srivastava festschrift.

104. Ajay Mitra Shastri, "New Vākāṭaka Inscriptions", *The Age of the*

Vākāṭakas, ed. Ajay Mitra Shastri, Harman Publishing House, New Delhi, 1992, pp. 233-34.

105. *Ibid.*, pp. 253-57.

106. V.B. Kolte, "Paunī Plates of Pravarasena II", *EI*, XXXVIII, pp. 53-56.

107. Ajay Mitra Shastri, "Māṇḍhaḷ Plates of Pṛithivīseṇa II, Years 2 and 10", *ibid.*, pp. 159-80.

108. V.B. Kolte, "Māhurzarī Plates of Pṛthivīṣeṇa II", *Annals of the Bhandarkar Oriental Research Institute*, LIII, pp. 183-94.

109. V.V. Mirashi, *CII*, V, pp. 80-81.

110. This correction was suggested by F. Kielhorn followed by V.V. Mirashi.

111. For the inscription, see Shobhana Gokhale, Hisse-Barālā Inscription of Devasena, Śaka 380, *eI*, XXXVII, pp. 1-4. For discussion, see G.S. Gai and S. Sankaranarayanan, "Note on the Date of Hisse-Borālā Inscription of the Time of Vākāṭaka Devasena", *ibid.*, 5-8; Ajay Mitra Shastri, *Dr. Umesh Mishra Commemoration Volume*, Ganganatha Jha Research Institute, Allahabad, 1990, pp. 617-27; *The Age of the Vākāṭakas*, pp. 246-47; D.C. Sircar, *Journal of Ancient Indian History, I*, pp. 94-98.

112. P.V. Parabrahma Sastry, "Hyderabad Plates of Vākāṭaka Devasena, Year 5", *JESI*, XIII, pp. 71-75; Ajay Mitra Shastri, *The Age of the Vākāṭakas*, pp. 248-51. We prefer to call the record as Bīdar plates after its real findspot.

113. V.V. Mirashi, "*Indological Research Papers*, I, Vidarbha Samsodhana Mandala, Nagpur, 1982, pp. 78-86. See for discussion, our paper in *The Age of the Vākāṭakas*, pp. 251-53.

114. See Ajay Mitra Shastri, "The Mudigere Plate of Siṁhavarman and Vākāṭaka-Kadamba Relations", *Indian Archaeological Heritage : Shri K.V. Soundararajan Festschrift*, eds. C. Margabandhu *et al*, Agam Prakashan, Delhi, 1991, pp. 317-19.

115. For a discussion of the date, see Ajay Mitra Shastri, "The Malhārā Plates of Ādityarāja: A Re–appraisal", *JESI*, IV, pp. 30-41; "The Date of the Malhārā Plates of Ādityarāja", *ibid.*, VII, pp. 69-75.

116. See Ajay Mitra Shastri, "Thālner Plates of Harisheṇa: A Re-appraisal" *ibid.*, XI, pp. 15-20.

117. Ajay Mitra Shastri, "Fresh Light on the History of Vishṇukuṇḍins", *Journal of Indian History*, XLIV (1966), pp. 683-91.

118. D.C. Sircar, Two Inscriptions from Guṇṭūr District: 2. Mañchikallu Inscription of Pallava Siṁhavarman", *EI*, XXXII, pp. 87-90.

119. Information kindly supplied by Shri Madhav N. Katti, Director, Epigraphy, Archaeological Survey of India, Mysore.

120. P.V. Parabrahma Sastry, "Babbepalli Plates of Pallava Kumāravishṇu", *EI*, XLII, pp. 44-54.

121. G.S. Gai, "Three Inscriptions of Rāmagupta", *EI*, XXXVIII, pp. 46-49.

122. M.C. Joshi and S.K. Gupta (eds.), *King Chandra and the Mehrauli Pillar*, Kusumanjali Prakashan, Meerut, 1989, We too contributed to the volume.

123. A.H. Dani in *Journal of Central Asia*, VIII (2), Dec. 1985, pp. 5-124. Some scholars are inclined against this identification, but there seems to be no valid reason for their opposition.

124. K.V. Ramesh and S.P. Tewari, *A Copper-Plate Hoard of the Gupta Period from Bāgh, Madhya Pradesh*, Mysore, 1990.

125. See our review of the book for some very important points, *JESI*, XVIII, pp. 126-31.

126. V.V. Mirashi, *Indological Research Papers*, I, pp. 88-97; K.V. Ramesh, "Three Early Charters from Sanjeli"; *EI*, XL, pp. 175-86.

127. K.V. Ramesh and S.P. Tewari, "Risthal Inscription of Aulikara Prakāśadharman", *JESI*, X, pp. 96-103. For the elucidation of some points, see our paper "Dravyavardhana of Avanthi, Royal Patron of Varāhamihira", *Prācī-Prabhā: Perspectives in Indology*: Essays in Honour of Professor B.N. Mukherjee; eds. D.C. Bhattacharya and Devendra Handa, Harman Publishing House, New Delhi, 1989, pp. 163-75.

128. Īśānavarman, known date AD 554 , was preceded by three chiefs beginning with Harivarman who may be placed in the last quarter of the fifth century AD.

129. B.C. Jain, "Shankarpur Plate of Budhagupta and Harivarman: Gupta Year 166", *JESI*, IV, pp. 62-66. The date was corrected to 168 by K.V. Ramesh.

130. B. Ch. Chhabra, "Bamhanī Plates of Pāṇḍva Bharatabala" *EI*, XXVII, pp. 132-46.

131. B. Sitaraman and M.J. Sharma, "Mallar Plates of Pāṇḍava Śūrabala, Year 8", *Studies in Indian Epigraphy (JESI)*, III, pp. 183-92.

132. D.C. Sircar and S. Sankaranarayanan, "Malgā Plates of Sāmanta Indrarāja", EI, XXXIII, pp. 209-14.

133. For a discussion of date and some other points, *vide* our "The Date of the Bamhani and Mallar Plates of Śūrabala Udīrṇavaira" *Bhārati-Bhānam: Dr. K.V. Sarma Felicitation Volume*, Vishveshvaranand Indological Research Institute, Hoshiarpur, 1980, pp. 439-43, and *Inscriptions of the Śarabhapurīyas, Pāṇḍuvaṁśins and Somavaṁśins*, Part I for the historical outline and Part II for texts of these records.

134. B.C. Jain, "Aḍhabhāra Plates of Mahā-Nannarāja", *EI*, XXXI, pp. 219-22.

135. M.G. Dikshit, "Senkapāṭ Inscription of the Time of Śivagupta Bālārjuna", *ibid.*, pp. 31-36.

136. For discussion of its historical significance, see our paper "Senkapāṭ Inscription of the Time of Śivagupta Bālārjuna: Some Observations", *Śrī Rāmachandrikā: Essays on Indian Archaeology, History, Epigraphy, Numismatics, Arts and Religion, Prof. O. Ramachandraiya Festschrift*, ed. A.V. Narasimha Murthy and I.K. Sarma, Book India, Delhi, 1993, pp. 145-52.

137. The records are yet to be published. But their contents have been abstracted and discussed by us in our paper "Bāleśvara-Bhaṭṭārkara: A Hitherto Unknown Śaiva Establishment at Śrīpura", *JESI*, XVIII, pp. 15-23.

138. A joint paper by us and Dr. Snigdha Tripathy is under publication in *EI*.

139. See K.S. Behera, "Bānpur Plates of Somavaṁśī Indraratha" *JESI*, XV, pp. 37-46, for the edition of the record as well as earlier references.

140. These include Degāon, Sambalpur University Museum, Sankhameri,

Kamālpur and Nuapatnā plates all of which have been included in our work on the *Inscriptions of the Śarabhapurīyas, Pāṇḍuvaṁśins and Somavaṁśins*, Part II.

141. K.V. Ramesh and S. Subramania Iyer, "A Fragmentary Inscription from Vidishā", *EI*, XLI, pp. 186-88.

142. K.V. Ramesh and S.P. Tewari, "An Inscription of Pratihāra Vatsarāja, Śaka 717", *ibid.*, XLI, pp. 49-57.

143. K.V. Ramesh and S. Subramania Iyer, "Malda District Museum Copper-Plate Charter of Mahendrapala, Year 7", *ibid.*, XLII, pp. 6-29. The record was actually found at the village of Jagajjībanpur in the Habībpur police station in the Sadar sub-division of the Māldā District in Bengal.

144. K.V. Ramesh, "Bhindon Plates of Rāshṭrakūṭa Karkarāja", *JESI*, X, pp. 30-35.

145. Most of the records of Dantidurga have been found in the Marāṭhwāḍā region, especially in the Aurangābād District.

146. For a list of the Maurya inscriptions, see *EI*, XL, p. 53, fn. 1

147. K.V. Ramesh, "Vala (or Vada) Inscription of Suketu-varman, Śaka 322", *EI*, XL, pp. 51-54.

148. For the gist of inscription, see our paper "Ayodhyā and God Rāma", *Purātattva*, No. 23, pp. 37 ff. Other scholars have also attempted to decipher this record. See Appendix by T.P. Verma*

149. *Yādava Inscriptions from Ambe Jogai*, Vishveshvaranand Indological Research Institute, Punjab University, Hoshiarpur, 1972.

150. The Department of Epigraphy at the Tamil University at Tanjavur is engaged in collection and publication of post-AD 1300 inscriptions as its primary aim. Besides the two volumes of the copper-plate charters and other inscriptions of the Marathas of Tanjavur and two volumes of palm-leaf records of the seventeenth and eighteenth centuries resembling earlier inscriptions in format and contents that have already been published, it has in press two other volumes on the copper-plates of the Tondaimans of Pudukkottai and Setupatis of Rāmanāthapuram. It is collaborating with Noburu Karashima of Tokyo University and some Indian scholars in a project on the revenue system of the Vijayanagar state, and the part relating to the Tamil inscriptions has been completed and a report published and that relating to Kannada and Telugu inscriptions in in progress. N. Karashima, Y. Subbarayalu and P. Shanmugam have published the report under the titile *Vijanagar Rule in the Tamil Country as Revealed thorugh a Statistical Study of Revenue Terms in Inscriptions*, ILCAA, Tokyo, 1988. Another project on a Historical Atlas of Tamilnadu mainly based on Inscriptions is in progress.

I am grateful to my esteemed friend Professor Y. Subbarayalu of the Department of Epigraphy at the Tamil University and presently Visiting Professor at the Tokyo University for this valuable information.

* For Copy of Inscription deciphered by T.P. Verma and A.K. Singh see Appendix

A Survey of the Study of Indo-Muslim Architecture

R. NATH*

Architecture is a source of history as well as a fine art and a discipline in itself. It constitutes a veritable chronicle in stone. The stamp of an age– and the people who lived in it: their tastes, beliefs, ideals, standards and skills– is most truthfully imprinted upon their monuments, without a knowledge of which the history of any period lacks that human interest with which it should be invested.

(a) Architecture: Lithic Record of History

History writ large on monuments can give, if and when deciphered, access to the spirit of the time which brought them into form. They preserve the most faithful and authentic records in stone, of the contemporary society and a study of architecture can open up "the enjoyment of contemplating buildings with an appreciation of their purpose, meaning and charm. Every structure conjures up the conditions of the past ages. It is one art with which we are all brought into daily contact, for it shelters us from the elements, gives us 'home' and enshrines the sacred symbols of all religions" [1]

World's greatest rulers have been patrons of architecture and have used it as a symbol of their power and glory, in faithful adherence to the dictum: '*Verily our relics tell of us.*' The History of Architecture is a record of continuous evolution of the respective civilization. "Architecture striding down the ages was evolved, moulded and adopted to meet the changing needs of nations.... A glance along the perspective of past ages reveals architecture as a lithic history of the events which are landmarks in the history of mankind; for as architecture is, in all periods, intimately connected with national life, *the genius of a nation is unmistakably stamped on its architectural monuments.* Throughout the history of human race, architecture – the mother of all arts – has supplied shrines for religion, homes for the living and monuments for the dead. [2]

Though less exciting and a little abstract, the silent history of architecture is a record of those tender feelings, sublime thoughts and sublime ideas which go to make a civilization, not of greed, vanity, duplicity, hypocrisy and cruelty of man, and not of those political intrigues and military conflicts which destroy it. It is the most monumental record of human creativity.

(b) Contemporary Record of Medieval Indian Architecture

Persian chroniclers who recorded the history of medieval India from the establishment of the Delhi Sultanate in A.D. 1192 to the capture of Agra and Delhi by the British in A.D. 1803 , concentrated mostly on the personal life of the king and court proceedings; grant of honours and awards; assignments, appointments and punishments; marches of armies, camps and battles; intrigues, conspiracies and assassinations; and bloodshed and change of dynasties. Their histories deal, by and large, with political, administrative and military matters and, but for few exceptions, there is practically no contemporary record of the

*2-G 11, Jawaharnagar, Jaipur–302 004

buildings which were raised before their eyes by their patrons to immortalize them.

The Quṭb Mīnār, one of the most important architectural relics of the Sultanate period, built at Delhi between A.D. 1200 and 1215, for example, has not even been mentioned by such contemporary historians as Ḥasan Niẓāmī in the *Tāj'ul-Ma'āthir* and Mīnhāj in the *Ṭabaqāt-i-Nāṣirī*, though the latter lived at Delhi for a long time and went to offer his Friday prayers in the adjoining Jāmi' Masjid (viz. the Quwwat'ul-Islām Masjid) at Mehrauli regularly[3]. Amir Khusrau just mentioned it in a passing reference to another mīnār which Sulṭan Alāu'd-Dīn Khaljī (A.D. 1296-1316) ordered to be built, in the same compound, on a larger scale. The Khaljī relic is now a despicable mound of rubble-masonry refuting the poet's eulogical description of the Sulṭān's architectural ventures. How scanty and deficient were the observations of these medieval historians even when they chose to record them, is also shown by a casual reference of Ibn Baṭūṭah, the Moorish traveller, who visited India (A.D. 1334-42), to the Quṭb Mīnār that its staircase was so wide that elephants could go up into it.[4] The magnificent tomb of Sher Shāh at Sasaram (A.D. 1545), another great building of the Sultanate period, has been similarly ignored by contemporary chroniclers. The Sultanate historian had, in fact, a different choice of subjects and architecture was practically excluded from it.

With the establishment of the Mughal rule in India in A.D. 1526, the scene changed, though not on a large scale. They were a cultured people and cultural things did not get such a rough handling in their histories as they did in the preceding ages.

Babur was an aesthete and he described, in his memoirs (viz. the *Tuzuk-i-Bāburī* or *Babūr-Nāmah),* the country and its fauna and flora; the people and their life and customs; and, of course, Fine Arts as poetry, painting, music and architecture. Several times did he allude to his building activities at Dholpur (precisely, Bari at Bāgh-i-Nīlūfar), Fatehpur Sikri (e.g. at the Jal-Mahal site), Agra and other places but these are just casual references.[5] He did not say a word about the mosques at Sambhal, Panipat, Rohtak, Maham, Sonepat, Palam, Pilkhuwa, Agra and Ayodhya which were built during his short reign from A.D. 1526 to 1530 and which popularly bear his name. It is owing to the absence of any authentic historical record that the mosque once built at Janmasthan in Ayodhya, which was called the Baburi Masjid, created such a dangerous controversy.

Through the contemporary historian Khwandamir describes Humayun's eccentric innovations such as the Floating Market, the Zodiac Tent and the Carpet of Mirth at length, his reference to the latter's buildings which he commissioned (A.D. 1530-40) is too brief even to help us to identify them. He mentioned the Dīn-Panāh, the most ambitious architectural project of Humayun, at Delhi but he did not refer to the Qal'ā-i-Kuhnā Masjid and the Sher-Maṇḍal, two most important buildings, inside it,[6] and we have no alternative except to study them stylistically and circumstantially.

Surprisingly, while the history of Akbar's reign (A.D. 1556-1605) was recorded in minutest details by competent historians, including Abū'l Faḍl, the official chronicler, and such a great encyclopaedic work as the *Āin-i-Akbarī* was produced they did not include architectural history in their subject matter and except for alluding to them casually, the great buildings commissioned by Akbar have been practically ignored. Thus they mentioned the Bengālī-Maḥal in the Agra Fort but did not describe it and such important buildings at Fatehpur Sikri (A.D. 1572-85) as the so-called Dīwān-i-Khāṣṣ *(Ekastambha-Prāsāda),* Panch-Mahal, Bīrbal's Palace *(Maḥal-i-Ilāhī)* and Buland Darwāzah, for example, have not even been mentioned, which is why a number of misnomers have been implanted upon them and their history has been fantasized.[7] History of Jehangir's reign (A.D. 1605-27) was also systematically recorded and he himself inscribed his own day-to-day Memoirs (viz. *Tuzuk–Jahāngīrī* or *Jehāngīr–Nāmah*) but architectural history was again practically excluded. Thus, for example, while his visits to Akbar's tomb at Agra (A.D.1605–12). were scrupulously recorded, the building itself has not been described and we do not know how it was planned and designed. Such a beautiful and marvellous monument as the Tomb of I'timad–ud–Daulah at Agra (1622-28) has been altogether ignored by the historians of Jehangir's reign, probably because building activity was then such a common practice that nobody considered it worthwhile to write on it. How and why such a unique and wonderful series of glazed–tile work as the Picture–Wall of Lahore Fort was produced (1612–19) has not been recorded, to cite another example of lacuna of medieval histories.[8]

'Abdul Hamid Lahauri is the first Persian historian who has, in his history of the first 20 years of the reign of Shah Jehan (1628–48), entitled *Bādshāh–Nāmah* (or *Pādshah–Nāmah*)[9], systematically described the contemporary buildings of Shah Jehan as a regular subject–matter of his narrative. He wrote on the Taj Mahal, for example, in Vol. I, Part–I, pp.385-89, 402–3, 487; Vol. II, pp.92, 322–30, 628–29 and 713–14 (= 22 pages) and this is, by far, the first detailed record of the construction of a medieval building. Other buildings of Shah Jehan have been similarly described. Though Akbar was also a great builder, architecture was the most important engagement of his grandson who maintained a full-fledged Building Department, (Dīwān–i–'Imārat) and spent most lavishly on its projects, which thus constituted the primary chronicle of his reign.

A large number of European travellers visited India during the medieval period, e.g. Fr. Anthony Monserrate and Ralph Fitch in the reign of Akbar; William Hawkins, William Finch, Thomas Coryat, Thomas Roe, and Francisco Pelasaert in that of Jehangir; and Fr. Sebastian Manrique, Peter Mundy, J.B. Tavernier and Niccolao Manucci in that of Shah Jehan.[10] Their observations contain valuable record of the monuments which they visited or which were being built contemporarily. Their accounts are useful in knowing these medieval buildings, though they have to be used extremely carefully not only owing to the limitations of these foreigners of language, culture and accessibility to correct information, but also because of their 'fancies' and 'biases' which filtered into their narratives unconsciously. They wrote primarily for their countrymen, and they had a particular standpoint to project.

(c) Narrative Literatures

Documentation and study of medieval monuments began with the establishment of the *de facto* British rule in India, in early 19th century A.D.. Firstly, a large number of War-Memoirs, Diaries, Travel Accounts, Gazetteers and Guide-Books were published in which these buildings were noticed or described, along with the personal narrative of the author. Essentially,these were ***'observations'*** and constituted a 'Narrative Literature', the utility of which lies mainly in the fact that they recorded information on these monuments for the first time in modern India, and laid foundations of a preliminary survey of the subject. Beginning with James Forbes' *Oriental Memoirs* (4 vols, London 1813) and Major Thorn's *Memoirs of War in North India* (London 1818), the other important works of this class are given in Appendix I under Narrative Literature[11].

Appendix I

(i) War-Memoirs, Diaries & Travel-Accounts (A.D. 1803-60)

Reginald Heber, Narrative of a Journey through the Upper Provinces of India (2 vols. London 1828)

James Tod, Annals & Antiquities of Rajasthan (2 vols. London 1829 and 1832)

Major Archer, Tours in Upper India (2 vols, London 1833)

Emma Roberts, Scenes and Characteristics of Hindustan (London 1837)

James Tod, Travels in Western India (London 1839)

W.H. Sleeman, Rambles and Recollections of An Indian Official (2 vols, London 1844)

D.C. Mundy, Journal of a Tour in India (London 1858)

W.H. Russell, My Diary in India (2 vols, London 1860)

The names of such authors in this class as Mrs Eliza Fay, Tiefenthaler, Honigberger, James Prinsep, and John Malcolm may also be recounted.

(ii) Official Gazetteers (1820-1930)

Calcutta & Agra Gazetteers (Calcutta 1820)

E. Thornton, Gazetteer of the East India Co (4 vols, London 1854)

F.S. Growse, Mathura : A District Gazetteer (1883)

E.T. Atkinson & F.H. Fisher, Statistical, Descriptive and Historical Accounts of North-Western Provinces of India, Vol. III (Allahabad 1884) and other volumes of this series

H.R. Nevill, Agra : A Gazetteer (Allahabad 1905) and other District and Imperial Gazetteers of India which were prepared mainly for administrative purposes but also included historical narratives and accounts of the existing monuments

(iii) Guide-Books (1850-1947)

Markham Kittoe, Illustrations of Indian Architecture from the Muhammedan Conquest Downwards (Calcutta 1838)

H.G. Keene, Handbook for Visitors to Agra and Neighbourhood (Calcutta 1854, 1862, 1869, 1874, 1878, etc.; ed. E.A. Duncan, Calcutta 1906)

H.G. Keene, Handbook for Visitors to Delhi (1874, 1882, 1899, etc.; Calcutta 1906)

Frederick Cooper, The Handbook for Delhi (Delhi 1863)

A. Harcourt, A New Guide to Delhi (Allahabad 1866)

James Fergusson & T.C. Hope, Architecture of Ahmedabad (London 1866)

J.T.N. Guide to the Taj at Agra (Lahore, 1854, 1862, 1869 etc.)

A.M. Cantrell, An Account of the Ruins of Bijapur (Bombay 1872)

Stephan Carr, Archaeology and Monumental Remains of Delhi (Ludhiana 1876)

H.H. Cole, Architecture of Ancient Delhi (London 1872, 1884)

Lepel, Griffin, Famous Monuments of Central India (London 1886)

H. Cousens, Bijapur Guide (Poona 1889)

S.C. Mukherji, Travellers' Guide to Agra (delhi 1892)

Syed Muhammad Latif, Lahore (Lahore 1892)

Syed Muhammad Latif, Agra, Historical and Descriptive (Calcutta 1896)

H.G. Fanshawe, Delhi, Past and Present (London 1902)

Ernest Barnes, Dhar and Mandu. A Guide (Bombay 1902)

Jawala Sahai, Dig. Its History and Palaces (Lahore 1902)

J.A. Devenish, The Bhawans or Garden-Palaces of Dig (Allahabad 1903)

G.R. Hearn, The Seven Cities of Delhi (Delhi 1906)

G.S. Sherman, A Comprehensive Guide to Agra and Its Historical Buildings (Agra 1907)

Major, Luard, Dhar and Mandu (Allahabad 1912)

H. Sharp, Delhi, Its Glory and Buildings (Bombay 1921)

Muhammad Fasihuddin, The Sharqi Monuments of Jaunpur (Allahabad 1922)

G. Yazdani, Mandu : The City of Joy (Oxford, 1929)

M.A. Chaghtai, Le Tadje de Agra (The Taj of Agra) (French) (Brussels 1938)

G. Yazdani, Bidar : Its History and Monuments (London 1947)

To this list may also be added such works as the Chronicles of the Pathan Kings of Delhi (London 1871) by Edward Thomas. Though, essentially, a work on medieval numismatics, and for that matter a basic work, it also notices the monuments and records their inscriptions.

(iv) Urdu Works (1846-1931)

Some very useful works of this class were also published in Urdu, the following being the most important of them:

Sayyid Ahmed Khan, Āthār'al-Ṣanādīd (Urdu) (First ed. Delhi 1846, revised and abridged ed. Delhi 1854) (tr. into English by R. Nath : Monuments of Delhi : A Historical Study (New Delhi 1979)

M. Muin'ud-Din, Muin'al-athar (Urdu) (Agra 1904) (Its English version was also published under the title Taj and its Environments. Agra 1905)

Muhammad Sa'id Ahmed Marehravi, Bostān-i-Akhyār or Tazkirā-Mashāhir Akbarābād (Urdu) (Agra A.H. 1331)

Muhammad Sa'id Ahmed Marehravi, Āthār'al-Akbarī (Urdu) (on the monuments of Fatehpur Sikri) (Agra 1906)

Bashiruddin Ahmed, Vāqiāt-i-Dār'ul-Hūkūmat (Urdu) (History of Delhi, The Imperial City) (3 vols, Hyderabad, 1919)

Muhammad Sa'id Ahmed Marehravi, Muraqqa'-i-Akbarābād or Tārīkh-i-Agrah (Urdu) (On the monuments of Agra) (Agra 1931)

By and large, it made up a faithful record of the monuments as they were noticed by the officers, travellers and scholars and, essentially, a beautiful ***Historical Literature***, mysterious and romantic, which the enlightened people were interested to read and enjoy. It was absolutely necessary to 'know' the people and their culture in order to be able to govern them and this also fulfilled an administrative need. The official policy of the British East India Co. to belittle the achievements of the medieval period had been filtering into these writings, but it was limited to those who worked on its pay-rolls.

(d) **Archaeological Data (A.D. 1862–1947)**

Unlike the guide-books which were essentially private ventuers, a systematic study of these monuments was also taken up on institutional and governmental level about the same time and, in fact, from an earlier period with the founding of the Asiatic Society of Bengal by Sir William Jones in 1784. It was not exclusive to ancient relics as *stūpas, vihāras, stambhas,* temples and Brāhmī inscriptions; medieval things as tombs and mosques were also covered, though, of course, emphasis was given to the former owing to the larger occurrence of these relics over the country. Thus, articles on medieval art and architecture frequently appeared in the *Asiatick Researches* (London/ Calcutta, Vol. I, 1788 to XX, 1839);*Journal of the Bengal Asiatic Society*, First Series, Vol. I (1832) to 75 (1904) and in its *Memoirs* and *Proceedings*. This set up a trend and the gentleman Englishman who was as honest and conscientious as he was cultured, soon channelised this study from the institution of the Asiatic Sooiety to the Government. With the appointment of Alexander Cunningham, as Archaeological Surveyor on 22nd Janurary1862, a Department of Archaeology came into being. Its objective had already been spelled out by James Prinsep in the *Bengal Asiatic Society's Journal* (1838, p.227) :

"what the learned world demand of us in India is to be quite certain of our data, to place the monumental record before them exactly as it now exists, and to interpret it faithfully and literally.

Thus began the era of the archaeoogical survey of Indian antiquities which, between 1862 and 1947, placed on record a vast literature on the subject which laid the foundations and prepared the plinth for this study. Cunnigham surveyed almost the whole of northern India and the vast data he collected was compiled in 23 volumes (vol. I, 1862–65 to XXIII, 1883–84) which included Muslim monuments. For example, the monuments of Delhi were treated in vol. I (pp. 131–231 by Cunningham) and vol. IV (pp. 1–91 by J.D. Beglar) and those of Agra in vol. IV (pp. 93–247 by A.C.L. Caralleyle). H.H. Cole's Reports from the year 1881–82 to 1884–85 brought a large number of medieval monuments on record. He also prepared several volumes on *Preservation of National Monuments*, including the monuments of Gwalior, Agra, Delhi, Lahore and other medieval sites. Other great archaeologists who pioneered the movement and collected the basic archaeological data which further advanced this study were James Burgess, J.B. Keith, Henry Cousens, A.Rea, H.K. Sastri, W.H. Propert, A.H. Longhurst, T.Bloch, D.B. Spooner, A.Führer, E.W.Smith. M.A. Stein and J.Ph. Vogel, for example.[12]

A series called the New Imperial Series comprising monographs on ancient and medieval sites was intitated in 1874, and by the year 1933, its 53 volumes were published. It included such basic archaeological works on medieval architecture as the following ;

Vol. III	:	*Bidar & Aurangabad* (by James Burgess, 1878)
XI	:	*Sharqi Architecture of Jaunpur* (Führer & Smith 1889)
XVIII	:	*Mogul Architecture of Fatehpur Sikri*, in 4 parts (E.W. Smith, 1895–98)
XXIII	:	*Muhammedan Architecture of Gujarat* (James Burgess, 1896)
XXIV	:	*Muhammedan Architecture of Ahmedabad* (Part–I) (James Burgess, 1896)
XXXIII	:	*Muhammedan Architecture of Ahmedabad* (Part–II) (James Burgess, 1905)
XXX	:	*Moghul Colour Decoration of Agra* (E.W. Smith, 1900)
XXXV	:	*Akbar's Tomb at Sikandara Agra* (E.W. Smith, 1909)
XXXVIII	:	*Bijapur & Its Architectural Remains* (Henry Cousens, 1916)

Another series of archaeological monographs known as *Memoirs of the A.S.I.* began in 1919 and in it, upto 1947, 69 volumes were published. This also included monographs on medieval sites, e.g.

No. 9 *Mosque of Shiekh Abdun–Nabi Delhi* (Zafar Hasan, 1921)

10 *Guide to Nizamuddin* (Zafar Hasan, 1922)

19 *The Jami' Masjid of Badaun* (J.F. Balakiston, 1926)

22 *An Historical Memoir on the Qutb* (J.B. Page, 1926)

52 *A Memoir on Kotla Firoz Shah* (J.B. Page, 1937)

In the meantime an enlightened Viceroy, Lord Curzon, took over the administration of the country and initiated a policy of systematic conservation of historical monuments. This inaugurated a new era of this study. A full-fledged Archaeological Survey of India (A.S.I.) came into being and John Marshall (later Sir) was appointed its Director General. *The Ancient Monuments Preservation Act* was enacted in 1904. Beginning with 1902–3, regular *Annual Reports* of the Survey were published and 34 voluminous reports from 1902–3 to 1936–37 brought on record a vast classified data on medieval as well as ancient monuments. Annual Reports of different circles, as for example, Bengal Circle from 1900–01 to 1904–5, thereafter renamed Eastern Circle from 1905–06 to 1920–21; Central Circle 1919–20 to 1920–21; Frontier Circle 1904–5 to 1920–21; Northern Circle 1905–6 to 1920–21; Punjab Circle 1889–90, 1901–2, 1902–3, thereafter renamed Punjab & U.P. Circle 1903–4, 1904–5; Southern Circle 1881 to 1921–21; and Western Circle 1889–90 to 1920–21, were also published simultaneously.

It is this archaeological data, in fact, which laid down the foundations of the study of ancient and medieval architecture of India, in right earnest and in required details. It provided all the necessary plans, sections, elevations and the most precise measurements, and even drawings of designs in scale, in polychrome, and there is hardly any doubt that, for this basic and vital data, we are immeasurably indebted to our pre-Independence archaeologists. They were honest, sincere and entirely devoted to the work they had on hand. They knew their subject. There were no financial worries and no administrative problems, no reservation and no incompetent officers and no corruption, and each one of them, from Cunningham to Marshall, dedicated his whole life to archaeology as a Śākta dedicates himself to his Devī. They saved our heritage for us in the hope that we would preseve it.

At times, of course,they have tried to interpret the things with which they were confronted but, essentially, it is *archaeological data.* Even when they have ventured to write *History* from this data, they have maintained the utmost possible impartiality and objectivity and all the time they have rigidly adhered to the technicalities of the matter. They have rarely indulged in surmises; and they had no fantasies to describe. The East India Co. policy to tarnish the glories of the medieval period in India had withered out, and this is entirely an unbiased study. They had no viewpoint and no preconceptions to impose upon their study and, by and large, this data is free from any deliberate attempt to give History any particular colour and complexion.

(e) **Critical Works on Art History (A.D. 1876–1947)**

James Fergusson who visited and surveyed the monuments *in situ*, both ancient and medieval, between 1835 and 1845, was the first scholar to write interpretative history of Indian Architecture and it was he who pioneered this study. After publishing some works on ancient relics, e.g. *On the Study of Indian Architecture* (London 1867) and *Illustrations of Various Studies of Indian architecture* (London 1869), he produced his classic : *History of Indian & Eastern Architecture* which was later revised and enlarged in two volumes by James Burgess. It included an expert and technical enumeration of Muslim monuments of India which he placed under several styles. He used racial and dynastic appellations, some of which like 'Pathan' were not correct. In one case, he went as far as to use the term 'bastard' for a style which, besides being in bad taste, was wrong; 'pietra dura' was also a misnomer which he used to denote Indian 'inlay'. He also suffered from bias– like his successor Sir Banister Fletcher *(A History of Architecture : On the Comparative Method,* in several editions)– that almost always prevailed in India; to him 'ornament' played a decisive role in the evolution of its architectural styles. He did not distinguish between the two fundamental divisions of all fine arts of India, viz. *Mārgīya* (classical) and *Deshīya* (regional or local). It was, in fact, too early in the middle of the 19th century A.D. to identify the sources of inspiration, the determinants and the evolutionary process, and Fergusson made mistakes. But he did not err much in the treatment of the techniques of '*spanning the space*' and '*roofing*', which developed in India, and in art–analysis he had no preconceptions and he had no policy to impose upon this study. He was a fair and impartial expert in his subject. That is why, even after more than a century, his work is indispensable.

Vincent A. Smith (*A History of Fine Art in India and Ceylon*, Oxford 1911) had his own limitations. He was an author, rather than a subject–expert and unlike Fergusson who knew the engineering technicalities alright and was more an architect than a historian. Smith was not conversant with his data and material, and he committed errors of omission and commission, though truly, he did not do this deliberately under a policy. E.B. Havell, on the other hand, was an avowed 'orientalist' who interpreted art–history with reference to, and in the context of the faiths and beliefs of the people and, in this respect, he extended A.K. Coomaraswamy's metaphysical approach in medieval architecture of India. There is no point in denying that he did it a little too zealously in his works published in the first quarter of the 20th centurye.g.

Ideals of Indian Art (London 1911)

A Handbook to Agra and the Taj (Calcutta 1912)

Indian Architecture : Its Psychology, Structure and History (London 1913)

Ancient and Medieval Architecture of India (London 1915)

A Handbook of Indan Art (London 1920)

However, there can hardly be any doubt as to his conviction and sincerity.

Several descriptive and narrative works, covering various aspects of medieval Indian architecture independently, were also written. C.M.V. Stuart's *Gardens of the Great Mughals* (London 1913) and J.Ph. Vogel's *Picture wall of the Lahore fort* (1921) (A publication of the A.S.I.) may be mentioned as examples. Such reputed journals as *Indian Art & Letters* (London) and *Journal of Indian Art* also regularly published articles and monographs with excellent illustrations (including colour plates)on medieval monuments. K.A.C. Creswell, an international authority on Islamic Architecture, published several important articles on *Indian solutions of the complex problem of roofing*, e.g. 'Indian Domes of Persian Origin' (*The Asiatic, Review*, New Series, vol. V, 1914); 'Lotus–Dome' (*The Indian Antiquary*, July 1915) and 'Vaulting System of the Hindola Mahal at Mandu' (*The Indian Antiquary*, Vol. XLVII, 1918). Medieval buildings were also noticed, or referred to, in the works of such historians of Islamic Architecture (of the world) as A.Choisy, M.S. Dimand, R.A. Jirazbhoy, E. Kuhnel, G. Marcais, L.A. Meyer, G.Migeon, D.T. Rice, E.T. Richmond, G.T. Rivoira and H. Saladin, but this was treated mostly as an appendix rather than in the form of an independent school. Precisely, its indigenous character which distinguishes it so overwhelmingly from the typical architectural styles of other Islamic countries, was almost always by-passed, or lost.

With all the vast archaeological data, including drawings and photographs, available to him, Percy Brown produced his classical work, in inimitable English, viz. *Indian Architecture* (Vol. I : Buddhist and Hindu Period; Vol.II : Islamic Period, Bombay 1942). He wrote this history of architecture with a fair amount of impartiality and objectivity, though, of course, he missed the things a number of times, firstly, because it was not physically possible for him to visit every monument he studied and discussed. Architecture is a visual art and without site study, which alone can tell us that a *chhatrī* shown in the photograph is hexagonal or really octagonal, justice cannot be done to it. And, secondly, even as late as that, he could not entirely get rid of the *colonial legacy* which weighed heavily upon every British author during British rule. He has a tendency to connect everything superb and sublime in Indian art with Athens, Florence, Venice, Milan and other centres of Greek, Roman and Medieval European civilizations; in fact, he viewed the medieval art from the point of view of the European Renaissance than of the Bhakti Movement which entirely changed the form and fabric of the life of the Indian people subsequent to the invasion of Tīmūr (Tamerlane) (A.D. 1398)

Percy Brown's *Indian Architerture* (Islamic Period, serveral editions) gradually became the *standard reference book* on this subject, on which almost all subsequent writers of books for tourists, or text-books for students freely drew. Thus, for example, A.L.Srivastava entirely borrowed from this book for writing on Akbar's architecture in his 3-volume series: *Akbar, the Great.* So did Z.A. Desai and others. There is absolutely no doubt that it was owing to its merits, both linguistic and scholarly, that Brown's work became basic and indispensable to a large degree for further studies on Medieval Indian Architecture.

Reference in this connection must also be made to Dr Mulk Raj Anand who edited 134 numbers of the *Marg* (Bombay), in about 35 years' time since 1947, regularly on a quarterly basis. The prestigious Journal was devoted to Indian Arts and Crafts, ancient, medieval and modern, and special numbers are dedicated to almost all major medieval sites and buildings. Besides the learned editorials, each such number, which is in fact a monograph, is written by a subject expert, i.e. the historian specialised in that field and, as such, each one makes a valuable contribution to the subject and updates this study. Above all is the fact of its exquisite production and *excellent visuals* prepared by D.H. Sahiar, assistant Editor, Anand and Sahiar did not do any number without visiting the site and verifying the data *in situ* and, along with scholarly contents and superb visuals, this is the other merit of these numbers of the *Marg*. For each number, Anand created an expert and dedicated *team* and perhaps no other institution or organization any where else could produce such a wonderful series on Arts and Architecture of India.

It must, however, be noted – and this has been generally complained – that Stella Kramrish's *The Hindu Temple* (2 vols, Calcultta, 1946 and subsequent editions) which is a classic on Temple Architecture, has no matching literature on Indo-Muslim Architecture. Yes, it is so and the reason is very simple: that mosque (*masjid*) or tomb (*maqbarah*) has no universal and standard theory of construction like the temple, and the mosque is no match to the temple theoretically. Even the Taj Mahal does not stand on the same *intellectual level* on which stands the Kandarīya Mahādeva Temple of Khajuraho.

(f) Propagandist Freelancing : (Post –1947)

It goes to the credit of the pre-Independence Muslim scholars that, though they produced excellent works on the subject, they were not biased and never tried to see things in the monuments which were not actually there. They carefully avoided symbolisation of the physical phenomena in terms of Islamic mythology. Even R.A. Jairazbhoy's study of Muslim architecture of India is balanced; though feelers and suggestions are at times proposed, he never imposed things extraneously. No religious fanaticism is reflected in their works. Even in such a stage of the study as the first half of the 19th century A.D., Sayyid Ahmed Khan in his *Athar al–Samadid* maintained an absolutely dispassionate and unbiased view of history and propounded the theory that the Qutb Mīnār was orginally built by the Hindus and the Turks converted it, subsequent to the establishment of the Delhi Sultanate.[13] He was wrong, no doubt, but he wrote what he believed, and there can never be any doubt as to the honesty and sincerity of these scholars.

The post–Independence era saw the rise of a band of self–styled historians taking up this study, as a hobby, with a view to undo the glories of the medieval period and its constructive role in the development of Indian culture and fine arts. Led by P.N. Oak (the President of an Institute of Rewriting Indian History, without any academic affiliations) they made the Muslim monuments their target and published booklets and pamphlets propagating the theory that all these monuments, including the Qutb Mīnār, the palatial mansions of Fatehpur Sikiri and the Taj Mahal, were originally Hindu buildings, and the Musalmans had only converted them and they never built anything new. In fact they have no grounding in history, historical method or historiography; they come from various professions, mostly Law. They have become historians without reading Persian, Sanskrit and Hindi sources (histories and literatures), or Travel Accounts, Inscriptions. They have not even consulted the archaeological and critical works cited above. Here and there, they come across a lotus, a *çakra*, a *swastika* and *kalaśa*, and only on the basis of the occurrence of a few motifs, they declared that the building was orginally Hindu. They are not aware of the evolutionary process : how the things have integrated and the medieval style has evolved

They are also altogether ignorant of the Śilpa–texts as for example, the *Samarāṅgaṇa–Sūtradhāra* (1018–54) and the *Aparājitapṛçchā* (c. A.D.1200), and do not know how a Hindu temple was built and whether a temple could be converted to the dimensions (on the vertical and horizontal axis) of the Taj Mahal, or whether the Hindus ever raised tapering *kīrti–stambhas* with *sopāna* (inner stairways) to support the theory of the conversion of the Quṭb Mīnār.

(g) Implanting of Islamic Symbolism

The most unfortunate aspect of this development is that a few foreign scholars (European and American), aided and abetted by some Indian art-historians,[14] have found in it an opportunity to implant their own biased views and theories upon the subject. Some books and articles have been recently published which attempt, on the one hand to defend and deny the early iconoclastic demolitions of the Hindu temples and their conversion into mosques, e.g. at Delhi and Ajmer;[15] and, on the other, to ascribe the development of the medieval art and architecture of India to the religion of Islam, read Islamic symbolism in it and interpret its various phenomena accordingly. It is more dangerous than the Oakian propaganda. If the British East India Company did everything to tarnish the medieval glories to incite the Hindus against the Muslims, this is an attempt to incite the latter to assume and assert an aggressive individuality and an independent identity by highlighting the same glories, this time in the context of orthodox Islam.

It must be noted that the nomad Arabs of Hidjaz had neither sculptors nor artists, nor architects nor schools of art.[16] Their way of life did not include the practice of arts. Their architectural resources, before they started on their career of conquest, was barely enough to give the rudest expression to their needs. Arabia constituted an almost perfect architectural vacuum. In its origin, what we call Islamic art a little loosely, was a "simple aggregate of constructional procedures and decorative formulae adapted by Islam from the techniques of the peoples under its domination,[17] and, precisely, it was a People's Art. Except for its choice and preference for certain designs and motifs, the religion of Islam had hardly anything to say in the evolution of this art, and it is wrong to give it such a religious connotation as 'Islamic', particularly in the context of its development in Medieval India where, instead, it must be given the social identification: 'Muslim' and it must be correctly denoted as 'Indo-Muslim Architecture'.

Writings of two American authors, the most representative of this class, Wayne E. Begley and Catherine B. Asher, may be briefly examined in this connection. The former obtained his Ph.D. from the University of Pennsylvania on the subject: 'The Chronology of Mahayana Buddhist Architecture and Painting at Ajanta' and published a book on Hindu iconography. But, without grounding in Medieval Indian History, Culture and Arts, he switched on to medieval architecture and calligraphy. Reference may be made first to his article: 'The myth of the Taj Mahal and a New Theory of its Symbolic Meaning'[18] in which he has tried to connect the Taj with the religion and mythology of Islam, with the help of a selective data, without taking into consideration the basic things of the matter. The Taj is primarily a 'rauḍa', i.e. a monumental tomb, and he has overlooked the fact that the idea of raising a monumental tomb is basically un-Islamic. The *Quran* does not mention *'maqbarah'* (tomb). The *Hādith* (traditions), on the other hand, forbids making of tombs with stone, or burnt brick, or to write a verse of the *Quran* upon it, and lay down that the grave (*qabr*), after the dead body is laid into it, should be filled in by earth, or, at the most, by unburnt *(kachchī)* bricks and levelled to the ground or raised to the height of a camel's back.

Thus, one Hadīth records: "Abū dā' ud related that Al-qāsim, the grandson of Abū Bakr came to 'Āyishah, the most beloved wife of the late Prophet and said, 'O Mother, lift up the curtain of the Prophet's tomb and of his two friends Abū Bakr (first Khalīfah after Muḥammad, 632-34) and 'Umar(second Khalīfah, 634-44)' and she uncovered the graves which were neither high nor low but almost one span in height and covered with red gravel".[19]

Ṣaḥīḥ'ul-Bukārī, one of the six greatest authorities on Hadīth, noted similarly : "Sufyan at-Tammar related that he saw the Prophet's grave and the top of it was like a camel's back." *Ṣaḥīḥ'ul-Muslim*, an equal authority on Hadīth, also noted: "Āmr b. Sa'd b. Abū Waqqāṣ told that Sa'd b Abū Waqqāṣ said during his illness of which he died: Make a niche for me in the side of the grave and set up (unburnt) bricks over me as was done in case of Allah's Messenger."[20]

And, "Faḍāla b. 'Ubaid said...' I heard the messenger of Allah commanding (us) to level the grave."[21]

And,...Alī said: "Should I not send you on the same mission as Allah's Messenger sent me? Do not leave an image without obliterating it, or a high grave without levelling it."[22]

And, Jābir said: "Allah's messenger forbade that the graves should be plastered or they be used as sitting places (for the people) or a building should be built over them".[23]

And, "Jabir said that he was forbidden to build pucca

graves"[24]

Erection of monumental tomb (*maqbarah)* over a grave is thus canonically ruled out under the Islamic Law and there cannot possibly be an Islamic symbolism of such a grand mausoleum as the Taj Mahal. There is absolutely no evidence in support of this view and the proposed new theory is, to use Begley's own phrase, "Patently absurd'. Nothing of such an architectural representation of a mythical thing is laid down in any text and the theological dicta are being implanted on the subject the way a round pebble is inserted into a square hole.

Begley entertains his own fantastic views of the Islamic Paradise (Arabic *Jannat;* Persian *Bahisht)* in respect to its incarnation at the Taj Mahal. The Quran refers to eight paradises as follows:

I. *Jannatu'I-Khuld* (The Garden of Eternity) IXXV.16)

II. *Dāru's-Salām* (The Dwelling of Peace) VI. 127)

III. *Dāru'I-Qarār* (The Dwelling which Abideth) XL. 42)

IV. *Jannātu'I-Adn* (The Gardens of Eden) (IX.73)

V. *Jannātu'I-Ma'Wā* (The Gardens of Refuge) XXXII-19)

VI. *Jannātu'n-Na'im* (The Gardens of Delight) V.70)

VII. *'Illiyun* (LXXXIII.18)

VIII. *Jannat'ul-Firdaus* (The Garden of Paradise) (XVIII.107)

Of these, the eighth viz. the *Jannat'ul-Firdaus is* the highest and the most prized paradise. Above all these is '*Arsh,* or the Seat of God. The *Quran* (e.g. LXXvI.12-22; LVI.12-39; LV.46-78 and XLVII-15) describes the paradise in profuse details. Summarily the Islamic paradise provides in the world beyond the following four things to the male believer (i.e. to the exclusion of women) in reward for their meritorious deeds they would do in this world:

1. Gardens and thier cool shades with flowing water through canals, rivulets and waterfalls;

2. abundant riches; pearls, jewels and diamonds; golden throne with precious stones, jars and cups of silver; carpets, cushions, silken robes and brocades;

3. fruits, meat (flesh of fowls, etc.), milk and above all, crystal-clear wine; and

4. free, exclusive and eternal sex with beautiful and virgin *houris* (heavenly damsels) and young lads.

Precisely, these heavens provided sensual (physical) pleasures and enjoyment of the things which were denied to the Arab by nature in his hard, unsettled desert life. Water was scarce in the Arabian desert, and garden was a myth. He lived on bare necessities and poverty was the way of life, robbery a profession and wealth was a dream. He lived on camel's milk and date-palm and pined for good things to eat and drink. And, finally, in the desert family life was rare. Sodomy was a Semitic practice, most prevalent in the desert, hence the repeated injunctions against it in the *Quran.* Sex offered, therefore, the greatest temptation.

All these sensual pleasures of the paradise had no meaning to the Mughals who had already made their provisions in their palaces. Obviously, Begley did not understand the outlook and attitude of the Mughals towards these Islamic things which were originally related to the Bedouin way of Arab life and for which they hardly cared. In fact, as the Persian inscriptions on their monuments amply show, they did not hesitate to belittle and outdo the Islamic paradise by bringing it on par with their own creations.[25]

Thus, Akbar's inscription in the Khwābgāh Palace at Fatehpur Sikri reads: "This Imperial Palace (Qasr-i-Shāhī) is in every way better than the Highest paradise (*Khulde-Barin)*; there is no doubt that it is the Highest Paradise. The room of the Emperor is beautiful, pleasant and lofty and comprises in its structure the Highest Paradise. The *rizwān,* the keeper of the paradise, made the floor of this palace as clean as a mirror and the Hur-ul'in (*houris)* use the dust of this palace like collyrium (*kājal or surmah)* in their eyes (it is so sacred and soothing). Whoever worships the dust of this threshold, as that of Heaven, obtains through the virtue of the dust a shining forehead like Venus (Zuhrā)".[26]

It is surprising that the palace of Akbar was not only designated as the Highest paradise and the *rizwān* (keeper) of the Islamic Paradise was employed herein as *farrāsh,* but the people were also advised to worship the dust of its threshold. Thus the mythical Heaven of Islam which had been promised to the believers as reward of their virtuous deeds has been belittled, surpassed and excelled by the palace of Akbar.

Jehangir also had similar Persian incriptions composed and inscribed on the tomb of his father at Sikandara, Agra. One on the facades of the main gateway reads that this building was more pleasant than the Garden of Paradise (*Bāgh-i-Bahisht)* and also loftier than the Divine Throne (*Arsh-i-Barin*), thousands of Paradises are situated in its garden and in its garden are employed thousands of *rizwāns* as servants (*ghulām*). It is the Garden of Eden (*Jannāt-u-Adn*) itself.[27]

The inscriptions of Shah Jehan have similar contents. The one in the Dīwān-i-Khāṣṣ of Agra Fort reads that the erection of this lofty place exalted Akbarabad to the Ninth Heaven (viz. '*Arsh)* and it embellished and adorned the sky; the sky lies beneath it like a shadow.[28] The Dīwān-i-Khāṣṣ of the Red Fort Delhi bears the famous couplet:

Agar Firdaus bar-rūye zamīn-ast,

Hamin-asto Hamīn-asto hamīn-ast.[29]

Literally, it means : if there be a heaven on Earth, it is here. But, the incarnation of *Firdaus* in the city of Shāhjehānābād is suggestive also the other way that is why to aspire for Heaven after death, in the world beyond (which may not exist at all) ? The Grand Mughal Emperor has created one on earth itself. Precisely, it means that instead of the mythical Paradise, it is the real Paradise here with all its provisions, viz. Garden and flowing water, wealth, wine and women.

The inscription of the Jāmi Masjid of Delhi also has similar contents, that its sacred arches and magnificent domes are comparable with the constellations of the heavens and, in fact, they are superior to them, and the *kalash* of its dome bestows radiance on the celestial lights of Paradise.[30] Similarly, the inscription of the Moti Masjid of Agra Fort reads that this bright ka'bah is the rival of the heavenly tabernacle ... its durable plinth is as high as the leg of the Divine Throne and its benefit-showering dome is arm in arm with the portico of Paradise, each of its gilt pinnacles is like a candle imparting light to the heavenly chandeliers; by the blessing of Emperor Shah Jehan's footstep the earth indulges itself in thousands of boastings over the heaven and owing to the abundance of these favours the Heaven has been subordinated to the earth.[31]

This is how the Grand Mughals belittled, in a certain degree ridiculed, the mythical heavens of Islam. In fact, they cared a fig for it, as all that it provided had already been brought about by them in these palatial mansions. It was not necessary, therefore, for one to die and go to *jannat;* he could enjoy all these sensual pleasures in his life-time at Agra and Delhi.

If bare similarity of a phenomenon, say the description of a garden with flowing water in the Paradise of Islam on the one hand, and its actual occurrence at the Taj Mahal on the other, could be an evidence in Begley's case, it can be equally applied in Oak's case, which would be absurd either way. History of Art is not a fanciful and subjective interpretaion but an analysis of the evidence vis-a-vis the evolutionary process. The garden and water-devices of the Taj Mahal are not there by accident at the suggestion of a Maulvi, but are a constituent of Mughal funereal architecture, the gradual development of which can be traced from Babur who introduced these features at his Bāgh-i-Zar Afshān at Agra, around a central building in a four-quartered *(chāhār-bāgh* or *Chār-bāgh)* scheme. He wanted it to be his tomb.[32] Had these features been inspired by the religion of Islam, pre-Mughal tombs, at least those of Fīrūz Shāh Tughluq and Sikandar Lodi, would also have had them. But this is not the case and, in fact, there is no Islamic symbolism in the idea of the Taj Mahal which marks the zenith of the development in Indo-Muslim Architecture. The religion had nothing to say in the matter of its evolution, simply because this religion is basically against the erection of monumental tombs. The Quranic verses have also been depicted against the Hadīth *prescription* which forbids making of tombs with stone brick, or writing a verse on it. Begley has no evidence whatsoever to support his hypothesis and he is trying to impose his own far fetched views on the subject. What he calls a new theory is in fact, a new misnomer.

Begley's second article, "The Symbolic Role of Calligraphy on three Mosques of Shah Jehan"[33] deals only with Shah Jehan's buildings, excluding those of Akbar, and from those he selects three public mosques of Delhi, Agra and Agra Fort only. Persian texts of the inscriptions of these three mosques were published in our work : Calligraphic Art in Mughal Architecture (Iran Society, Calcutta 1979) as follows :

Jami Majid, Delhi, pp. 64–66,

Jami Masjid, Agra pp. 62–63,

Moti Masjid, Agra pp. 67–68.

Their English translations had also been given, vide Appendix–Q, pp. 47–48A; Appendix–P, pp. 46–47 and Appendix–R, pp. 48A–48B respectively, and commentary on pp. 29–31. Yet, by omission or commission, Begley does not refer to it and laments: "Their contents have never been systematically analysed", just to show, in a typical American style, that he was going to break new ground. How could one afford to ignore Sayyid Ahmed Khan's *Āthā al-Sanādīd* (Urdu, Delhi 1846, rep. 1854) (tr. by this author : *Monuments of Delhi : A Historical Study*, New Delhi 1979) or Aziz' ur Rehman's *History of Jami Masjid, Delhi* (Delhi 1936) and write on the inscriptions of the Jami Masjid of Delhi, for example ?

He exerts on the hypothesis that these inscriptions are analogous to iconographic depictions on monuments and these words have been used like images. He discussed their contents under three heads : factual, political and religious, in each literal and allegorical (?) meanings. All this is academic acrobatics. He cities no evidence. What he has conveniently ignored is the fact that the very idea of using images is a taboo in Islam and that these are not Quranic verses but Persian eulogies in lavish praise of Shah Jehan and his daughter Jehanara in which, as discussed above, the Islamic theological Heaven has been belittled, if not actually ridiculed: "This bright Ka'bah is the rival of the Heavenly tabernacle... Its durable plinth is as high as the leg of the Divine Throne, and its benefit–showering dome is arm–in–arm with the portico of Paradise....each of its gilt pinnacle is like a candle imparting light to the Heavenly Chandeliers. Verily it is an exalted place of Paradise made of single resplendent pearl...the breeze of Paradise craves the dust of his heaven–exalted court.[34] These are panegyrics pure and simple, and Begley is trying to see things which are not there.

He has used only selective portions of these inscriptions, of his choice and convenience. Other contents of these inscriptions which are technically outrageous to the Islamic religious and political theory, including Shah Jehan's assumption of 'The Divine Right of Kingship' in contravention to the basic concept of Islam of a world *Khilāfat*, have been ignored by Begley.

There is no inscription, Arabic or Persian, in any of the three white marble private mosques of Shah Jehan, viz. the Mīnā and the Nagīnā Masjid in Agra Fort and the Mīnā Masjid in the Red Fort Delhi. If calligraphy was to play a 'symbolic role' in the mosque architecture of Shah Jehan, these could not have been altogether devoid of it. Is it that the 'symbolic role' was not personally relished by Shah Jehan and it was meant for public consumption only ?

Begley has no evidence whatsoever to refute that calligraphics in Mughal buildings, besides being historical document, have been used as architectural ornament and, hence, at the outset of his article he proclaims: "We may immediately dismiss as patently absurd the popular notion that the role of the calligraphy is primarily decorative. The inscriptions were meant to be read, they possess content and meaning". Thereby does he imply that architectural ornaments are not to be seen, read or understood and they do not possess content or meaning? This is a curious, albeit casuistic, way of argumention. Is there no content or meaning in the Devānganā sculptures which have been used ornamentally universally in the Hindu temple architecture and are they not meant to be seen, read or understood. The phrase 'patently absurd', besides being in extremely bad taste, is applicable to Begley's own belief and argument that all ornaments are pure design, not meant to be read, and that they do not possess content or meaning.

In such cases as this our primary objective is to examine the *raison d'etre* of its use: Why it is there? And what is its relation to the building? Firstly, has it been used as a historical document? Or, secondly, has it been used to add to its asethetic effect in accordance with its complexion, i.e. is it an *ornament?* Or, thirdly, is it pure and simple, a leaf from the Quran, only to be read and adored from the religious point of view? Has the calligraphic art grown with some symbolic meaning in view or has it developed as an ornamental scheme in the Muslim buildings, e.g. in Syria, Iraq and Iran ? Can Begley interpret such a symbolic meaning in any other country, or is it only in the Indian context that a 'symbolic meaning' can be imposed.

Several beautiful styles of writing Arabic script make up the Art of Calligraphy developed gradually, for example, from Kufic to Naskhī to Nastālīq, to bring about the best aesthetic impression, rather than to add to the meaning of the contents, or to add any symbolism to this meaning.

That this art either in book-writing (i.e., with respect to the manuscript) or in monuments was primarily used for ornamentation is shown unmistakably by the growth and development of intricate and almost unintelligible artistic compositions which are rated among the gems of calligraphy. One from the mosque of al-Moyyed which looks to be a geometrical pattern is really a Quranic verse. [35] It is a befitting design for mural surface decoration, as al-Gayet aptly commented: Unable to convey the nuances it became formulated for the Islamic artist "more visibly, written in actual letters at the head of the murals; there it unrolled palpably; he then applied it in the same way as the ancient Egyptians, to bringing the writing into the sphere of his compositions. For that he chose from among the verses of the Quran the principal articles of the Muslim faith; he arranged them in squares where a phrase such as *Iawakkaltu-al-Allah* (I have faith in God) is four times repeated around a common letter." [36] A similar artistic composition was sometimes employed to ornament a frieze or other mural surface with mosaics. [37] *Kalma,* the Islamic creed, has been used in a variety of artistic compositions of Kufic for mural ornamentation. Recourse to calligraphic art for architectural decoration was taken on a very large scale in Egypt, Syria, Iraq, Iran and Central Asia, during the whole medieval period. [38]

The most ingenious of these compositions, traced in Kufic, is the frontispiece of a manuscript. With its domes and minarets, it appears to represent the *Ka'bah* but in fact it is an artistic composition of the *Kalma.* While demonstrating the skill of the calligrapher who could devise this wonderful method of artistic presentation of a religious formula, its use on the frontispiece of a manuscript unequivocably confirms that it was for ornamentation rather than for anything else that this composition was made. The *raison d'etre* of use of Calligraphic Art both on manuscripts and monuments was ornamentation and no symbolism was intended to by conveyed. **It was an art of calligraphy rather than a *philosophy* of calligraphy.**

That calligraphic art was employed in India, right from the establishment of the Delhi Sultanate. Similarly surface decoration is shown by the examples from the main arcade of the Quwat' ul-Islām Masjid, Delhi (A.D. 1192–97); the Qutb Mīnār (1200–1215); Tomb of Iltutmish (c. 1236); 'Alāi Darwāzah (1311) and the Barā-Gumbad Masjid (1494) Delhi. [39] All these are Quranic verses and have been depicted for ornamentation, pure and simple. It was with the same objective that Quranic verses, in beautiful compositions, were used in the Mughal monuments from Babur to Shah Jehan, e.g. in the Qali' ā-Kahnā Masjid, Delhi (1535); Jāmi' Masjid, Fatehpur Sikri (1563–64 to 1571–72); vestibule of Akbar's tomb at Sikandara, Rauda Agra (c. 1638) and the Taj Mahal [40] (1631–48), on the *miharabs,* portal-*īwāns* and mural panels in carved, glazed-tiled, painted and inlaid schemes.

The Persian inscriptions are rare in the monuments of the Sultanate period and these were primarily as historical document, though architectural ornamentation was also an objective of the builders. Afif, the author of the *Tārīkh-i-Fīrūzshāhī,* for example, recorded that Sulṭān Fīrūz Shāh Tughluq (1351–88) had, besides Quranic verses, a number of ethical instructions, good principles of government and his own policies inscribed in Persian on the great dome of the palace of Firuzabad [41]. He also had his autobiography, the *Futūhāt-i-Fīrūzshāhī,* inscribed on eight slabs which were fixed on the octagonal drum of the dome of the Jāmi' Masjid of Firuzabad. He has again noted that Fīrūz Shāh was greatly interested in history. Barni had died and no other historian came to his notice, he had his exploits, drafted in his own words, inscribed on the sides of the dome of the *Kushk-i-Nuzūl* and the *Kushk-i-Shikār* and also in the building of the Stone Mīnār so that the people might know of these things and learn. Precisely, these inscriptions were used as historical documents and no symbolic representation was involved.

The Persian inscriptions in the buildings of Akbar at Fatehpur Sikri (1572–85, 1601) have been noticed above.[42] These are panegyrics and record of history, and have been used for mural embellishment. Exactly similar is the case at the Gateway of his tomb at Sikandara, Agra, the palatial mansions of Shah Jehan at Agra and Delhi and his three mosques under survey, viz. the Jami' Masjid, Agra (1648), the Motī Masjid, Agra Fort (1654) and the Jāmi' Masjid, Delhi (1656). *These panegyrics have been as record of history, i.e. a historical document, in calligraphic art, i.e. ornamentally, and there is no Islamic symbolism whatsoever.* It is an art, pure and simple, the various stages of the development of which can be systematically traced and it is absolutely wrong to connect this art with any symbolism of the religion of Islam. The consistency with which he is using this explanation in his other writings indicates that he is doing this deliberately. Following him, a few other American authors have also started writing similarly, which shows that this is being done under an organized plan and policy.

Catherine B. Asher follows the same plan and policy in her magnum opus: Architecture of Mughal India which is Part–4 of Vol. I of the Series : The New Cambridge History of India (Cambridge University Press, Cambridge, 1992). For example, she notes that the Quranic inscriptions in the tomb of Iltutmish at Delhi commence, "in India the tradition of paradisical imagery for tomb construction" which was used later "in the entire conception of the monument" (p. 5). Not only is she following Begley, she is also even advancing his 'thesis' to the whole monument. This interpretation of the use of calligraphy of the depiction of Quranic verses on tomb, as discussed above, and even a bold lie cannot alter the truth. These are, in my opinion design, pure and simple, like geometrics and arabesques, and no Islamic symbolism can be legitimately ascribed to them.

Though she is very averse in using the term *'Hindu'* because, she says, it is a "sectarian connotation" (p.6), she freely uses the term *'Islamic'* in the whole text, probably because, she thinks, 'Islamic' is not a sectarian connotation. In fact, she uses the word 'Islamic' most frequently (e.g. thrice on p.l only) to denote anything and everything related to the medieval period. She uses it indiscrimaintely with dynasties which were, in fact, Turk or Afghan and, obviously, her preference is to use and popularise this religious connotation istead of the *correct racial one.* To her, again, it was the Islamic conquest of India in A.D. 1192 (p.l) and it was not a Turkish conquest. This is to deny the *political content* in the campaign of Sulṭān Shihābu'd-Din (Muī'zu'd-Dīn) Muḥammad Ghorī (Muḥammad bin Sām) and to invest it with a religious mission, which it did not have. This is distortion of history.

She has used the term 'Islamic Architecture' to denote the Muslim Architecture of a period or a region of India and, all along, she avoids the use of *correct social connotation: 'Muslim'*, and prefers to use the religious one, viz. 'Islamic' which is, in fact, a misnomer in most of the cases, e.g. in Gujarat, because the religion of Islam had absolutely nothing to do in the evolution of this regional style, so much so that in some buildings there is not even an arch. Likewise, she preferes to designate Sultanate period buildings *'Islamic structures'* instead of indentifying them regionally, socially or racially, which are always more decisive considerations in the evolution of an art in all ages and in all countries. How a Sultanate period building: the Qutb Mīnār-iZarrīn of Koṭlā Fīrūz Shāh and numerous *serāis,* canals, bridges, bunds and tanks, for example, could be 'Islamic' and not Muslim; or Ilbarī, Khaljī, Tughluq or Sūr? It is all but deliberate. The phrase 'Indo-Islamic' is her motivated choice which she uses instead of 'Hindu-Islamic' or 'Hindu-Muslim'. If she wanted to avoid a sectarian connotation honestly, as she professes, the phrase '*Indo-Muslim*' could have been the only correct term.

It is pertinent to note that the historians of this class and their Indian supplicants are not conversant even with the language of the people and the region where the respective architectural style grew and developed, or of the artisans whose forefathers built these medieval relics, and all along, they have been using a wrong terminology in place of the correct denotary *'chhatrī'* and *'chhaparkhaṭ'* and almost always use the former for the latter, e.g. Asher notes in respect of the Jaunpur bridge : "It consists of ten arched openings supported on massive pylons; *chhatrīs* (sic) line either side of the top" (p. 87). These are not *chattris*, but *chhaparkhaṭ. Chhatrī* (from the Skt. root '*chh* = to cover; overspread) is never rectangular (oblong) and it is always square, hexagonal or octagonal – with equal sides. *Chhaparkhaṭ* (from *chhappar* and *khāṭ*) is always built on oblong or rectangular plan and is used to crown the archways, portals or in a similar ornamental way, though in this case, it is also fulfilling a structural need of placing heavy weight on each pier-buttress to add to its massivity. *Chhatrī* with a four-sided triangular, pyramidal and sloping, roof is technically *chaukhaṇḍī* [46]. 'Bārahdarī' is a square or rectangular, spacious pavilion with 3 openings on each side (thus having 12 openings or 'dar'), generally with a *chaukhaṇḍī* roof. Hence it is also sometimes called '*Chaukhaṇḍī*'. But these historians do not distinguish between these different elements and use the common term *'chhatrī'* for everything; *chhatrī, chhaparkhaṭ, chaukhaṇḍī* and *bārahdarī,* indiscrimately, creating insuperable confusion and misunderstanding on the one hand, and undermining a correct appraisal of the style on the other. By and large, they are not able to distinguish between the usual *misnomers* we have inherited from early British writers and such correct and denotary terms, prevalent in northern India for example, as *āmalaka, āṅgan, baiṭhak, bārahdarī, burj, chabūtarah, chandovā, chaubārā, chaupar, chejā, chhaijā, chhājan, chhakkā, chhaparkaṭ, chhatrī, chowk, chowk chaukhaṇḍī, dālān, dar, darwāzah, dāsā, ḍāṭ, duchhattī, ḍyoḍhī, gachkārī, gaukh, havelī, jālī, jhajjharī, jhārā, jharokhā, kaṅgūrā, khaprel, kalash, koṭ, koṭha, kuṇḍ, kursī, lahara–vallarī, maḥal, maḥal, mahāpadma, māṇḍ, maṇḍpa, muṇḍair, osārā, parkoṭā, paur, pol, raddā, rāoṭi, rehanṭ, rekhā, saḥn, sāybān, tarahbandī, ṭhāns, tibārā* and *ṭoḍā,*[47] which make the warp and woof of this study.

Moreover, there is no attempt by these scholars to investigate, analyse and interpret its technical aspect : the solutions evolved in this stone art to tackle the problem of load, for example, how, with the use of two slabs, an arch is reduced to an ornamental accessory without the dreaded lateral thrust (which led Fergusson to coin the phrase : 'arch never sleeps'); how corbelling (kaḍalikā-karaṇa), or a single stone beam pendentive is used in the phase of transition to support a dome; and how *'lado'* is not a vault, though its stone ribs are placed in position by scaffolding *(ḍhūlā)*; and the aesthetic aspect of this study – how mass and volume are organized on mural surface to bring about pleasant 'shadows' which are key to aesthetic perception in such a tropical country as India; how facade and superstructure are composed and skyline and silhoutte are organized to bring about a beautiful architectonic effect as a whole as at the Taj Mahal. Unfortunately, they are also not aware that a wide variety of flat *Paṭṭīdār,* triangular *Bānglādār,* and composite (Ribs-and-Panels) *Chaukhaṇḍīdar, ladāo-dār and Chandavādār* stone ceilings – without any problem of lateral thrust *(thāns),* which was an indispensable accompaniment of arcuate construction, were evolved and used in India during the medieval period. In fact, instead of knowing, admiring and vindicating the 'skills', 'feelings' and 'ideas' of the people who brought these monuments into form, these historians are imposing their own biased, half–baked or fake theories upon this study the way four blind men did to an elephant. One wonders if an architectural style can be studied and explained without correctly analysing the sources of its inspiration; the course of its evolutionary process; and Geo-Physical, Historico-Cultural and Personal determinants of this evolutionary process. There is no doubt that they can write as they please. They have unlimited financial resources at their disposal and they are assisted by uptodate and most advanced library, photographic and other mechanical equipment, and it is mostly by the *sheer force of their excellent means of research* that they have assumed 'scholarship' of this subject. They are trying, once again, to reduce this study to a compendium of romantic tales, fanciful anecdotes and hearsay legends, instead of a discipline of Art History, like the earlier European travellers and, probably like them, they are also writing solely for their countrymen, without a universal appeal or application.

(h) An Assessment of the Style

A brief assessment of the style of 'Indo–Muslim' Architecture may be made. With the establishment of the Delhi Sultanate, around the close of the 12th century A.D., the Turks began to feel the need to build. They requisitioned the traditional, native stone-masons (śilpīn; silāwaṭ) who came with their simple tools (viz. *Aṣta-sūtrakam*), the available material and their own techniques, norms and concepts of architecture. They worked under the overall guidance of their new patrons who could, at the best, provide plan and design of the proposed building on paper. The things from the two different cultural milieu and the two different architectural styles, thus, gradually began to coalesce and integrate. To this process of evolution which lasted for several centuries, the Indian setting and environment was one of the most forceful determinants.

With new vigour and energy, outlook and standpoint and freedom to incorporate extraneous inspirations, the foundations of a composite style were laid and this style began to take shape gradually. Regional sultanates of Gujarat, Malwa and the Deccan, for example, made their own contribution to this evolutionary process. It was, however, during the period of Mughal ascendancy (1526–1707) that Indo–Muslim Architecture reached the zenith of its development and assumed an individuality and personality of its own, in fact, the status and dignity of a National Style as far as non-sectarian architecture was concerned. Arch, vault and dome were adopted in various forms and were ultimately absorbed in the main stream. An arch was made up of two stone-slabs like brackets; it was engrailed (cusped) or had a fringe of lotus-buds; the dome was made plain *'piyājiyā'. 'kharbūjiyā', 'tarbūjiyā',* or *'kamarakhī'* (so-called popularly according to its form), or its was fluted (*'dhārīdār'*). It was built on pendentives instead of squinches and on the corbelling system, and it was invariably crowned by such traditional features as *mahāpadma, āmalaka* and *kalasa.* Geometricals and calligraphics were intermixed with *swastika, padma çakra* and other auspicious symbols, used as ornamental motifis, and glazed-tiles with stone-carving. Indigenous elements such as *stambha* (*khambhā*, pillar), *madala* (ṭoḍa, bracket) (which developed into strut), *chhajjā, qaukh* (projecting balcony), *jharokhā, chhatrī* and *chhaparkhaṭ* were compounded with arch, *īwān* (portal), dome and pinnacles with such uniformity and homogeneity that it was impossible ultimately to distinguish one from the other. It was this way that the facade and superstructure each became unitary and homogeneous compositions in Medieval architecture.

Stone is abundantly available in India and it was the chief building material also during the medieval period. Stone carving in various modes of relief is the associated form of ornamentation. With it, the emphasis shifted from line and colour, and surface decoration of typically Muslim Art, to the treatment of *mass and* volume of stone in the third-dimension, and the organization of pleasant 'shadows', which is the key to architectural aestheticism in India. Muslim art introduced beautiful geometrics, calligraphics and arabesques which were used together with indigenous motifs. With the help of this vast material, the ingenious Mughal artist created a thousand stylized designs.

The things gradually moved from Medapāṭa (Mewar), via Gopādri (Gwalior) to Agra, Fatehpur Sikri and Delhi, in the Jumuna–Chambal region. The Mughal age, with the greatest impetus from Akbar, tremendously accelerated this process. With the emancipation of the State from the theocratic point of view, and of the artisans from the Śāstric dogmas, the emphasis in architecture shifted from sectarian to purely artistic considerations to which the indigenous repertoire of stone-art could provide inexhaustible resources. Thus, with these characteristic features, came into being a National Style of Architecture towards the close of the 17th century A.D.

It is remarkable that the development of Architectonies in India belongs to the medieval period. The Hindu temple symbolised the idea of the Mountain–and–the Cavern, but the Muslim architecture was an art of silhouette on the skyline. It is the masterful organization of the superstructure – mass and volume of the structure rising imperceptibly into the sky, combining some graceful curved lines, e.g. at the Taj Mahal, to leave, like a painting, beautiful rhythmic shadows on the canvas of horizon. This is its unique contribution to Indian art.

Indo–Muslim Architecture was essentially a court (darbārī) art which reflected the personal moods, whims, likes, tastes, beliefs, choices and preferences of the patron. With the disappearance of the Mughal Court as the decisive factor, it became a people's art and it filtered into the Indian life at large. The Mughal idioms : tapering fluted pillars with broad over-hanging *chhajjas* supported on exquisitely designed three-tiered brackets; curved roof and bent cornice; *jharokhā* windows; *duchhattī* and *chhappar* compositions; *chatrīs* and *chhaparkhaṭs* set with fluted domes crowned prominent *mahāpadma* and *kalaśa* finials on the skyline, determined the form and fabric of regional styles, for examples, palatial mansions, havelīs and *chhatrīs* (Rajput tomb-structures) of the rulers of the princely states of Rajasthan, the erstwhile manṣabdārs. It was essentially with these constituents that non-sectarian buildings from Kashmir to Kanyakumari and Okha to Guwahati were raised during the whole of the 18th and 19th centuries and this style, in fact, lasted – if the buildings of the Albert Hall Jaipur and St. John's College Agra, both designed by Col. Swinton Jocab, can be an indication – till Independence. This style was national in character and it cannot be identified as Hindu or Muslim. The mosque too has freely drawn on it; it also went into the maṇḍapa of the Hindu Temple as is unmistakably illustrated by such examples as the Jagat–Shiromani Temple of Amer (Jaipur) and Govindadevji Temple of Vrindaban, of late 16th century A.D., though its *mūlaprāsāda* comprised of *garbhagṛha* and *śikhara*, remained unchanged. It was the people's Art, in letter and spirit. The process which began in the late 12 th century A.D., thus, found its culmination and climax in the late 19th century A.D. and it is the story of the evolution of an art in a country of such diversities as India, during seven centuries' time.

REFERENCES

1. Fletcher, Sir Banister. 1956. *A History of Architecture* (On the Comparative Method) (16th ed. London) Preface, p. XI and p. 4.
2. *Ibid.*
3. Nath, R. 1978. *History of Sultanate Architecture,* New Delhi, pp. 20-37.
4. Husain Mahdi. 1953. *The Reḥla of Ibn Baṭūṭah* (tr.) Baroda, p. 27.
5. Nath, R. 1982. *History of Mughal Architecture,* Vol. I, New Delhi, pp. 77-126.
6. *ibid,* 127-86.
7. Nath, R. 1988. *History of Mughal Architecture,* Vol. II and *Architecture of Fatehpur Sikri : Forms, Techniques & Concepts,* Jaipur.
8. Nath, R. 1993. *History of Mughal Architecture,* Vol. III, New Delhi.
9. Ahmad, Kabiruddin and Abdul Rahim (Ed.) the *Bādshāh–Nāmah (Pādsāh–Nāmah)* ed. Bibliotheca Indica Series, Calcutta, Vol. I 1866, Vol. II 1867. It is a voluminous work, Vol. II containing (Part–I, pp. 1-544 and Part–II, 1–359 =) 903 pages and Vol. III 759 pages, with total 1840 pages of printed Persian.
10. Nath, R. 1990. *India As Seen By William Finch* (1608-11), Jaipur, Introduction, pp. 1-24.
11. Here only the most important works have been listed, and this is not an exhaustive Bibliography, which has been prepared by the present author in his : *Athar's al-Hind : An Annotated Bibliography of Indo-Muslim Architecture* (under publication).
12. For details of progress of Archaeology in India, reference may be made to C.R.Markham, *A Memoir on the Indian Surveys* (London 1871) and C.E.D. Black's work of the same title from 1875 to 1890 (London 1891); James Burgess, 'Sketch of Archaeological Research in India during Half a Century' *Journal of the Bombay Branch of the Royal Asiatic Society* (1905) 131-148; Ghosh, A. 'Fifty Years of the A.S.I. ' *Ancient India* (New Delhi) No. 9, pp. 29-52; S.N. Ray, 'Indian Archaeology from Jones to Marshall' *Ancient India* (New Delhi) No. 9, pp. 4-28.
13. *Monuments of Delhi: A Historical Study* (tr. of Sayyid Ahmed Khan's *Athar'al–Sanadid,* 1846 and 1854 ed.) (New Delhi 1979) pp. xviii-xix.
14. Z.A. Desai on whom a detailed Historiographical Critique has been prepared and is being published by this author under the title: *The Munshī–Nāmah.*
15. As Fritz Lehmann did. For a full historiographical critique on his writings reference may be made to this author's article: 'On the Study of Indo-Muslim Architecture' *Indica,* Bombay, Vol. 22 No. 1 (March 1985) Section (i) 'Defending Iconoclastic Demolitions' pp. 38-46.
16. Creswell, K.A.C. 1932. *Early Muslim Architecture,* Vol. I, Oxford, p. 154.
17. Godard, Andre. 1965. *The Art of Iran,* Heron & Rogers London, p. 254.
18. *The Art Bulletin* , (March 1979), pp. 7-37.
19. *Mishkat,* V. 6.1., cf. Hughes, T.P., *A Dictionary of Islam* (London, 1885) pp. 46, 48, 150, 183, 635, etc.
20. *Ṣaḥīḥ–Muslim* (tr. of *al–Jāmi'–uṣ–Ṣaḥīḥ* of Imām Muslim by Abdul Hamid Siddiqi) Vol. II (Lahore 1987) 347-2112, p. 458. Also see ftn. 1292. This is also confirmed by *Mishkat.*
21. *Ibid,* 348-2114, p. 459 & ftn. 1295.
22. *Ibid,* 348-2115, p. 459 & ftn 1296; *Mishkat* gives this *Hadīth* as follows : Abū'l Haiyāj al-Asadi related that 'Alī (cousin and son-in-law of Muḥammad and the fourth Khalīfah, 656-61) said to him : "Shall I not give you the orders which the Prophet gave me, i.e. to destroy all pictures and images, and not to leave a single lofty tomb without lowering it within the span from the ground."
23. *Ṣaḥīḥ–Muslim,* ibid, 349-2116 and 2117, pp. 459 & 460. This is confirmed by *Mishkat.*
24. *Ṣaḥīḥ–Mislim,* ibid, 349-2118, p. 460.
25. Nath, R. 1979. *Calligrahic Art in Mughal Architecture,* Calcutta, Texts and translation of the Persian inscriptions of the Mughal monuments of Agra, Fatehpur Sikri and Delhi have been published, along with a commentary in each case.
26. *Ibid,* 18, 39-40 and 50.
27. *Ibid,* 42 and 52-53.
28. *Ibid,* 45 and 61.
29. *Ibid,* 28-29.
30. *Ibid,* 47-50 and 64-66.
31. *Ibid,* 48-A and 48-B and 67-68.
32. Nath, R. 1988. *History of Mughal Architecture,* Vol. I, pp. 109-119.
33. *Kalā–Darśana,* ed. J.G. Williams (New Delhi 1981) 7-18.
34. Nath, R. 1988. History of Mughal Architecture, Vol. I, p. 48A.
35. *Ibid,* 3.
36. *Ibid,* 4.
37. *Ibid,* 4.
38. *ibid.* 4-6.
39. *Ibid,* ps. IX, X, XI, XII and XIX to XXI respectively.
40. *Ibid,* ps. XVII- A; XXVIII-XXIX and XXXI to XXXV; XLII; XLV-XLV-A; LVII-LVIII; and LX, LXIV-LXV respectively.
41. Rizvi, S.A.A. 1957. *Tughluq-Kaleen-Bharat,* Vol.II, Aligarh, 1957, p. 51.
42. Nath, R. 1988. *op. cit.,* Vol. I, pp. 13-20.
43. Ibid, 20-21.
44. Ibid, 27-31, ps. L to LVI.
45. A full review of this work is under publication.
46. Nath, R. Chaukhaṇḍī in Mughal Architecture, *Journal of the Pakistan Historical Society,* Karachi (in press).
47. Nath, R. 1985. *Jharokhā : An Illustrated Glossary of Indo–Muslim Architecture,* Jaipur.

A Journey of Sulphur Oxides in Atmosphere

B.B. CHAKRAVORTY*

The subject of sulphur oxide pollution has drawn much attention due to a lot of media exposure on the issue of Taj Pollution in recent past. The various processes and changes sulphur oxides undergo during their journey from the time of release into atmosphere till they meet a receptor, are still not fully understood. Many world-wide studies were carried out in the seventies and even today a lot of indepth scientific studies, researches are being carried out, but conclusions on the subject seem to be still a far cry. So when people talk of sulphur dioxide emission and its effect on far and near flora-fauna and human beings, these are not essentially based on established scientific findings especially in a tropical country like India. Most of the studies so far have been carried out in USA, UK, Canada and Western Europe where the atmospheric conditions, extent of industrialisation, and weather are quite at variance with those in India. Unfortunately in our country, no comprehensive scientific studies on sulphur oxides in atmosphere, air pollution and its effect on flora-fauna and human beings have so far been taken up. However, one such study report from USA and Canada gives enough insight into the transportation, conversion and deposition process of sulphur oxides. This report also deals with research studies on the health effect on flora-fauna and human beings. These would be dealt separately.

We bring out here the salient features of the findings from these studies to improve our understanding.

A. Transport and Mixing

The first step in the atmosphere cycle, i.e. pathway of SO_2 from source to ultimate return to the earth's surface, includes transport and mixing. This process is largely dependent upon the prevailing meteorological conditions following the release of the pollutant into the atmosphere. The residence time of a particular pollutant in atmosphere depends on the regional as well as local meteorology, concentration and ambient conditions.

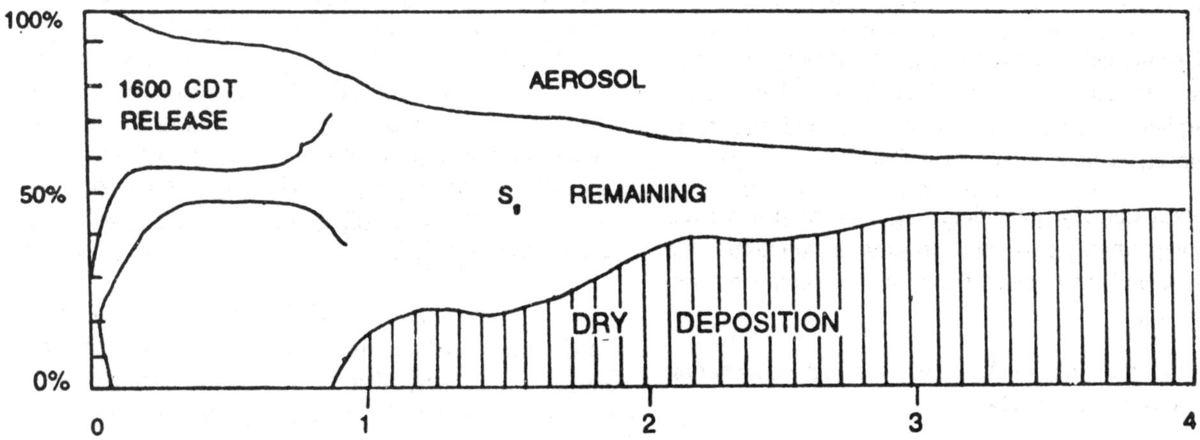

*Indian Oil Corporation Limited, New Delhi

In some instances with short stack heights, removal at the earth's surface occurs within a short time after release and within close proximity of the source. Such conditions are not favourable for chemical transformation in the atmosphere. But with taller stacks, conditions are more favourable for efficient mixing, longer residence time which permit chemical transformation to occur.

There exists a number of proven computer models to study the transport mechanisms. These are used in India also for regulatory purposes. Present studies are focussed on determination of deposition of SO_2 in gaseous state. This is generally valid for shorter stack release. With tall stacks the transport and residence time increases considerably. Therefore, the present model estimate of SO_2 in gaseous phase will not determine the actual phase deposition of pollutant. This leads to over-estimation of ground level concentrations. A typical estimate of sulphur budget for a power plant plume over a 4-day period is indicated in the figure on the previous page.

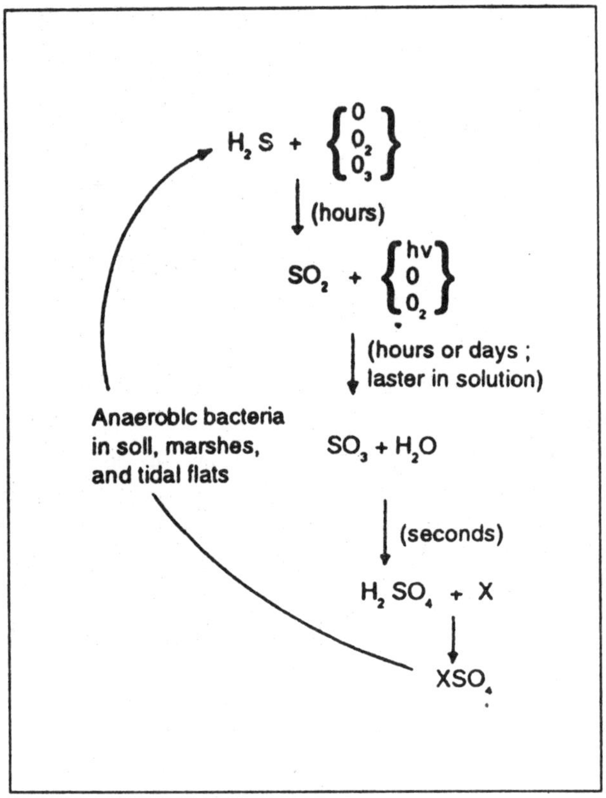

B. Chemical Transformation

Sulphur dioxide, a primary pollutant undergoes chemical reaction in the atmosphere that lead to a change in its oxidation state, most common to sulphates. The change is accompanied by a gas-to-particle conversion process having particular sulphur, a secondary pollutant, as an end product. Evidence is accumulating that the major effects of sulphur dioxide (those on health, terrestrial and aquatic ecosystems, visibility, weather and climate) are associated more with the reaction products than with sulphur dioxide itself.

Due to inadequate knowledge of quantitative aspects of the conversion of sulphur dioxide to sulphates in the atmosphere, model calculations of down-wind impacts are still unsatisfactory and inconclusive.

Oxidation of sulphur dioxide in the absence of promoting compounds is slow and temperature, humidity, solar radiation and other natural factors may influence the conversion rate.

Four mechanisms work at varying degrees in atmospheric sulphur dioxide conversion

1) Indirect Photo-oxidation : This is a major route for conversion of sulphur dioxide to sulphate in the troposphere. The sulphur dioxide is oxidised after gas-phase collision with strong oxidizing radicals such as HO, HO_2, O_3 & CH_3O_2, etc. The source of these radicals in the polluted atmosphere is hydrocarbon NO_x emissions and radicals which are produced by photo-chemical reaction during day time. The rate of conversion varies from 0.5 to 5% per hour. During winter, the conversion rate is reduced due to reduced sun-light intensity and duration. The conversion usually takes place within 2 to 3 hours of release.

2. *Catalytic Sulphur-Dioxide Oxidation :* It takes place due to presence of high concentration of metal catalysts such as iron, manganese in the atmosphere. However, unless metal concentration and PH substantially differ from those in the rain water, this process is unlikely to be of any significance.

3. *Oxidation in Liquid Phase by Strong Oxidants :* This takes place due to presence of ozone and hydrogen peroxide in the atmosphere. The rate of oxidation is comparable with the rate of indirect photo-oxidation. However, further studies are necessary to establish this conversion process.

4. Surface-Catalyzed Oxidation of sulphur dioxide in collision with solid particles : This phenomenon has been studied in laboratories. Elemental Carbon (Soot) appears to be particularly effective in this regard.

The average oxidation rate over the life-time of SO_2 is about 1 to 2% per hour as determined by model studies. Day time actual conversion varied between 1 to 4% per hour whereas the night time value was less than 0.5% per hour. Various reactions invoving sulphur dioxide, particulate matter and other pollutants are given.

C. Removal of Sulphur Contents from the Atmosphere

Overall removal has four major components viz., dry removal of sulphur dioxide, wet removal of sulphur dioxide, dry removal of sulphate radicals and wet removal of sulphate radicals. The residence time and the transport distance of atmospheric sulphur are determined by the overall removal rate of sulphur components from the atmosphere. Dry removal of sulphur dioxide and wet removal of sulphate radicals appears to be major components.

Dry Deposition : Dry removal of sulphur dioxide is a mass transfer process. Sulphur dioxide is first transported to a surface by turbulent and molecular diffusion and then removed by adsorption or absorption at the surface.

Wet Deposition : Wet deposition of sulphur compounds proceeds through a combination of in-cloud and below cloud scavenging by precipitation (rain and snow). Sulphur dioxide emission in eastern US has resulted in increased deposition of sulphur dioxide and sulfate aerosols (Sulphuric Acid, ammonium biosulphate and ammonium sulphate). Overall dry and wet removal rates were 55% and 30% respectively, as per the study carried out in Northern Europe. It has been found, based on the overall study , wet removal rate of 2 to 4% per hour. The characteristic residence time for sulphur dioxide is about a day. According to the study report the sulphate residence time is 3-5 days. Wet deposition rate is greatly influenced by the local humidity, suspended particulate matter at various layers in the atmosphere. In India, wet deposition rate could be rather higher than that in USA or Canada. Both dry and wet deposition go on simultaneously along with formation of H_2SO_4 aerosols and other sulphur compounds.

We shall now describe the effects of sulphur oxides and related compounds on flora-fauna and humans. We also bring here some observations related to effects of sulphur oxide and its compounds on buildings, materials, stones and marbles which are also important in view of growing threats to the historical and cultural heritages due to increasing pollution all around.

In the presence of certain promoting compounds and pollutants solid particles, sulphur-oxides undergo chemical reactions to produce secondary pollutants like suphuric acid aerosols and droplets, ammonium bi-sulphate, ammonium sulphate which deposit on to the surfaces of the receptor like buildings, structures, stones, etc. Sulphuric acid and sulphite compounds are more reactive than the sulphates. Gas phase absorption affects the plants, animals and humans. Dissolved SO_2 and sulphuric acid precipitation contaminate water bodies and soil resulting in deforestation in the long run. Examples are available in the eastern USA and Scandinavia where excessive sulphur dioxide emission is prevalant.

Effects of Atmospheric Sulphuric Oxides and Related Compounds on Vegetation: Many sulphur oxide induced changes have been found in metabolic or physiological processes and status of plants such as changes in the sulphur content, PH of the cellular milieu, metabolities, activities of enzymes, respiration, transportation and photo synthetic carbon dioxide fixation. Effects on the vigor, structure and composition of the flora and changes in the PH and sulphur contents of soils and water of plant communities have been reported. Several possible mechanisms have been suggested to account for the interactive effects of sulphur dioxide on diseases of plants. It has been observed experimentally that there are four variables which can affect the plant's response to sulphur dioxide. These variables are concentration of sulphur dioxide, duration of exposure, number of exposures and intervals between exposures. Further, effects are also related to four phenomena : (1) entrance of gas into leaf tissues, stomatal effect and gas exchange characteristics, (2) membrane as the primary site of action, (3) changes in plant chemical constituents resulting from exposure and (4) speculation on the mechanisms of plant response.

Foliar injury is the most commonly observed response of the plants on exposure to sulphur dioxide. Of the different kinds of effects, the occurrence of foliar injury may be regarded as typical of short-term range and exposure of 12 hours or less. Reduction of growth of yield may be viewed as a representative of mid-term effect and associated with cumulative result of short term effects such as reduction of photo-synthesis. For orchards, forests and eco systems, the time scale is lenghtened and cumulative effect of many seasons must be considered. Plants differ in their inherent capacity to convert the more toxic sulphite to the less harmful sulphate. Therefore, vascular plants absorb sulphur dioxide through stomata and generally are less sensitive to sulphur dioxide, whereas non-vascular plants (such as lichens) are generally more sensitive to sulphur dioxide because gas absorptions occur over the entire surface.

On several studies, it has been observed that sulphur dioxide concentration on an average of 44 microgm./m^3 had chronic effect on forest growth and the same was not observed where the SO_2 annual concentrations averaged 21 microgm./m^3. Epythytic lichens are affected by sulphur dioxide concentration over 52 microgm./m^3. However, the survival of lichens was better where the sulphur dioxide levels were less than 26 microgm./m^3.

Differences in sensitivity are often compared to the extent of SO_2 uptake and thus stomata activity. Sulphites are photo-toxicants for acute plant injury. In case of some plants, called tolerant varieties, there has been net increase in both photo-synthesis and transpiration at low SO_2 concentration for short periods. Both metabolic processes and enzyme activities are increased by exposure of plants to low of SO_2 and decreased by higher concentration. It is believed that chronic exposure at low SO_2 levels can be far more detrimental than acute exposure of high low level SO_2 for short time.

Effect of Sulphur Dioxide on Human Beings : The sulphur dioxide is so soluble in the mucous of the airways that only a small fraction less than a few percent of the inspired concetration, penetrates further than the larynx especially during quiet breathing. The nose is a more efficient scrubber of sulphur dioxide than the mouth. With increasing activity, as in exercise, a person switches from nasal to oral breathing and loses some of this protective absorption. Not all sulphur oxide absorbed by the mucous lining is retained by the body. A small fraction, estimated at about 12% is absorbed and conversion of sulphites to sulphates probably acts to protect tissues and to confine the effects of inhaled sulphur dioxide to respiratory system. Long term exposures of animals, including subhuman primates have generally been associated with adverse effects when the concentration ranged upto about 5 ppm (13,000 microgm./m^3).

The acute exposure to low concentration of sulphur dioxide may have no effect on pulmonary function. Eleven persons were studied on 1 ppm of concentration and exposure duration of 15 minutes. The study indicated increase in the nasal flow resistance. Sulphur dioxide at 0.3 ppm elicitated no functional changes. In a study with 0.5 ppm concentration of sulphur oxide for a period of 3 hours, the subject showed no functional changes that could be judged adverse.

Exercising individuals and asthmatics are more sensitive to sulphur dioxide than healthy subjects at rest. In the clinical study conducted to-date clear effects have not been observed on healthy subjects exposed for brief periods of concentration for sulphur dioxide less than 2600 microgm./m^3. Natural breathing of sulphur dioxide can cause some asthmatics to experience symptoms and increased airway resistance at concetration as low as 1000 microgm./m^3. The health effects of exposure to sulphur dioxide have been enhanced by combined exposure with either water vapour, sulphuric acid aerosols or inherent dust. It it believed there exists synergistic effects of sulphur dioxide, ozone and nitrogen dioxide. The taste and odour threshold for sulphur dioxide in human beings ranges between 780 and 2600 microgm./m^3.

Based on the review of the available data from observational studies, it was concluded that effects of pulmonary function and increases in respiratory diseases in children and adults had been observed in population exposed to a mixture of pollutants, where the concentration of sulphur dioxide exceeds 100 microgm./m^3.

On a study in the later part of eighties, CPCB found that most of the cities and towns in India have ambient air SO_2 concentration much below 100 microgm./m^3. It is obvious that in rural India the SO_2 concentration in ambient air would be further less. Normally background concentration levels are in the range of 4 microgm./m^3 or less.

Effect on Materials and Structures : Moisture, atmospheric oxygen, carbon dioxide, sun light, temperature fluctuations and the actions of micro-organisms all contribute to the deterioration of materials. Acidic pollutants, whether they are present as primary pollutants (i.e. SO_2 and NO_2 gases) as fully oxidised acids (i.e. SO_4, H_2SO_4, HNO_3), assets (i.e. sulphates and nitrates) or in the form of acidic rain, have adverse effect in the building materials, specially the stones and marbles which are basically inorganic compounds.

In view of the threat to Taj marbles due to SO_2 concentration prevalent in Agra area, it would be desirable to know about the studies carried out on such materials by experts else where in the world. It is accepted that building stones, marbles are also damaged by chemical actions of sulphur oxides and other acid gases. Types of damages are surface erosion, soiling, black crust formation. Yellowing is generally due to deposition of sand, dust and particulate matter, whereas blackening is generally due to acidic attacks and attacks by algae and micro-organism. Laboratory chamber studies are unrelated to the actual environment and field conditions. So these studies did not present the true picture of the pollutants under conditions of long-range transports in the atmosphere.

The attack of sulphur dioxide on carbonate stones has been studied over a century now, unfortunately, no quantitive relationship has been developed between ambitient SO_2 levels and resulting material damage.

Stones and marbles are attacked in all modes of SO_2 deposition, i.e. gaseous, dry and wet liquid aerosols, droplets and particulate sulphates. However field studies revealed that humidity plays a vital role in all aspects of interactions of SO_2 with stone. This is due to greater uptake of SO_2 at higher humidity.

In USA, measured rates of marble deterioration have generally been small and this is substantially lower than in case of stones exposed in urban areas in Europe. However, this physiochemical activity on stones and marbles are generally very slow and gradual.

Though primary air pollutant causing damage to stones are sulphur compounds but nitrogen compounds, carbon dioxide particulate matters and moisture play vital role in the comprehensive decay mechanism of stones and marbles of all origins. Damages due to attack of micro-organism, algae, etc. are quite widespread, more so in tropical countries like ours. This is very much evident where old temples in rural areas (having no industries) are found to have become black with dead organic deposits.

Chalcolithic Walki - the Satellite Settlement of Inamgaon: A Study by X-Ray Diffraction of Pottery

VISHWAS GOGTE & VASANT SHINDE*

Introduction

The village Walki (Lat. 74° 18'E, Long. 18° 35'N) is located in Daund Tehsil of Pune district, Maharashtra. It is roughly 60 km to the east of Pune city and 32 km west of Inamgaon, the largest Chalcolithic settlement located on the right bank of river Ghod in the Bhima basin. The ancient site. roughly 2 km to the north of the present village, is situated on the right bank of river Bhima near its confluence with Mula (Fig.1). The site is very small in size, measuring not more than 2 ha with hardly 60 cm thick habitation deposit. It was occupied only during the Chalcolithic period in the latter half of 2nd millennium B.C. Considering the surrounding ecological conditions, it's size and the thickness of habitation deposit, it was hypothesized that Walki was a farmstead, which was seasonally occupied by the people from Inamgaon (Shinde 1989; Shinde 1991).

Altogether 106 architectural features were exposed in the course of the excavations at Walki. Most of the houses were circular in plan and they were found to form distinct clusters. Each cluster consisted of five to six units, among which one was a large mud platform rammed hard, identified as a threshing floor and one or two were probably used as shelters to sheep and goats at night. One or two huts with better floors could have been occupied by people. Besides these, there was a circular pit-silo plastered with lime, probably to store grain. Most of the circular huts were devoid of walls and the fire-pit was usually located in the open, which suggest that they were probably not occupied during the rainy season.

Dept. of Archaeology, Deccan College Post Graduate & Research Institute, Pune

A few permanent, large rectangular mud structures, with low mud walls, were found in the central part of the habitation. They were perhaps occupied by the owners of the farmstead who lived there throughout the year (to look after the farmstead). The excavation also yielded 13 burials, of which 12 were child burials and one adult, the feet of which were chopped off. The owners of the farmstead probably brought labour with them to work in their fields, and the clusters of circular huts were occupied by them. A large proportion of grain produced at Walki could have been transported back to Inamgaon (Shinde 1989). The hypothesis that Walki was a farmstead of Inamgaon was based on the fact that Inamgaon was the largest known settlement in the vicinity. Besides, the excavations carried out for over two seasons yielded ceramic assemblage, which in all respect, resembles the one found in the Jorwe levels at Inamgaon and an adult burial with chopped feet, the custom prevalent at Inamgaon (Dhavalikar *et al.* 1990). In order to test our hypothesis, a more reliable scientific method of X-Ray Diffraction analysis of pottery and the modern clay samples from Walki and Inamgaon were carried out. The following account gives the details of analysis and results obtained.

Discussion

From the view point of materials science, pottery is seen as nothing but a product of clay with a certain form, whereas the archaeologists perceive it mostly from its external features, namely, colour, shape, thickness, slip applied on the pot etc. It has been observed that the morphological features of pottery of any particular culture collected from various sites are found to be identical. No further information can be obtained particularly about the interrelationship of various sites of the same culture. Simply by observing the provenance of the pottery. Some of the large archaeological sites such as Inamgaon and Daimabad have produced the evidence of pottery kilns, suggesting thereby that the majority of pottery was locally produced. However, in the case of smaller sites like Walki, it becomes difficult to know the source of pottery. At this stage, the scientific methods such as chemical analysis with neutron activation or atomic absorption and the analysis of minerals by X ray diffraction can profitably be used. All these analyses are directed to understand the basic raw material of the pottery i.e. the clay.

(a) clay minerals such as montmorillonite, kaolinite, illite and chlorite.

(b) associated clay minerals forming a large list of minerals such as quartz, plasioclase, felspar, calcite and mics. Quartz is present in varying amounts in practically all clay deposits.

The clay is formed by disintegration of underlying rocks due to weathering. The clay therefore varies from region to region depending upon the corresponding rock formations. The clay mineral, illite, for example, occurs in the soils of the Gangetic plain while montmorillonite is present on the Deccan Trap. Although for a given geological region the main mineral composition of clay is the same, there are minor but distinct difference in the clay composition from place to place so much so that characteristic chemical and mineral patterns can be assigned to various deposits in that region. This had a great significance in archaeological studies of pottery. The pottery produced at different production centres can be distinguished on the basis of the mineral and chemical compositions of clays of these centres. The X-Ray Diffraction analysis is used to determine the mineral composition. At times, a simple visual comparison of the XRD patterns without even identifying the minerals is sufficient in sorting out pottery of different origins (Gogte 1992).

In the present study, the pottery of the small Chalcolithic site of Walki is studied by XRD analysis. The hypothesis that the Chalcolithic site of Walki as the satellite settlement of Inamgaon has been tested by comparing the XRD patterns of the pottery and the modern clay samples collected from both the sites. The pottery and clays of Daimabad and Nevasa, the other major contemporary sites in Western Maharashtra, are also compared with those of Walki.

The modern clay samples of Walki contain albite, Na Al Si3 08, as the major associated clay mineral with small amounts of quartz. As against this, the pottery excavated from the Chalcolithic site of Walki, consists of anorthite, (Ca, Na) (Si Al) 4 08, and small amounts of quartz and augite. As the mineral patterns of clays and pottery are different from each other, the pottery could not have been produced at Walki. As against this the Figs:1 and 2 show clearly that the XRD patterns of, both, the Jorwe Ware and Coarse Ware contains higher amounts of augite than that in the Jorwe Ware at both sites. The difference in the mineral patterns of clay from Inamgaon and Walki can be attributed to difference in alluvial deposit brought by rivers Ghod and Mula respectively. The clay and pottery from Daimabad and Nevasa have in general a similar mineral pattern with that of Inamgaon and Walki as all these sites belong to the same geographical zone of the Deccan trap. The clays collected from Daimabad and Nevasa, however, contain very high amount of augite as compared to that in the pottery of Walki.

From the XRD analysis it is evident clearly that the Chalcolithic people of Walki procured the required pottery from Inamgaon. Considering the short distance between Inamgaon and Walki (32 km), it is quite likely that the people from Inamgaon could have established a seasonal settlement at Walki for exploiting the fertile tracts of black cotton soil lying in the confluence of two rivers near the site.

REFERENCES

Dhavalikar, M.K., Vasant Shinde and S.M. Atre. 1990. Small Site Archaeology: Excavations at Walki, *Bulletin of Deccan College Post-Graduate and Research Institute* 50:197–228.

Gogte, V.D. 1992. XRD Investigations of Megalithic Pottery from Raipur, in *Megalithic Raipur* (G.B. Deglurkar and Gouri Lad Eds.), Deccan College Post–Graduate and Research Institute, Pune.

Shinde, Vasant. 1989. New light on the Origin, Settlement System and Decline of the Jorwe Culture of the Deccan, Indian, *South Asian Studies* 5:59–72.

Shinde, Vasant. 1991. Craft Specialization and Social Organization in the Chalcolithic Deccan, India, *Antiquity* 65 (249) : 796–807.

The Alloying Traditions of Protohistoric and Historic India: Some General Trends and Their Ethnographic Dimensions

NAYANJOT LAHIRI*

The purpose of the present paper is twofold. First, it surveys the extant archaeometallurgical and literary evidence to produce a synthetic picture of the alloying traditions of protohistoric and historic India. From this survey emerge two conclusions. One is the presence of multiple alloys across the entire spectrum of Indian archaeological data. This variegated picture requires us to recognize that a cultural trajectory which conforms to a stage-wise evolutionary model of metallurgical development cannot be usefully offered for subcontinental alloy traditions. The second conclusion relates to the compositional variation within alloy groups. Elemental variation, in artifacts ranging from domestic tools to royal coinage, is present in disparate chronological and geographical contexts. The widespread occurrence and persistence of this trend suggests that it cannot be explained, as has generally been the case, as being merely a reflection of craft and alloy metal deficiencies.

Secondly, an attempt is made to understand these trends within a framework based on the nature and techniques of alloy production of the traditional metal craftspersons of the Indian subcontinent. Within that frame, the diversity of Indian copper based metallurgy is shown to fit in with what we know about the range of pre industrial alloy types in India, an aspect that is underlined in some literary texts as well. The variations in the element composition of alloyed artifacts are also explained, not in terms of technological determinants/constraints but as products of the tradition of recycling disused/multiple/scrap metal.

On the whole, the history of copper alloys in India is not a mere inventory of typological traits and technological features that can be simplistically collapsed within evolutionary paradigms appropriate for West Asian and European metallurgy. It embodies a much more complex reality than has been realized so far which, as the paper argues, can be more pertinently explained within a subcontinental referential context.

I. The Data

1. Archaeological data on alloy diversity and elemental variation.

From the technical analyses data, tabulated in Charts I-II[1], the range of alloys produced from the 3rd millennium BC till the historical period, as also their differential distribution is evident. Briefly, these were of low and high grade tin, arsenic, lead, zinc, nickel and a variety of mixed alloys which ranged from mixtures of two metals/minerals as alloys (cf. tin and lead, tin and nickel, lead and arsenic, lead and nickel, zinc and lead) to combinations of three metals/minerals (zinc-tin-lead, lead-tin-arsenic, tin-lead-nickel). The continued presence of the tradition of working in pure copper in such alloy producing contexts is also an important element of the Indian metallurgical tradition, but has been discussed elsewhere[2]. At this point, only an assessment of some dimensions of early Indian alloy types, evident in the tabulation contained in Charts I-II is called for.

First, metal craftspersons in the ancient context produced a range of diverse alloys. This diversity is strikingly present in the Harappan phase itself, and every type of binary alloy subsequently found in the historical record is present in

*Reader, Dept. of History, South Campus, Delhi University.

the metal working tradition of that civilization, including deliberate alloying in zinc; the copper-zinc objects in Gujarat, where the concentration of zinc in one object from Lothal (6.04%) and four artefacts from Rojdi (1.00 - 1.54%) constitute, in fact, the earliest evidence of zinc alloying in India. The importance of Harappan metal working in understanding the roots of later patterns of alloying is also evident in the extensive presence of mixed compositions, mainly ternary alloys (copper-lead-arsenic, copper-tin-lead, copper-tin-arsenic, copper-lead-nickel, copper-tin-nickel), and the occurrence of a copper-lead-nickel object at Sohr Damb, Nal in Baluchistan suggests that this pattern of alloying may even have had pre-Harappan roots. This diversity exists at the micro-level as well; at most of the Indus civilization sites there is a variety in the range of copper based alloys, and such heterogeneity is present at the major cities as also at the smaller centres.

This diversity exists in other protohistoric horizons as well. While in the Gandhara Grave Culture specimens from Timargarha (1st millenium BC) only one type of alloying (that of copper-zinc-tin) could be detected, in general, however, there is a plurality in the alloying traditions of different regions and cultures, whether it is Rajasthan where lead and arsenic alloying is evident at Ganeshwar (3rd/2nd millennium BC), or Maharashtra, where despite the preponderance of bronzes, leaded copper objects also occur, as at Chandoli, or even the Copper Hoard material of the Gangetic *doab*, in which three types of alloys-copper with arsenic, copper-lead-arsenic, and copper-lead-tin-arsenic are present. Equally significantly, the hoard material from Rewari (in Haryana) contains all three compositions. There are diverse alloying practices in the different cultural provinces of historical India as well. While there was a preference for tin alloys in the Potwar plateau in the north-west as in the Ranchi area to the east, lead and zinc mixtures are also present in both these areas. Additionally, there were as many as five mixed alloy groups at Taxila. Moreover, in the Indo-Gangetic *doab*, three types of alloys are known to exist even with reference to one category of artefacts, i.e. coins, and, of the two analysed Punch Marked specimens from Ahichchhatra, one is alloyed with lead while the other is of leaded bronze.

Secondly, the different types of alloys are not regionally or culturally circumscribed. In the Harappan context, tin and arsenic alloyed copper artefacts occur in Gujarat, Sind and the Punjab, while copper-lead and copper-nickel are found in the first two of the above mentioned regions. The spatial distribution of most of the different groups of mixed alloys are equally wide. Subsequently, the distribution continues to remain broad as testified to by the continuance of zinc alloying in such diverse protohistoric horizons as the Gandhara Grave Culture graves and among the villagers of the Painted Grey Ware settlement at Atranjikhera, while the range of tin alloying extended over Birbhum in Bengal, Gujarat, Malwa, Maharashtra and Karnataka. Copper-lead alloys are also present in Maharashtra, Rajasthan and Central India, among other areas. The data on historical India are admittedly limited, but are suggestive of a similar transregional spread.

Finally, Charts III-IV underline the element of variation in the proportion of different additives/alloying metals in the analysed artefacts of early India. This remains, infact, a constant attribute of alloyed objects. To take the example of tin, if at Mohenjo-daro the proportions vary from 1.04 to 26.9%, at historic Taxila the range, which varies between 8.28-24.85%, is also significantly wide. The range of variation in the ternary (three metal) and quaternary (four metal) alloys of all periods is also uniformly broad. Usually this variation is taken to be a reflection of the alloying skill of the metalworkers, and while there may have been some points in the protohistoric and historical periods when such elemental variations could have been the result of what Mackay called "incomplete knowledge of mixing", at the same time, it needs to be recognized that the *constant* presence of such variations in objects over many millennia demands a cultural explanation—this paper argues that an alternative, ethnographic explanation for this variation is possible (see Section II).

2. Textual Evidence on Alloys

Although a detailed analysis of the literary data is not within the purview of the present paper, it may be briefly pointed out that there are certain terms in Indian literary texts which denote copper based alloys. The interpretation of such terms in the earlier texts, however, is seldom free from doubts, as for instance, the references in the Vedas. The *ayas* in the Rigveda is commonly understood as denoting metal in a generic sense, that includes copper and its alloys,[3] and in the Taittrîya Samhita recension of the Krishna Yajurveda has been translated as bronz[4] although,

CHART I— COPPER ALLOYS OF PROTOHISTORIC INDIA

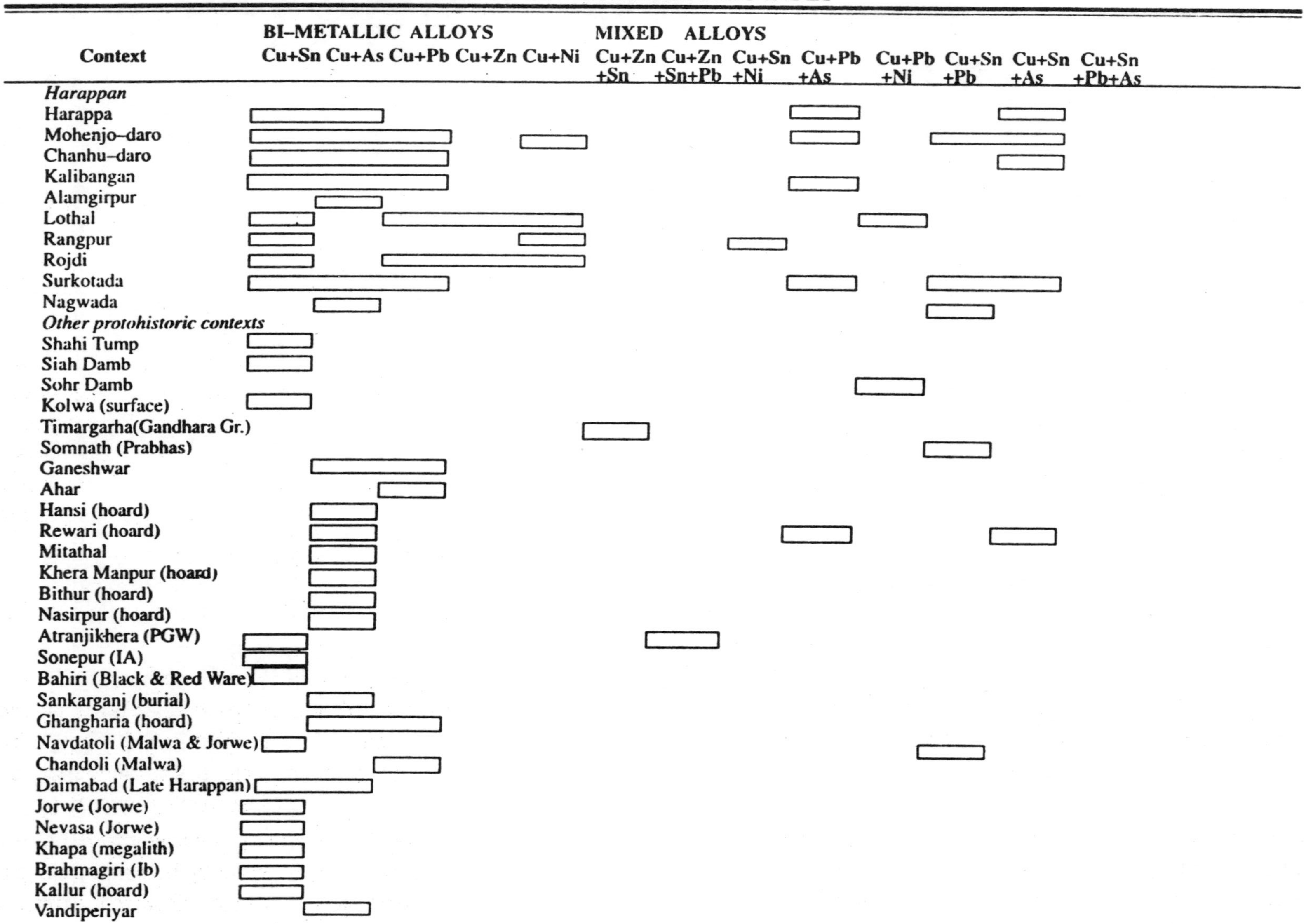

CHART II—COPPER ALLOYS OF HISTORICAL INDIA

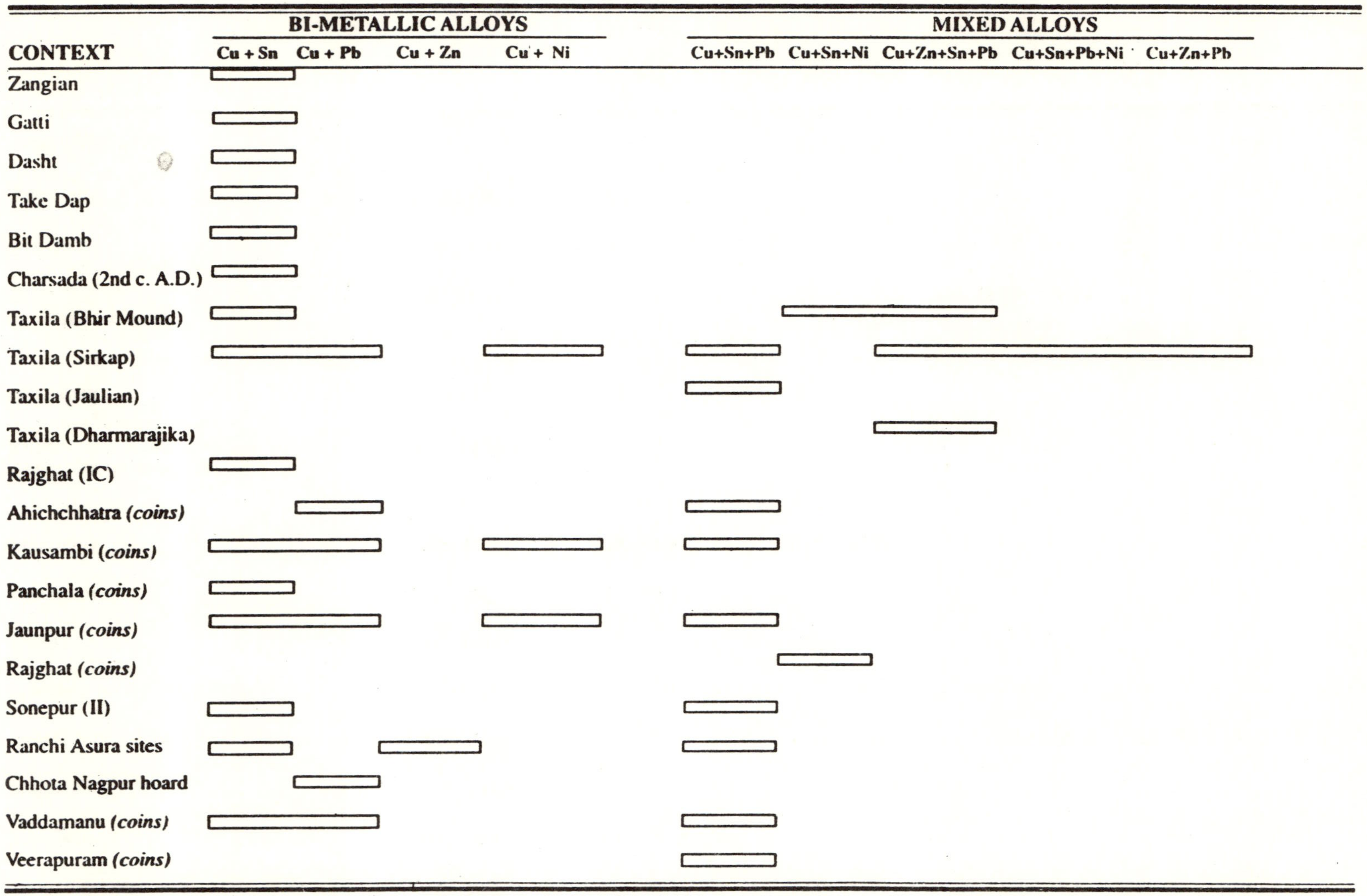

CHART III—RANGE OF ELEMENTAL VARIATION IN BI-METALLIC ALLOYED ARTEFACTS IN EARLY INDIA

Contexts & sites	Cu-Sn	Cu-As	Cu-Pb	Cu-Ni
Harappan contexts				
Mohenjo-daro	1.04—26.9	1.30—4.42	1.08—2.20	1.04—9.38
Harappa	1.02—10.45	1.19—1.40		
Kalibangan	2.21—3.48			
Lothal	1.09—13.80		1.30—3.60	1.50—2.48
Rangpur	2.69—6.94			
Rojdi	1.23—11.00			
Chanhu-daro	1.42—10.74	1.27—3.24		
Surkotada	1.26—4.68	1.00—1.87	1.12—20.23	
Other protohistoric contexts				
Kolwa	8.70—19.30			
Daimabad	4.58—6.51			
Historical contexts				
Taxila	8.28—24.85			18.88—21.35
Rajghat	1.82—13.99			
Asura sites	4.96—23.80			
Vaddamanu coins	5.95—22.73		1.45—10.33	

CHART IV—RANGE OF ELEMENTAL VARIATION IN MIXED ALLOYS IN EARLY INDIA

Site	Cu–Sn-Ni	Cu–Zn-Sn	Cu–Zn-Sn-Pb	Cu–Pb-As	Cu–Sn-Pb	Cu–Sn-As	Elemental variation
Harappan contexts							
Harappa				2			Pb:2.80–3.72; As:2.96–6.58
Surkotada					6		Sn:2.46–8.08; Pb: 2.28–3.26
—do—				2			Pb:1.04–1.33; As: 1.49–1.87
Rangpur	2						Sn:2.60–11.07; Ni:1.80–2.10
Mohenjo–daro						4	Sn:1.76–13.21; As: 1.17–2.10
—do—					4		Sn:1.20–22.1; Pb:1.4–14.9
Other protohistoric contexts							
Atranjikhera (PGW)			2				Zn:6.28–16.20; Sn:11.68–20.72
Navdatoli					3		Sn:3.26–4.37; Pb:2.28
Timargarha (Gandhara Gr.)		3					Zn:4–12; Sn:8–12
Historical contexts							
Taxila–Sirkap					4		Sn:2.12–15.03;Pb:2.59–7.06
Taxila–Dharmarajika			2				Zn:12.88–13.07;Sn:2.58–3.58 Pb:3.22–6.33
Vaddamanu Coins					6		Sn:5.11–18.52;Pb:1.30–9.97
Veerapuram Coins					2		Sn:10.42–24.46;Pb:1.54–1.83

in the relevant references, it remains uncertain as to whether it is copper or one of its alloys that is being denoted. The meaning of *ayas* in the dscription of Mitra-Varuna's chariot at sunset (Rigveda V.62.8)[5] which suggests a reddish metal can be translated as either copper or bronze, and similarly, the allusions to the thunderbolt of Indra "gold hued, gold coloured, very dear and yellow in his arms" (Rigveda VI.71.4)[6] or to the cheeks of Savitar, the Sun God (Rigveda X.96.3), [7] are to a yellow metal, which could be brass, although there is nothing in the references which would preclude them from being translated as gold since *ayas* is a generic term for metal in the Rigveda.

The other term used for a copper alloy in Vedic literature is *kansa*, which occurs in the Brhadaranyaka Upanisad (6.4.13; 6.4.24)[8] but the particular alloy that is being specified is not obvious from what precedes or follows the reference. This also holds true for the usage of this term in the *Sutras* and consequently, the relevant translations of different texts belonging to this genre render *Kansa* (Hindi = Kansa) alternatively as bell metal, brass and even white copper. In the Astadyayi, while there are two general categories under which alloys could be classified i.e. *ayas*, used as a generic term for metal[9] and *kupya* (3.1.114), translated as a base metal other than gold and silver, [10] the spcific term is *kansa* (4.3.155) and here also, Katre's dictionary seems to consider it as an umbrella term that could denote white copper, bell metal, and brass.[11] *Kansa* is also the only word used in the Pali canon to designate a copper based alloy, and the reference in the *Suttavibhanga* section (LVII.2.3) of the Vianaya Pitaka to its dark green colour-*Kansanilam* - suggests that possibly it meant bronze, patinated, of course, in the above mentioned reference.[12] However, in the various other references to *Kansa* bowls and vessels (Culavagga V.9.1:[13] Majjhima Nikaya I.5 (volume I), II.77 (volume II), I.105 (volume III), [14] shoes (Mahavagga V.9.1-3),[15] cow horn tips *(kansu-padha-ranani;* Maha Sudassana Suttanta II.5),[16], goods and dealers in such goods *(kansabhandam and kansapattharika;* Culavagga V. 28.1),[17] and bronze as a medium of exchange (*Tulakuta - kansakuta- manakuta pativirato Samano Gotamo*, Brahma-jala Sutta (1.1.10), [18] the nature and composition of the alloy being alluded to remains unclear.

Possibly this lexical uncertainty may have been less problematic if it was clear as to what *kansa/kansya* came to subsequently denote. Although *kansya* in the Rasa-Jala Nidhi, a medieval alchemical text, is definitely an alloy of copper and tin, [19] and even today is popularly understood as referring to bell metal (a mixture of copper and tin), many 19th century usages of *kansa* in north and east India indicate that the term was also used for designating zinc based alloys.[20] The only conclusion that can be arrived at, then, is that *kansa* in early literature is a term which denotes an alloy, although its specific character remains unclear.

The same ambiguity holds true for the term *raityanam* (5.114) which is mentioned in the Manusmrti. Buhler and Doniger and Smith translate it as pewter (an alloy of copper containing a high percentage of tin,)[21] although the references do not give any indication of the specific alloy that is being denoted. R.L. Turner considers *riti* which is derived from *raitya* to be 'yellow brass, bell metal' [22] while V.S. Apte's entry reads: 'brass, bell metal, rust of iron. The oxide formed on the surface of metals'; [23]; however, he explains the meaning of *riti pushpam* as calx of brass.[24] Monier Willams considers *riti* to be 'bell metal, brass, pale brass, calx of brass, rust of iron, scoria of any metal or oxide formed on the surface of metal by exposure to heat'.[25] *Raityanam* may well have been brass, bell metal or even iron rust.

Finally, the terms *arakuta* and *tala* in the Arthasastra merit attention, although *kansa* also continues to be used (2.12.23).[26] The text itself is silent on the composition of these alloys, although Kangle translates *arakuta* as brass, *kansa* as bronze and *tala* as bell metal and, in this note, argues that *arakuta, kansa* and *tala* are alloys of copper with tin or zinc in various proportions[27]

It is obvious then that, while there are a number of terms and references to copper alloys in the early literary texts, such terms were used ambiguously in antiquity. The absence of specific data for the purposes of reconstructing the metallurgical history of alloying in early India in what is primarily religious literature is understandable but even here, it is worth pointing out that these texts sometimes contain explicit references to artisanal activities; the details on gold extraction and working in the Anguttara Nikaya is one such example. What is more surprising is that, the Arthasastra which considers Sulbhadhatusastra or the science of metals as being integrally linked to statecraft, since 'the treasury has its source in the mines'

(22.12.37),[28] does not refer to the alloys that come under the purview of the Director of Metals in greater detail. Clearly, the range of terms used suggests the existence of different alloys, especially where such terms occur together, but such literary testimony is rendered mute by the complete silence on the character of the alloys being referred to.

The only body of texts which is specifically useful for answering questions about the nature of early alloys is medieval alchemical literature, because precise compositions were considered necessary in alchemical receipes. For this reason alone, it is worth drawing attention to these data even though most of the relevant texts fall outside the chronological parameters of the present paper. In alchemical formulae, there are three kinds of alloys; (a) a copper-tin alloy called *kansya*[29]; (b) a brass called *Raja-riti* made up of copper and zinc,[30] and; (c) a number of alloys of mixed composition. These mixed alloys include *Vajrasanghata* (Brhat Samhita LVII.8):[31] 8 parts of lead, 2 of bell metal, and one of iron rust; Nagaghosa *(Rasarnavakalpa)*[32]: amalgam of lead and bell metal; *Brahama-riti* (synonym: *kaka-tundi; Rasa jala nidhi*[33]988): an alloy consisting of copper, zinc and lead; *Varta loha* (synonym: *pancha loha; Rasa-Jala Nidhi;*[34] *Rasaratnasamucchaya*[35]) an amalgam of bell metal, copper, brass, iron and lead. While most of the alchemical texts are medieval, possibly they are part of a much earlier alchemical classificatory scheme which, however, came to be formally codified at a later date.

II. Possible ethnographic dimensions

To briefly recapitulate on the major themes that have emerged in the preceding section, the production of diverse copper alloys in many areas of the Indian subcontinent, as is evident from the Harappan repertoire, was well underway during the 3rd/2nd millennia BC. Moreover, this tradition of producing multiple copper based alloys, i.e. types of bronzes, brasses as well as mixed alloys containing tin, zinc, lead, arsenic and nickel, did not end with the eclipse of that civilization but continued in different protohistoric regional pockets and cultures, and remained the hallmark of early historic India as well. Variations in the elements present in different alloy groups from the Harappan till the historical period are also constant. As for literary allusions, the terminological range is fairly wide and the referenes to *kansya, raitya, arakuta, vartaloha,* and *tala,* among others, hint at the existence of diverse alloys. The identifications that have been suggested for these alloys, however, can only be provisional, not merely because of lexical uncertainties but because of the absence of any details in the texts on the composition of such metals. Systematic evidence of alloy compositions is, however, available in alchemical literature, and there the distinctions that can be discerned among the alloy groups-*Vajrasanghata, nagaghosa, Raja-riti, Brahama-riti, Varta-loha and kansya*-also suggest a similar diversity.

This emerging archaeological picture complemented by whatever unambiguous literary evidence that is available may now be explained with reference to the rich history of the diverse ways in which alloys have been handled in the premodern past of the Indian subcontinent. Information on the major elements of traditional copper alloy working is available in the various monographs that were prepared under the aegis of the Government of the British in India and among the more recent works, Meera Mukherjee's study - *Metacraftsmen of India* is the most comprehensive extant anthropological survey on the different copper based metalworking traditions. It is this ethnographic tradition that provides the most suitable context for understanding and explaining some of the major themes that have emerged on the copper alloy traditions of early India.

1. Range of Alloys

One can perhaps begin with terminology where the textual evidence suggested the possibility of more than one kind of metal being designated by one term. Interestingly enough, the ethnographic data broadly support this generality in nomenclature. If *kansa* in the Grhysasutras and Dhamasutras has been understood as alernatively denoting bell metal, brass or even white copper, it is not very dissimilar from the varied compositions which passed off as *kansa* in the 19th century. *Kansa* was synonymous with a copper-sinc alloy in many parts of the former North-Western Provinces and Oudh, althouh, in Aligarh it was applied to bell metal.[36] An analogous situation existed in the east where in Bengal *Kansa* denoted a copper-tin alloy, although a lead and brass mixture was called by this name in some places in Bihar.[37] Similarly, in the context of Rajasthan, in his discussion of the anklet casting tradition of Sawai Madhopur, T.H. Hendley described as *kansi* or bell metal ... composed of sixteen parts of brass and six of zinc."[38]

Can the composition of the principal alloys of the subcontinent in the 19th century throw any light on their ancient prototypes? Obviously, there is not much point in attempting a one-to-one correlation, since many of the archaeologically documented early Indian alloy groups such as copper-arsenic and copper-nickel, if one goes by the ethnographic literature, do not seem to have been manufactured in the recent past, although one is aware of the existence of medieval images of such composition. As for the copper-tin group, the percentage of tin in such alloys in the 19th century was follows:

Punjab,[39] North-Western provinces and Oudh: 20-40%;[40] Bengal: 10-28.57%[41] Central India: 25%[42]. In general, the percentage of tin in early Indian objects is much lower although some objects at Mohenjo-daro and in historical Taxila and Baluchistan contain a higher percentage of tin which would be well within the elemental ratios of *phul* or *kansi* as the copper-tin group of the north in the 19th century was called.

A more useful correlation is, however, possible with regard to the wide, almost bewildering group of compositions that are passed off as mixed alloys in archaeological writings. Some of the early mixed alloy groups are fairly similar in composition to traditional Indian types. For instance, the mixed alloy artefact from Atranjikhera which is made up of 54.42% copper, 20.72% tin, 9.77% lead and 16.20% zinc, is compositionally very close to an alloy group that was called *bharat* in the Punjab area. There *bharat* was made of copper, zinc, tin and sometimes a small proportion of lead.[43] There was also a mixed alloy manufactured in Bengal called *bharan* or *toul* which was made by adding either some zinc into pure bronze or some tin into brass.[44] The composition of the copper-zinc-tin objects from the Gandhara Grave cultural context at Timargarha could be validly placed in this group. Sometimes a small quantity of lead was added to the above mentioned *bharan* objects to increase their malleability[45] and it is noteworthy that compositionally similar objects are present at the Bhir Mound, Sirkap, and Dharmarajika sites at historical Taxila.

Literary allusions can also be marginally correlated with the archaeological and ethnographic data. A composition similar to *Brahma-riti,* consisting of copper, zinc and lead can be recognized in some Taxila objects and is not dissimilar to the above mentioned *bharan* composition. The ratio of copper and zinc in *Raja riti* is identical to one type of *pital* or brass of the former North-Western provinces, which was made of 2 1/2 parts of copper to 1 zinc.[46] Finally, what also deserves notice is the presence of iron or iron rust in *Vajrasanghata* and *Varta loha/pañcha loha* since many ancient and medieval artefacts are known to contain iron as a major element.

2. Compositional Diversity within Alloy Groups

Striking regional diversities in the elemental compositions of the various copper based metals is a noticeable feature of traditional crafting in alloys in the Indian subcontinent and, in general, in the 19th century, the composition of an alloy could vary from region to region, sometimes from locality to locality and occasionally from artefact to artefact. The bell metal made in Bengal[47] was different from that made in Punjab[48] and in other regions.[49] Even within one region, different provinces wrought articles in alloys which differed in their element compositions; apparently in Sagar itself, there were three or four different varieties of zinc alloys.[50] The best and most malleable was that made of 3 parts of copper with 2 parts of zinc. A lighter coloured alloy was made from 20 parts of copper and 16 of zinc. A still lighter one, usually for manufacturing cooking pots, was made of 16 parts of copper and 18 of zinc. An even more cocnentraed zinc alloy was called tora, greyish in colour and used for ornaments, manufactured from 16 parts of copper and 20 parts of zinc. Such variations in metal composition, incidentally, continue to persist as is evident in Mukherjee's book which reveals, for instance, an area-wise variation in the composition of brass in Orissa.[51] There, at Ghantimunda, brass is made of 7 parts of zinc to 10 parts of copper, while at Kantilo and Rengali the mixture is 20 parts of copper with 16 parts of zinc, and at Katapalli, brass is composed of 80 tola (0.93 kg) of copper to 64 tola (0.74 kg) of zinc.

In fact, different alloys can also be manufactured by the same community for producing different types of objects, as at the Oriya village of Pitala, where the Khoruras, for making brass utensils like *handi, mathia* and *dhara,* use 10 kg of copper alloyed with 6 kg of zinc, while the *kathua* is manufactured by them from a mixture made up of 700 gms of copper, 420 gms of zinc and 80 gms of lead. Additionally, the same type of artefact is also known to have been manufactured by the same metalcrafting community using different elementalmixtures. In Rajasthan, a group of metal cratspersons of Sawai Madhopur, for instance, used to employ three different mixtures for the manufacture of *sanths* (anklets).[52] The first was composed of 16 parts of brass and 6 of zinc. The second was made of 16 parts of the first mixture with 4 additional parts of zinc. A third consisted of old and broken anklets.

This variegated picture seems to suggest that traditional alloying practices cannot be reductively compartmentalized on the basis of region, culture or artefacts. Incidentally, in the wide geographical and historical range of early India, it is a similar diversity that is encountered, right from the beginning of the Harappan Civilization. For instance, within Harappan Gujarat, there are five binary alloys - bronze of a low and high grade, copper-arsenic, copper-lead, copper-zinc, and copper-nickel- as also five ternary alloys. Five of these alloy-groups are present at Lothal itself, and what is even more striking is that in the eight artefacts analysed from Rojdi, four alloy groups were detected. The variety of copper alloy-groups at Taxila in the early historical period also emerges quite strikingly from the elemental compostion data and a reading of the relevant section in Marshall's excavation report. Additionally, the work done by C.L. Reddy[53] on alloy types in relation to attribution groups of statues from the north and northwestern parts of the Indian subcontinent underlines such variations within one area. Only 57.1% of the relevant statues could be correctly classified using alloy differences, and according to Reedy, "the probable reasons for this lack of success are the large range of variation in types of alloy used within a single regional attribution group and the fact that a particular alloy type is never unique, but may be found in two or more groups." [54]While the lack of texts prevent ancient historians from any focused perception of the sociocultural dynamics of early Indian alloy-workers, what can be suggested within the context of the archaeological evidence is that perhaps, the same group of craftspersons could have produced goods in different copper based alloy metals which was the pattern in the more recent past. That, in any case, is what is suggested by the presence of metals of differing compositions at the same site and even at the same locations within it. Possibly, such variations merely illustrate the antiquity of this aspect of the preindustrial metalworking traditions of India.

3. Multiple/Disused/Scrap Metal usage and its Technological Implications

First, the use of different kinds of primary copper at some major metalcrafting centres in the 19th century needs to be noted. There is at least one documented instance of more than one kind of primary copper being used for the production of metal articles. In Rewari, Johnstone noted that one seer (slightly less than a kg.) of a very superior kind of copper called pisa, that used to come from Khetri Singhana in north-western Rajasthan, costing about Rs. 50 per maund (40 secrs) and procured in very small quantities, was added by the local braziers to every maund of their alloys.[55] In copper poor regions, the procurement of raw material from a variety of sources was much more extensive. In the case of the former North-Western Provinces and Oudh, in 1984, five different qualities were imported[56]: *Zafarani*: considered to be the most superior, its name was derived from the Arabic Za'afara, meaning "be dyed with saffron"; *Jajhar*: this was the copper remaining from the sheets from which pice had been cut in the Bombay and Calcutta mints; *Lodhra*: Japanese copper; *Jahazi*: old copper plates, broken from vessels. One is also aware that at different points of time, Russian and Nepalese copper used to be imported into this region.

The more consequential aspect of metal procurement for the production of alloyed artefacts in the 19th century is the use of old and broken metal articles. Dampier's observation[57] on the presence of this tradition in north-west India is evocative of the scale of this practice:

> "There is hardly any limit to the number of times old metal can be worked up into new vessels, and in some districts the collection of old metal for export to the chief centres of the brass manufacture forms quite a trade by itself. Old and broken vessels in this country are never thrown away, as is the case so often in England, but are either sold to the itinerant dealers who perambulate the country collecting old metal, or in districts where threre are large manufactures of brass ware, as in Mirzapur, the purchaser of a few vessel gives the old vessel as part price of his few purchase."

Such transactions in metal scrap are documented from most parts of the subcontinent, while the objects that were made from them were also morphologically diverse. In the northeast, for instance, while among the Ao Nagas, broken and unserviceable brass was used for making bracelets, women's head rings and heavy neck rings[58], in Manipur, such metal was used for producing the bell metal currency, coined by the Raja: 'the metal is obtained chiefly from Burmah, and consists of gongs, etc. some of it is also procured from the British provinces'.[59] Disused/scrap metal was probably preferred for alloy production because it was cheaper than new metal; in the Punjab whereas old *kansi* was priced at Rs. 30 per *maund*, the price of new *kansi* per *maund* was between Rs. 40 and 45.[60], and this is also why the indigo factories in Gorakhpur bought old metal in large quantities for making nuts, etc.[61]

This tradition of using old metal still continues, whether it is in Ramareddi where Lambadi gypsy ornaments are produced from old bell metal utensils[62], or Nabadib (Bengal) and Gondia (Orissa) where different untensils are among the variety of objects manufactured from old brass and bell metal scrap.[63] In fact, the present scale of old metal usage can be gauged from the case of the Kaseras of Raipur, who in manufacturing the Raipur Gondi, a kind of pitcher, use machine rolled brass circles that come out of a factory in Dhamtari, near Bastar.[64] These cirlces are made in the factory by melting old pitchers and other brass scrap with 10% of prime copper and 4% of prime zinc.

What could be the possible ramifications of multiple scrap metal usage on the technical composition of the final products? A preliminary study with a view to investigating this question was done by me in September, 1992 and the results of that survey, given below, hopefully demonstrate that at least one of the possible results of this metal recycling tradition would be an elemental variation in the artefacts produced.

Sri Shyam Dhan Jhara and his wife, Indra Jhara, who are tribal metal crafts persons, domiciled in Raipur, Madhya Pradesh, spent the monsoon on 1992, giving various demonstrations and selling their artefacts, at Pragati Maidan, New Delhi. Winner of a National Award in 1986 for *Jhara Dhatu ki Dhalai*, Shyam Dhan is of Oriya background, originally belonging to Bargampalli village in Sambhalpur. He was brought to Ektaal village in the Raigarh *zillah* of Madhya Pradesh by a District Officer, and since then a large number of his family members have also settled there. The raw material used by them seems to be primarily broken metal, from which a variety of artefacts ranging from grain measures to religious figurines are produced. The term used for designating scrap is *phuta pital*, whichis bought at Raigarh, 20 km's away from their village. *Phuta pital* itself can be of various categories, and the cheaper one is that from which glasses are made while *chandari pital*, the metal of plates, water pitchers etc. isRs.5/- more expensive than the others.\Two artefacts, a bird figure and a *dvipa*, bought from these craftspeople were sent to Hindustan Copper Limited, Research and Development Department, Khetri, for chemical analysis. The results are as follows:

Sl. No.	Description	Cu	Pb	Sn	Ni	Zn	Other traces
1.	Dvipa figure	65.0	15.0	nil	5.2	13.2	Balance
2.	Bird	70.0	6.6	7.5	tr.	13.9	Balance

Two points about the above mentioned chemical analyses are woth considering. First, there is a noticeable discrepancy in what the craftspeople considered to be the metallic composition of their artefacts and the chemical report. According to Shyam Dhan Jhara, the objects were of a copper-zinc alloy or *pital*. The analyses, however, reveal that the first object is a copper-lead-nickel-zinc alloy while the second object is a copper-zinc-tin-lead alloy. Secondly, there is a considerable variation in the percentages of three elements, the range being as follows: lead: 6.6—15.0%; tin: nil—7.5%; nickel: traces—5.2%. Our surmise is that if disused and broken metal scrap is used for casting purposes, such variations would be quite logical since the proportions of different elements cannot be controlled, except in a most general way.

Such variation in the compositions of objects produced by the traditional metalcasters of India have, infact, been consistently noted by perceptive observers. For instance, J.L. Kipling opined that "nothing could be more variable than the Oriental idea of proportions in these matters. There is often a wide and apparently unaccountable discrepancy between the habitual practice of a workman and the receipt or *canoon* he thinks he goes by, and is ready to quote".[65]

What has perhaps not been understood, as Kipling's remarks make reasonably clear, is the reason behind this "unaccountable discrepancy" between the perceived and actual composition of traditional alloys. The present section has hopefully demonstrated that the widespread practice of using scrap metal may account for the variations in the ratio of different alloys. Obviously, in assessing the technology of different cultural groups, the intentions of the artisans themselves need to be considered. The practice of using old and broken metal objects expresses the values and preferences of craftspeople sensitive to economic constraints, albeit, and as a consequence, producing artefacts which in their elemental composition were at variance with 'scientific parameters' of alloy mixing.

Clearly, old metal was also being used in the ancient period. The literary allusion in the Srivanija Jataka describes such a practice[66] in its tale of the hawking pattern of two dealers (*Kacchaputa vanijo*) in pots and pans, one of whom is the Bodhisattva. Their method of trade involved the exchange of old and broken utensils for new ones. The two dealers in the above mentioned Jataka seem to be the ancient prototypes of the itinerant vendors of later centuries. The repertoire of metal objects in metal working areas at some early sites also suggests such recycling. For instance, at Mohenjo-daro and Harappa there are a number of 'hoards' where copper lumps, unfinished, broken metal objects along with numerous pieces of copper are found together - it is likely that such artefacts were intended for resmelting and reuse.[67] Obviously, in situations, where old metal was being used, the proportions of different elements could not be strictly controlled-this may be a plausible explanation for the variations that are so often highlighted in ancient metal objects. Moreover, when old metal was being used, as also in those cases where more than one kind of copper was employed, the elemental composition of ancient objects also cannot be considered as being indicative of the source areas of the ore. This dimension must be given serious thought in provenance studies to make provenancing a more meaningful exercise.

An assessment of early Indian metallurgy cannot be made from a unidimensional, technologically deterministic perspective alone. The present paper hopefully demonstrates some ways in which literary data as well as ethnographic sources can be employed for contextualizing more meaningfully the varied components of the subcontinent's rich copper based alloying traditions.

REFERENCES

1. In Charts I-II, most of the elemental analyses data, excluding images which are generally medieval in date, are compiled; where coin analyses are cited, it is specifically indicated. The charts have been compiled on the basis of the elemental analyses results contained in the following works: M.S. Vats, *Excavations at Harappa*, Delhi, 1940; J.H. Marshall,, *Mohenjodaro and the Indus Civilization*, London, 1931; S.R. Rao, *Lothal A Harappan Port Town*, New Delhi, 1979-85; S.R. Rao, Excavations at Rangpur and Other Explorations in Gujarat, *Ancient India* 18 & 19 (1962 & 1963); S.K. Bhowmik, Chalcolithis Protohistoric Period Copper Metallurgy of Gujarat-A Preliminary Survey, *Museum Bulletin* XXV (1973-74); G. Kuppuram, *Ancient Indian Mining, Metallurgy and Metal Industries*, Delhi, 1989; R.C. Gaur, *Excavations at Atranjikhera*, Delhi, 1983; P. Yule, *Metalwork of the Bronze Age in India*, Munchen, 1985; H.D. Sankalia & S.B. Deo, *Excavations at Takalghat and Khapa*, Nagpur, 1970; H.D. Sankalia, S.B. Deo and Z.D. Ansari, *Chalcolithic Navdatoli*, Poona, 1971; H.C. Bhardwaj, *Aspects of Ancient Indian Technology*, Delhi, 1979; F. Coarelli, The Bronze Handles at Charasada, *East and West* (1966); J. Marshall, Taxila, Delhi, 1975 (reprint); H.C. Bhardwaj, Review of Metallurgical Studies of Ancient Indian Coinage, *Numismatics & Archaeology* (ed. P.L. Gupta & A.K. Jha), Nasik, 1987; B. Chakravarty, Chemical Composition of some Copper Coins from Jaunpur hoard, *The Journal of the Numismatic Society of India* LIII; K.S. Caldwell, The Result of Analyses of Certain Ornaments found in Asur Sites, *Journal of the Bihar and Orissa Research Society* VI (1920); R. Seshadri, The Composition and Smithery Techniques of Copper Artefacts from Nagwada-A Preliminary Study, *Man and Environment* XVII (1992); R.C. Agrawala,

Aravalli, the major source of copper for the Indus and Indus related cultures, *Frontiers of the Indus Civilization* (ed. B.B. Lal & S.P. Gupta); P. Yule, *The Copper Hoards of the Indian Subcontinent Preliminaries for an Interpretation*, Mainz, 1989; H.D. Sankalia, *Excavations at Ahar 1961-62*, Poona 1969; S.B. Deo & Z.D. Ansari, *Chalcolithis Chandoli*, Poona, 1965; H. Hargreaves, *Excavations in Baluchistan...Sohr Damb, Nal*, New Delhi, 1981 (reprint); A.H. Dani, Timargarh and Gandhara Grave culture, *Ancient Pakistan 3 (1967)*.

2. N. Lahiri, 1993, Some ethnographic aspects of the ancient copper-bronze tradition in India, *Journal of the Royal Asiatic Soviety of Great Britain and Ireland* (3)
3. For a recent discussion of *ayas* in the Rigveda see D.K. Chakrabarti, 1992, *The Early Use of Iron in India*, Delhi, pp. 96-99.
4. A.B. Keith, 1914, *The Veda of the Black Yajus School*, I, Massachusetts, p. 381; A. Weber, *Die Taittriya-Samhita*. Leipzig, 1872, p. 404. *Taittriya Samhita* 4.7.5 refers to iron as *syamam*, copper as *loham*, and thus *ayasa* in this passage has been translated as bronze, although there is nothing in the reference that suggests that may not be another copper based alloy.
5. Tilak, 1933, *Rigveda Samhita*, Maharashtra University Poona, II, p. 934-5; R.T.H. Griffith, *The Hymns of the Rigveda*, Benares, 1896-7, I, p. 534.
6. *Ibid.*, p. 693.
7. *Ibid.*, II, p. 531; Tilak Maharashtra University, *op. cit., p. 648.*
8. S. Radhakrishnan, 1953, *The Principal Upnaisads*, London, pp. 325, 329.
9. V.S. Agrawala, 1953, *India as Known to Panini*, Lucknow, p. 231.
10. S.C. Vasu, 1962, *The Ashtadhyayi of Panini*, Delhi, p. 392.
11. S.M. Katre, 1968, *Dictionary of Panini*, Poona, p. 170.
12. 'There are two kinds of dark green: the dark green of bronze' *(nilam namma dve nilani kansanilam)*. H. Oldenberg, *The Vinaya Pitakam*, IV, London, 1882, p. 120; I.B. Horner, *The Book of the Discipline-Vinaya Pitaka, II, London, 1957, p. 408.*
13. H. Oldenberg, 1880, *op.cit*, II, p. 112; I.B. Horner, *op. cit., V, 1952, p. 152.*
14. V. Treckner, 1888, *The Majhima Nikaya*, I, London, pp. 25, 15?; R. Chalmers, *The Majjhimanikaya*, II, London, 1954, p. 32;, *ibid.* II, 1957, p. 216; *ibid.*, III, 1959, p. 44.
15. I.B. Horner, 1951, *The Book of the Disipline-Vinaya Pitaka*, IV, London, p. 253.
16. T.W. Rhys Davids & J.E. Carpenter, 1890, *The Digha Nikaya*, London, p. 188; T.W. Rhys Davids, *Dialogues of the Buddha-Digha Nikaya*, II, London, 1910, p. 221.
17. H. Oldenberg, 1880, *op.cit.*, II, p. 135.
18. T.W. Rhys Davids, 1899, *op.cit.*, II, p.6; T.W.Rhys Davids & J.E. Carpenter, *op.cit.*, I, 1890, p.5.
19. B. Mookerji, 1984 *Rasa Jala Nidhi*, III, Ahmedabad, (reprint), p. 147.
20. G.R. Dampier, 1894, *A Monograph on the Brass and Copper Wares of the North-Western Provinces and Oudh.* Allahabad, 1894, p. 22; T.N. Mukharji, *A Monograph on the Brass, Bronze and Copper Manufactures of Bengal*, Calcutta, 1894, p. 282.
21. The relevant line in original reads: *tamrayah kamsya raityanam trapunah sisaksya cha*-J.Jolly, 1887, *Manava Dharma-Sastra*, London, p. 108. For translations, see G. Buhler, 1886, *The Laws of Manu*, Oxford, p. 189 and, W. Doniger & B.K. Smith, 1991, *The Laws of Manu*, Middlesex, p. 111.
22. R.L. Turner, 1966. *A Comparative Dictionary of the Indo-Aryan Languages*, London, 1966, p.
23. V. S. Apte, 1890, *The Practical Sanskrit-English Dictionary*, Poona, p. 913.
24. *Ibid.*
25. M. Williams, MXCCLXXII, *A Sanskrit-English Dictuionary*, Oxford, p. 847.
26. R.P. Kangle, 1960, *The Kautilya Arthasastra*, I, Bombay, p. 59.
27. *Ibid.* 1960, II, Bombay, p. 124.
28. *Ibid.*, p. 126.
29. P.C. Ray, *op. cit.*, p. 185. In the *Rasaratnasamuchchaya*, *kamsya* issupposed to be made by melting together eight parts of copper and two parts of tin; *Rasa jala Nidhi* (ed. B. Mookerji), III, p. 147. Here *kamsya* has an identical composition to

the above mentioned reference.

30. *Ibid*,. p. 142. Here *Raja riti* consists of two parts of copper and one part of zinc.
31. V.S. Sastri, 1947, *Bharat Samhita*, I, Bangalore, p. 503.
32. M. Roy & B.V. Subbarayappa, 1976, *Rasaranvakalpa*, Indian Science Academy Monograph No. 5, p. 143.
33. *Op. Cit.*
34. *Ibid.*, p. 150.
35. *Op. Cit.*,p. 185
36. G.R. Dampier, *op. cit.* Dampier noted the composition of *kaskut*, *Bharat*, and *kansa* as being of 1 copper to 1 zinc. He also noted that "this alloy varies little in composition, though much in name all over the province, and appears from its proportions to correspond with what is known as Prince's metal in England. It is variously known as *Kaskut*, *Bharat*, or *Kansa*, though this latter name is in some districts, such as Aligarh, applied to bell metal.
37. T.N. Mukharji, *op. cit.*
38. T.H. Hendley, 1909, Jewellery of Rajputana and Malwa or Central India, *Journal of Indian Art and Industry* XII p. 37.
39. D.C. Johstone, 1888, *Monograph on Brass and Copper Ware in the Punjab*, Lahore, p. 1.
40. G.R. Dampier, *op.cit.*, p. 22.
41. T.N. Mukahrji, *op.cit.*, p. 281.
42. *Monograph on the Brass and Copper Ware of the central Provinces*, Bombay, 1894, p.6.
43. D.C. Johnstone, *op.cit.*
44. T.N. Mukharji, *op.cit.*
45. *Ibid.*
46. G.R. Dampier, *op.cit.*
47. T.N. Mukharji, *op.cit.*, pp. 281-82.
48. D.C. Johnstone, *op.cit.*
49. E.B. Havell, 1890, The Industries of Madras, *The Journal of Indian Art and Industry* III p. 15.
50. *Monograph on the Brass and Copper Ware of the Central Provinces*, p. 6.
51. M. Mukherjee, *Metalcraftsmen of India*, Calcutta, 1978.
52. T.H. Hendley, *op. cit.*
53. C.L. Reedy, 1986, Technical analysis of medieval copper alloy statues for provenance determination (Ph. d. thesis), University Microfilms, Ann Arbor, 184-85.
54. *Ibid.*, p. 227.
55. D.C. Johnstone, *op. cit.*, p.2.
56. G.R. Dampier, *op. cit.*, p. 21
57. *Ibid.*, p. 23
58. J.P. Mills, *The Ao Nagas*, London, 1926, p. 99.
59. T.C. Hodson, 1975 *The Meitheis*,Delhi, (reprint), p. 36-37.
60. D.C. Johnstone, *op. cit.*, *p.2.*
61. G.R. Dampier, *op. cit.*, p.23.
62. M. Mukherjee, *op. cit.*, p. 259.
63. *Ibid.*
64. *Ibid.*, p. 167.
65. J.L. Kipling, 1886, The Brass and Copper Ware of the Punjab and Kashmir, *The Journal of Indian Art I* p. 7.
66. V. Fausboll, 1877, *The Jataka*, I, London, No. 3; E.B. Cowell, *The Jataka*, I, Cambridge, 1895, No.3
67. CF. N. Lahiri, 1992, *The Archaeology of Indian Trade Routes upto c. 200 BC*, Delhi, pp. 74, 87-88.

NOTES AND NEWS

Iron Working in Ancient India with Special Reference to Excavations at Khairadih

Little attention has so far been paid to the reconstruction of ancient iron working in India. In view of the limited archaeo-metallurgical researches in the country, it is quite understandable. Excavations rarely reveal only furnaces, much less smiths' workshops which can lead to a proper and full understanding of ancient iron working. An attempt has, nevertheless, to be made to collect the scattered data and put them together in one place for understanding the technology that was anciently practised in India. The excavations conducted at Khairadih- district Balia in Uttar Pradesh, by the Banaras Hindu University revealed several furnaces and even workshops of blacksmiths. It is aimed here to study the prevalent technique of iron making at different cultural levels as exhaustively as possible with special reference to Khairadih excavations. The archaeological data would be substantiated with ethnological evidence to see whether it corroborates the deductions. Only through such an approach a worthwhile reconstruction of the furnaces and the process and mode of production of iron can possibly be understood.

Archaeological Evidence

In India iron working has been traced in the Chalcolithic *milieu* from sites of eastern and central India, Rajasthan, etc. At Pandu Rajar Dhibi[1] iron slags and ash pits identified as iron furnace have been reported along with restricted number of iron objects from Chalcolithic level (Period II) dated by 14 C between 1045 ± 55 B.C. and 920 ± 50 B.C. On the basis of examination of slags, it has been deduced that smelting was done here at a rather low temperature, below 1100°C. There is no clear cut evidence for the use of tuyeres. Some of the samples belonging to post-Chalcolithic level (Period III) have a high percentage of fayolite (iron silicate) rendering the object brittle and naturally indicating an elementary knowledge of iron smelting. Seeing the early context of occurrence, it is quite understandable to conclude that the knowledge of the technique had just been acquired.

At Jodhpura in district Jaipur, Rajasthan, pits associated with slags and ashes have been noticed at Painted Grey Ware level.[2] The details of working or shape of the furnace, etc. have not been discussed by the excavators. But more recently some light was thrown on the evidence of smelting furnace at Noh, again at the PGW level (in the Seminar on New Archaeology and India held by ICHR in New Delhi in October, 1988). According to Lal the ' furnance with a side hole into which the nozzle bellows could have been inserted' was found at Noh.

Atranjikhera, an important site of Upper Ganga basin having a rich collection of iron right from the earliest levels of the Painted Grey Ware culture, yielded a pear-shaped fire pit from the upper phase of PGW culture. In the words of the excavator[3] "in some cases the openings for introducing nozzles of the bellows for pumping air into the furnace there could be clearly seen. Inside these pits were found rounded tapering clay-lumps and finished iron tools. A pair of tongs, which might have been used by the blacksmiths, lay outside the pit along with iron slags and charred animal bones". The significance of charred bones in the context of a furnace is not very clear and led Gaur to assume that some of these pits might have been community hearths. Nevertheless, the occurrence of slags, finished iron objects and smiths' tools is significant indeed. At Jakhera some iron–working was evidenced in the Painted Grey Ware level. The details of the same, however, are not yet known. Iron working has also been evidenced at Ujjain in layers assignable to 500 B.C. The shape of the furnace is not very clear. Use of lime as flux has been suggested.

Megalithic cultures of south India and Deccan were very rich in iron and local smelting has been attested to from several sites. Most valuable evidence to date has come from the excavations at Naikund in the Vidarbha region of Maharashtra. It has been dated on the basis of Radiocarbon dates to 700-400 B.C. (690 ± 110 B.C.) A careful excavation with the help of resistivity meter led to the discovery of an iron smelting furnace.[4] The furnace at Naikund was a small one with a diameter of 30 cm and height of 25 cm. It was built with circular clay bricks. The walls were tapering towards the opening at the top. A hole was provided at the bottom for tapping the slag. Two tuyeres of 16 cm length and 2.5 and 3.6 cm thickness in heavily vitrified condition were recovered. Nearly 40 g of slag and cinder were found in the trench. A corroded iron rod was also noticed in the vicinity. Gogte[5] has reconstructed the furnace and a model has been prepared. A large number of finished and well-prepared iron objects were found in excavations at Naikund. This excavation provides us with a model to work on. The evidence of iron working at Dhatwa in Gujarat (Surat Dist) is significant indeed.[6] It has yielded slags, ores, finished iron objects along with evidence of iron working where crucible shaped furnaces with bellows were in use.

At Khairadih three furnaces have been found in a row. Though heavily damaged (it could have been destroyed by the ancient smelters themselves while working) but it may be reconstructed. Underground pits with flat base were excavated; they were 39 cm deep and had a diameter of 20 cm. The clay lining of this pit is thinner than the furnace top. At this level a superstructure was raised above ground, the shape appears to be akin to the shaft furnace. Clay mixed with straw and sand was used for the furnace walls. Although no tuyere could be found, bamboo plastered with clay might have been used. A thick burnt bamboo has been found *in situ* just at the level of the top of the undergound pit. The slag ran through a channel provided for it at a lower level. A close observation of slags reveal that they flowed out of the furnace in a liquified form and dropped down as drippings on the lower level. A large amount of slag (over 30 kg) was picked up nearby leaving the rest *in situ* indicating a fairly heavy working in the area. Being partially underground, the furnaces must have been more efficient than the Naikund example which was completely above ground level. Such an inference is possible on the basis of ethnological evidence in Orissa.

The entire northern side of the site was occupied by the artisans or metal workers. In another trench (CC 6 and the adjacent trenches) similar evidence has come forth. Traces of glass making and iron smelting have been located in the same area. A mud-floor with earthen lamps and other household accessories along with pestle, quern (a four legged oblong platform and a straight short handled rounded pestle) of fine grained grey sandstone, used probably for breaking the ore, a crucible, etc. were found in association with lots of burning activity. Whitish ash slags and finished iron objects and glass beads were also recovered from this complex. The exact shape and size of the furnaces could not be traced in this trench despite best efforts. It appears to be a multiple furnace area with working in several pyrotechnologies. The associated pottery belongs to somewhat later stage of Northeren Black Polished Ware culture. Most of the objects found were of wrought iron. However, some of the iron objects analysed at Banaras Hindu University (Department of Metallurgical Engineering) show a uniform pattern of pearlite cementite, thus, pointing to a high standard of smithy at Khairadih; carburization has also been attested to.

The types of furnaces described above were in operation at different cultural levels in India. In chalcolithic Bengal, at the time of introduction of iron technology, simple bowl furnaces without tuyeres appear to have been used (Pandu Rajar Dhibi). The yield in these furnaces is generally very small and the quality poor as shown above on the basis of analysis of slags and finished products. This kind of technical knowhow shows a very limited use of iron and thus will have little impact on the cultural set up. Nevertheless, introduction of iron was made, howsoever limited its use. An improvisation on this simple bowl was the introduction of bellows and tuyeres) with a dome-shaped superstructure to which additional charger of ore and charcoal could be added as smelting progressed. At Atranjikhera and Noh the 'oval pits' with provision for tuyeres and bellows could be classified under this category. Additional and a more careful retrieval of data on metal working may confirm this. The comparatively large number of iron tool repertoire and their good quality could be possible in this kind of operation. The slag in the form of drippings collected at those sites may suggest that provision for tapping slag was made in these furnaces. As compared to the most elementary bowl furnaces, comparatively a larger bloom can be obtained here.

The shaft furnace is of the most evolved kind. It appears at a slightly later stage of technological growth. At Khairadih this has been found (as discussed above) only at late NBP culture stage. In fact the number of iron objects show a marked improvement from early NBP to late NBP level at the site. Archaeological evidence may be well substantiated with ethnological evidence available in India.

Ethnological Evidence

Due to largely prevalent destructive method of iron working and also due to the problem of survival of superstructure of furnaces as archaeological remains, ethnological evidence of iron working is a great asset to the proper understanding of smelting-forging processes that was traditionally followed. Till the capture of market by the British pig iron in the beginning of 20th century, iron was being locally manufactured in small quantities in almost every part of India particularly near ore deposits. The quality of iron thus produced was very high and does not require any elaboration. A variety of furnaces are known to have been in operation in each region. Certain furnaces used by pre-industrial societies are well comparable with furnaces found at Khairadih.

Recently, Vikash Bharati, a regional centre for appropriate rural technology, traced Asur Birjia tribes in Gartha Harup village on Netarhat Plateau (near Bishunpur on Lohardaga - Netarhat Road, Ranchi in Chotanagpur Division of Bihar and studied their working process.[7] They also tried to get iron production restarted and make it economically viable for the iron workers. It is noteworthy, however, that the modern metallurgical engineers could not suggest any improvisation in the basic technology of iron-working adopted by these traditional workers.

A vertical shaft furnace is used at Bishunpur. Lumps of iron ore and charcoal of sal wood are the raw material. Twin bellows, held down by a stone are used for air blast. The same opening at the base was used for inserting the tuyere and was sealed with clay and charcoal mixed together. At the conclusion of the smelting the bloom was removed through this hole. Two shallow pits were provided on both sides of the front opening for catching the outflowing slag.

The temperature in the tuyere region was found to be as high as 1500°C but was measured to be lower on the inside of the shaft region. Sponge iron of 96% purity is obtained in this process as a result of reheating and beating of the bloom. The carbon content varies from 0.01 to 0.04%. Similar furnaces were used in Bastar region with only one basic difference that a platform was added at the opening through which additional charge could be slid into the furnace occasionally.

A similar furnace with slight variation was used in Orissa in Koraput region (near Baipariguda in Jeypore subdivision of Koraput) and Sambalpur. It was also in use, though on a smaller scale in several other districts like Kalahandi, Bolangir, Sundergarh, Keonjhar and Dhenkanal. There are some minor variations in the designs of furnace, viz., the Sambalpur furnace was built above the ground and while that at Koraput was located underground and was claimed to be more effective.[8]

In some furnaces near Rourkela limestone was used as flux, indeed a significant evidence. Some analysis was conducted at Rourkela Steel Plant. Carbon 0.3% was found to be present in this iron though in a non-uniform pattern. Carburization was also prevalent in a limited scale for imparting hardness.

The process of iron working has thus been understood fully with the help of experimental metallurgy based on the pre-industrial model. It has been conducted by the team of metallurgists at SAIL, Ranchi and Rourkela. Actual production of iron has been successfully attempted at both the centres above. While it has thrown light on the most intricate details of the technique of iron working at these places, this experimental metallurgy by engineers at the modern steel plants also has highlighted the traditional

Indian technology, preserved and practised by these ethnological groups. They represent the knowledge acquired through generations and thus may be a true legacy of traditional Indian iron working.

Interestingly, it may be observed that most of these societies live in close proximity to ore deposits. This automatically removes the necessity of long and tedious transportation of the mass of ore to the work place. No wonder that a somewhat similar situation prevailed in ancient days too. It may be demonstrated by an indepth study of resource zones in connection with specific cultural centres.

The other observation which may be made on the basis of an evolution in furnace design - from simple to more complex - is that the technology was developed indigenously on the basic pattern of existing copper smelting technology. It is clear, however, that since the newly acquired metal could be produced only in a very limited quantity because of the small size of furnaces iron was put to use only for very special purposes, like hunting (a favourite sport of the elite) and warfare. However, it paved the way for innovations in the field of technology.

REFERENCES

1. De, Sudhir and Chattopadhyay, R.K., 1989. Iron from Pandu Rajar Dhibi: Archaeometallurgical Studies, *Steel India* 12.

2. Agrawala. R.C. and Vijay Kumar, 1976. The problem of PGW and Iron in Northern Rajasthan. In *Mahabharat Myth or Reality*. ed. S..P. Gupta and K.S. Ramachandran, New Delhi , pp. 241 – 244.

3. Gaur, R.C., 1983, Excavation at Atranji khera, New Delhi, pp. 128.

4. Deo, S.B. and Jamkhedkar. A.P., 1982. *Naikund Excavations*, Bombay.

5. Gogte, V.D. 1982. Report on Iron Working and Furnaces in Deo, S.B. and Jamkhedkhar A.P. (above) pp. 11, 56 - 59, 52 - 55.

6. Hegde, K.T.M. 1973. A Model for understanding Ancient Indian Iron Metallurgy, *Marg*, Vol.8, No.3 (September), pp. 416 - 421.

8. Srinivasan, N.R. 1991. Revival of rural Iron making in Orissa. Paper presented at National Seminar on Indian Archaeometallurgy, October 2 - 4, B.H.U.

7. Agarwala, B.B., Prasad, K.K. *et al.* 1991. Evaluation of earlier Iron making processes and their relevance in Indian context. Paper presented at the National Seminar on Indian Archaeometallurgy, B.H.U. October, 1991.

Dept. of Ancient History & Archaeology, Banaras Hindu University Varanasi-221005.

VIBHA TRIPATHI

Buddhist Remains in Maldives

Maldives, a coral archipelago, in the Indian Ocean, is having a large number of Buddhist remains. These were first noticed by Naval officers, Lieutenants I.A. Young and W. Christopher in the year 1834-35[1]. Subsequently, Mr. H.C.P. Bell, Retired Archaeological Commissioner, Archaeological Survey of Ceylon, brought to light a number of Buddhist remains at Gāṇ and Fuā-Mulākū Islands of Aḍḍū Atoll, South Maldives in 1922[2]. This work created a cultural awareness in the National Council of Maldives. Consequently, Mohammad Ismail Didi was deputed to undertake the clearance of Buddhist remains at Toḍḍū and Ariaḍū Islands in 1958[3]. Later these Buddhist structures were surveyed by Mr. Thor Heherdahl in 1986 who, at the behest of Govt. of Maldives, visited various Islands and conducted excavations at Fuā Mulākū and Gāf Islands in south Maldives and Nilandu Island in north Maldives in the company of Mohammad I. Loutfi, Director, National Centre of Linguistic and Historical Research, Māle. [4]

The islands lie 450 nautical miles westward of Sri Lanka and 300 miles southwest of Cape Comorin (Kanya Kumari) in India. They encompass a total of 1195 atolls.

The islands covering Buddhist relics from north to south across the Republic include Lāṇdū, Miḷḷadū, Kareṇḍū, Kariḍū, Goiḍū, Toḍḍū, Kuramathi, Ariaḍū, Nilaṇdu, Kuḍāhuvādū, Islū, Dambidū, Gāṇ(1), Gāḍū, Kon̄dy, Kaḍeḍḍu, Gān(2), Fiorī, Fuā Mulāku, Gāṇ(3) (Fig. 1). Buddhist remains are found in these islands hidden under coral stones. They occur in the form of stūpas, monasteries, water tanks and enclosure walls. Most of them are now in complete ruins. Moreover, some of the structures are converted into mosques. Besides, a good collection of Buddhist antiquities is kept in the National Museum, Māle the capital of Maldives.

(i) Kuramathi

The island is stretched towards northwest of Māle. It is learnt that here a Buddhist establishment was in existence until a few years ago. The site is found located near the beach in the midst of palm trees. A minor excavation at the site has revealed an alignment of dressed stones in two courses at a depth of 50 cm. These stones in fact form the walls which are in east-west orientation. They measure from 27 cm. to 48 cm in length, 38 cm. to 45 cm in width and 10 cm to 25 cm in thickness. A few broken dressed stones carved with geometrical designs were noticed during the excavations. They appear to be the components of the basement of the structures as they retain vertical mouldings. Hence, it can be surmised that these may be the last remnants of the Buddhist complex left after destruction (P1. I). No antiquity has been recovered in the small dig. However, a number of potsherds of red ware were found scattered nearby. It is worth mentioning here that a few years back contextual antiquities, including different types of beads made of agate, carnelian, coral, crystal, etc. and silver and gold rings, gold foil, cowries, conch, and a terracotta ram figurine were found encased in a relic chamber of sandstone. These antiquities are now housed in the National Museum, Māle.

(ii) **Kuḍāhuvādū**

It is situated south–south–west of Māle. There are remnants of a Buddhist tank noticed here. Numerous stray dressed-stones are found near a mosque. The mosque is constructed of dressed stones, most likely taken from some Buddhist ruins. A solitary finding of the site is a lamp *(deepmālā)* of bronze now kept in the Primary School of the island.

(iii) Ariaḍū

It is said to have had several Buddhist structures. But only two ruined structures have survived, now lying south-west of seashore. The large structure, measuring 3 m in height and 9 m in diameter is a stūpa. The other one also seems to be a stūpa. Measuring 8 m in diameter, it occurs in the form of a dilapidated structure. It is learnt that there were other Buddhist structures here, including a tank, monasteries, etc. Ironically, they were destroyed in the pretext of clearance work undertaken by the native excavator of the land.

(iv) **Toḍḍū**

It is located northwest of Māle. The stūpa-site lies to the northwest of the island. The stūpa stands in a better state of preservation in comparision to the other Buddhist remains referred in this article (Pl.II). It is built of dressed stones of beach rock. It is lime plastered. The stūpa, measuring 5.25 m in diameter, is raised over a circular drum. Its dome is missing. The drum of the stūpa, characterised by vertical mouldings evidently consisted of various tiers. The drum is built on a square stepped platform. An inset stone-railing is seen around the entire lime plastered drum (Pl. III). The edifice faces east. A sculpture of Buddha head, now kept in the National Museum, Māle, was reported to have come from this very place.

(v) **Nilaṇdu North**

It lies south-west of Māle. The site is found to have a square platform which consisted of eight courses of dressed stones. It is enclosed all around by a wall. The platform was partially exposed by Loutfi and Heherdahl during their excavations in 1986. It is noticed that here parts of the Buddhist structures have been utilised in the construction of the mosque and houses of this island; the mosque is situated close to the Buddhist remains.

(vi) **Lāṇdū**

This island is located towards the north of Māle. A high mound measuring 30.0 × 30.0 × 7.00 m is noticed here. It appears to be a stūpa (P1. IV). There are a number of smaller stūpas lying near it. All these dilapidated structures are found covered with coral stones and marshy vegetation. Potsherds of red ware and Chinese Celadon ware were also recovered from the surface of the site.

A trial dig towards the northeast of the mound has revealed an entrance comprising of basement decorated with mouldings. The basement is characterized by retaining stone casing which is an abutment to the square platform of the stupa unexposed tell now. Both the walls of entrance, running north-south, contain damaged offsets of tiles and dressed stones. Towards south of the entrance, two broken stone slabs are found placed at right angle to the basement on either side. The staircase is buried under debris. The pathway leading to the stupa measures 6.00 m in length and 2.00 m in width. Its walls, having seven courses of dressed stones, are found 40 cm. in thickness. The pathway finally terminates in an unexposed square platform (PI.V).

The noteworthy finding from the trial dig is a shard of Celadon Ware bearing floral designs on its lip part. It seems to be fragment of a bowl.

(vii) Milladū

It is said that a relic chamber containing cowries (shells) and conch was found here during the demolition of Buddhist structures. Presently, only dressed stones are found scattered at the site which lies on the seashore.

(viii) Ceramics

The occurrence of pottery in the coral archipelago is significant as there are no clay deposits. Probably they were imported either from India or Sri Lanka. Import of pots from other countries also can not be ruled out; after all the Celadon ware was of Chinese origin.

A large number of pot sherds of red ware and Celadon Ware were collected from Kuramathi, Kuḍahuvādū and Laṇdū islands during explorations and minor excavations. The shapes of the ceramics include carinated bowl, jars, handis and lid. The redware shards are devoid of any slip or any other colour; the decorative designs are bound incised. However, shards of glazed ware and Celadon ware show floral decorations.

Antiquities Exhibited in National Museum, Māle.

The change in religion appears to have had its impact on the Buddhist remains. In the process, a number of antiquities were encountered, which are now housed in the National Museum, Māle. A few of them are described below.

(i) *Votive Stūpa on coral stone*

It is hemispherical in shape, measuring 36 × 22 × 3 cms. with a socket on top wherein was fitted a miniature stupa. Its lower part is broken. There are four Buddha figures engraved in four cardinal directions on the exhibit. It was recovered from Biḷḷaḍū island.

Besides, a large number of votive stūpas are exhibited in the porch of the museum. They all are in cylindrical shape, tapering towards the top which has a circular socket in the crown for fixing the spire. Some of these stūpas are marked by circular mouldings in the middle.

(ii) *Fragments of Railing*

There are various architectural member of stūpa displayed in the museum. Among them a part of a railing is noteworthy. It is a limb inset into the lower circular part of the dome. In fact, it is a part of basement attached to the stūpa as seen in Toḍḍū. The railing comprises of cross-bars which are intersected with vertical bars. These (railing) uprights are devoid of any figure. They contain concentric circular medallions. These fragments are reported from Gāfdāl and Gān islands.

(iii) *Bracket figures*

Four dwarf figures carved in coral are displayed. They are in crouching posture. Among them two seem to be mythical lions while remaining two are human beings. These crouching human figures show a close affinity to the sculptures of Ratnagiri. [5]

(iv) *A Buddha figure in Bronze*

The image is seen seated in Dhyānmudrā. It is characterized by a flame on the top of the heard. It has elongated ears. The eyes are half open. A piece of cloth is seen on its body as an upper garment (P1. VI). It measures 10 cm in length and 8.5 cm in width. The figure is brought to the museum from Gāḍḍu island. Strikingly, it has similar features with the Buddha images discovered at Kāñchipuram.[6]

(v) *Avalokiteśvara figure in Bronze*

The image is also found seated on a lotus throne. His both hands are rested on respective hips. It measured 10 × 5.5 cm is dimension.

(vi) *Casket*

A soapstone casket containing knobbed lid is exhibited in the museum. The upper part of the lid is decorated with incised floral designs. The contents of its bowl is said to have had a golden ring. The height of the casket is 8.5 cm.

(vii) *Demon figure*

It appears to be related to the Vajrayāna. The figure has four faces above a single face of awesome appearance with bulging eyes and protruding tongue. Its faces, with hanging ear-rings, and crowned head, show contentment due to exposed fangs. There are two inscriptions in Maldivian characters on top of the faces.

These Buddhist ruins suggest the prevalence of Mahāyāna form of Buddhism, which came to the coral archipelago either from southern India or Sri Lanka probably in the 16th century; later it, was transformed into Tantric form of the same religion. However, there is no evidence found in Maldivian referring or indicating to the advent of the Buddhist religion. There are however historical records in an ancient script which need decipherment. The ceramics, notably the Celadon and the glazed ware, encountered in investigations, suggest a very late phase of Buddhism in Maldive; post-11th century. Moreover, a bronze Buddha figure (Pl. VI) kept in the museum points towards its close affinity with the Buddha image of Kāñchipuram. The sculpture of demon seen in the museum also corroborates the Vajrayāna pantheon which can not be assigned prior to 7th century A.D. Conclusively, it can be stated that Buddhism survived in Maldive till A.D. 1152. Afterwards, the sudden embrace of Islam by the king in A.D. 1153 and his subjects led to its rapid decline and final disappearance after a few hundred more years.

REFERENCES

1. *Memoir on the Inhabitants of Maldives Islands*, 1936-38 (Transactions of the Geographical Society), Bombay.
2. Bell, H.C.P., 1940. *The Maldives Island: Monograph on the History, Archaeology and Epigraphy*, Colombo.
3. Didi, Mohd. Ismail, 1958. A personnel report in Dihevi Language.
4. Heherdahl, Thor 1986. *The Maldive Mystry*, London.
5. Mitra, D. 1981. *Ratnagiri*, Memoir No. 80, Vol. I, 1958-61, New Delhi : 165. Pl. CXIV.
6. Mitra, D. 1971. *Buddhist Monuments*, Calcutta : 194, Photo 122.
7. Taj-uel-din, Qasi Hasan, *Tarikh of Maldives III*: Muslim Chronicle.

Archaeological Museum Amaravati - 522020.

S.S. Gupta

Rock Paintings from Hazaribagh, Bihar

The Chota Nagpur Plateau comprises the hilly region of eastern central India. It encompasses parts of the modern states of Bihar, Uttar Pradesh, Madhya Pradesh, Orissa and West Bengal. Rock pictures from this area have been reported off and on since the early years of this century. The better known sites from this region are Singhanpur in the Raigarh district of Madhya Pradesh and the Vikramkhole shelter in the Sambalpur District of Orissa. Both sites have been subjects of publications during the twenties and thirties of this century. Singhanpur featured in a well illustrated monograph on rock art sites in Central India by Manoranjan Ghosh, while the engravings and paintings of the Vikramkhole shelter were in the center of a long running discussion on the meaning and origins of these ancient pictures.[1] Although these notices came quite early in Indian rock art research, they did not cause any long standing interest for the archaeologists, which is rather surprising, considering the fact that prehistoric finds were frequently referred to in ethnographic studies or monographs on tribal cultures, and it is the Chota Nagpur plateau where many of the famous ethnographic studies during the first half of this century originated. Only during the seventies and eighties further rock pictures were observed by archaeologists in the districts of Sambalpur and Sundargarh in Orissa.[2] Therefore it was not much of a surprise when the findings of several rock painting sites from the fringes of the Hazaribag plateau were announced in 1991.

The first reported site—Isko—was brought to the notice of a school teacher, who heard about these "Khowar Cave" from his students, living in the village close by. The information ultimately reached an environmentalist from Hazaribhag — Bulu Imam — who not only announced the find to the press, but together with his son and friends explored several of the hill ranges. In the course of his exploration he found several more rock art sites as well as other archaeological remains.

The finds of these antiquarian remains came at a time when large parts of the Chota Nagpur plateau were facing environmental destruction by large scale open cast mining for coal. This environmental havoc is caused under the term "development projects" which are invariably enforced against the interest of the local population, which, not incidentally, belongs to the weakest segment of the society.

The rock art and antiquarian remains are often rallying points of a growing national or ethnic self-consciousness, a form of ancient "title deeds" to the land and resources. No wonder that often new mythologies spring up as soon as these sites are "discovered" by archaeologists and visited by city based antiquarians. Within a short period of the first press reports on the discovery the site of Isko enjoyed considerable influx of visitors from far and wide, accelerating the precariousness of the preservational condition of these pictures.

The Painted rock shelters

The shelters are situated at the base of slopes of gorges formed by nullahs or water channels at fault lines in the sandstone massif and sometimes under the towering rock structures marking the cliff like periphery of elevated plateaus, which form a typical feature of the Chota Nagpur Plateau. The rock walls suffer from heavy exfoliation , which seems to be mainly caused by climatic de-stabilization of the chemistry of the exposed rock-surface. Particularly the fluctuating humidity seems to accelerate the formation of mineral salts and with it the structural weakening of the rock surface. Fungal growth in turn serves as base for higher organism and insect infection which load the micro fissures of the rock surface with organic material. The shrinking and expanding of the organic matter accelerates the physical detachment of large flakes from the rock surface. The sandstone in this region is deposited in horizontal bands. It is rather heavy grained and quite heavily pigmented towards red. The individual bands are often separated by layers of conglomerate. Indeed, only few of the available shelters house paintings, and the few painted panels are in particularity well protected spots, suggesting that of the originally painted surfaces only the most well protected have survived.

The paintings in Isko are under a shelter formed in a narrow fault-gorge hardly more than five metres from top to bottom and hardly ten metres wide. This miniature gorge channels the runoff water from one part of a several kilometre-long sandstone monolith, which slopes gently to a height of no more than 100 m above the surrounding landscape. The lower part of the monolith is shaven clean from top soil and vegetation therefore is only found at the higher reaches of the hill. The gorge channels the surface water as well as the sub-soil water towards a small swamp, which holds water perennially, although in summer the water is fit only for animals. Ultimately bordering the rocky hill lies the beautiful park-like country of agricultural fields and pasture land, intersected by clumps of *mohua* trees under which the houses of the tribal population are set. Indeed, several houses from the wide spread hamlet of Isko use parts of the flat bare rocks as their back-yard where they spread their paddy to dry. Higher up the hill is covered with vegetation, although the more valuable timber trees are butchered to mere brushwood, and no new shoots of the trees are allowed to grow higher than three metres. It is almost unbelievable that only a few years back these regions were under some of the best forests of India, where tigers, bears, elephants and all the large bovides and cervides abounded. Nowadays the forests are destroyed to the point of no return, turning into large stretches of lantana bush-jungles.

The paintings at Isko virtually cover a long stretch of the rock face. The main panel is one of the most impressive painted rock surfaces known in India. The most eye-striking features of the paintings are the overwhelmingly geometric patterns with intricate designs on many variations (19,-37) Most of the paintings are done in red and white, the red pigment is used in several shades from a deep purple to an almost yellowish brick-red. Within the mass of geometric patterns only very few figures of an anthropomorph or zoomorph character can be made out (10-16). Depictions of man indeed are virtually absent, save four or five figures showings the basic features of an anthropomorph, upraised arms and rudimentary legs (14-16). Zoomorphs, although not much more frequent, are in several instances well executed, and the best examples can easily be compared to the animal depictions known from the mesolithic pictures in the Vindhyan Hills (12). Anthropomorphs as well as zoomorphs are found invariably only in the lower strata of paintings. The upper — later — layer of paint is invariably taken by geometric figures. These patterns are in most cases squares or trapezoids, rarely triangles, circles or ovals (20,23-24) etc. The geometric designs in the earlier paintings, where they appear side by side with animals, are often decorated with concentric repetitions of the outline. Sometime the square designs are partitioned diagonally, so that triangular segments appear, which are filled in with concentric triangles, very much like body decorations of mesolithic animals from the Vindhyas (24,43,44). Although there are several patterns from the Vindhyas, the intricate labyrinth spiral or honeycomb patterns are rare — although not absent — in the paintings from the Hazaribag district. Most of the designs are done in two colors–red and white.

As already mentioned, the earlier paintings contain almost all the animal figures, the geometric designs are rather small and scarce, if compared to the wall fillings mass of geometric designs of the later layer of paintings which virtually fill whole shelter walls, particularity so in Isco and Raham. Two shelters situated at the top of the plateau of the Satpahar Hills show well preserved groups of animals. In one shelter (Satpahar 2) is a group of animals, bovides, antelopes, monkeys and tiger which are arranged in a long procession (65, 55a-5). In front and at the rear are diminutive figures of hunters armed with bow and arrow. The awkward style of the hunters and their diminutive size stand in contrast to the vivid naturalism of the animals. But we, of course already know the strict conceptual dimorphism of depictions of animals and men in the mesolithic rock art of the Vindhyas. The animals are drawn in elegant single outlines with out any attempt of further decoration or infilling. since the rock here is pigmented in deep red, the rather thinly applied pigment stands well in contrast. Close to the panel of the animals are several square designs executed in red and white. In a shelter near by (Satpahar 3) is a further group of animals (54). Here four fawns with spotted flanks are shown. These animals are particularly fine examples of the vivid style and artistic accomplishment of the earliest paintings in this region. These animal depictions are at par with the finest animal portrayals known from the early rock art in the Vindhya Hills. On account of the scarcity of animal depictions in the rock art of the Hazaribag District the observation of stylistic analogies to the better known also from the shelter Satpahar 1, where also polychrome paintings of animals are available (52,53). These pictures are strikingly similar to the depictions of polychrome paintings at Katni, one of eastern-most sites in the Vindhya Hills. The shelter Satpahar 4 is situated close to the river-valley which dissects Satpahar into two. The unique painting in this shelter is the detailed depictions of a moth (56). Portrayals of insects are altogether rare in rock art. I know of only one other example[3] — found in the southern Deccan — in which several locusts are shown. Indeed, the only insects shown in rock art are bees, which are invariably show as a mass of dots indicating the swarming insects

Another very interesting shelter is situated under a projecting rock right at the top of the cliff wall which forms the southern periphery of the Satpahar massif (1-9). This avant situation allows an extraordinary view over the plain towards the Ranchi Plateau in the south. The surface of this rather small shelter is extremely uneven and pock marked with fist-size holes and depressions. Indeed these miniature "shelter" in the rock surface was taken by the artist as surface for their often diminutive creations of figures. These figures are sometimes recognizable as animals or human beings, but more often the figures are best described as metamorphosis of anthropomorph and zoomorph features. Some of the anthropomorph figures even seem to have members transformed into vegetation (5,6,8). A few figures of fish are the only depictions of animals whose family can be understood with some degree of certainty (7). In these paintings we find again the "anthropomorph" figures with square shaped bodies upraised arms and legs wide apart, so that the whole figures could also be described as frogs (6). A small hole between the legs of one of these figures is transformed to female genitalia (?). The figure of a diminutive feline is placed in one of these minute hollows, the tail encircling the edge of the depression (4). This feline (?) faces the figure of a hunter holding a microlithic arrow in one hand.

The most prominent figures in this rather confusing panel are three mushroom-shaped anthropomorphs, whose one leg seem to metamorphose into vegetation (6,8,9). Several other depictions of anthropomorphs seem to be related to the extremely minimalist human figures of the earliest mesolithic style in the Vindhya Hills. Already in the paintings near Chhenga Pahar in the Hemgiri Reserve Forest of Orissa, I observed a small panel of three figures, one of them a person holding a bow and a microlith-beset arrow, which were quite[4] unique (Neumayer, E., 1993: Fig.:268), and since these three figures were not related to any of the other paintings in this area, their relative-chronological position could not be ascertained. Here, in the paintings of the Satpahar Hills, is quite clear that this style belongs to the earliest face of rock art in this region.

Conclusion

The paintings in the district of Hazaribag are stylistically related to the paintings known from the sites in the Hemgiri Reserve Forest and the site Usakothi in the Sundargarh district as well as some sites from the Sambalpur district of Orissa (Neumayer, E., 1993). Further stylistic analogies can be shown[5] with the mesolithic art in the Vindhya Hills, particularly the vivid style of the animal depictions and some of the intricate design patterns. The prominent depiction of geometric designs in the later stylistic group are obviously a continuation of the earlier style. Since geometric patterns are to be found already in the earlier strata of painting as well, although there the designs are never placed so prominently. It should be remembered that early Indian rock art contains a large amount of "abstract" designs which is not placed in any obvious narrative relation to "naturalistic" depictions. Surprisingly, there are no figures of animals or men to be found in the later paintings.

The paintings in the Hazaribag district — although very well preserved — form a very limited sample. Altogether only eight shelters were found till now, and almost all of them in the small area of the Satpahar Hills. So it is not so very surprising that all the shelters have more or less paintings of the same patterns. Surprising is that there are no pictures of later styles, like paintings of cattle or other rock domesticated animals which are invariably present at other rock art sites, as indeed they are also available at the sites in the Hemgiri region in Orissa. There is only a single ancient inscription in the Tirthangi shelter, giving the *aksharas* for "MA" enclosed by a shaped frame(51).

Since the paintings contain no chronological material, nor do they show any narrative "scene pictures" it is indeed difficult to place these pictures with any chronological certainty. On account of the stylistic analogies of the paintings from the Hazaribag district and the mesolithic paintings in the Vindhya Hills. I believe that the paintings here as well belong to mesolithic hunting and gathering cultures. However, the discovery of these paintings is a further important step for rock art research in the eastern parts of India.

NOTES AND REFERENCES

See Illustrations from pp. 99

Khowar is the term for the beautifully painted nuptial rooms in the traditional houses in the countryside of Bihar. Several rock art sites in the northern Vindhyas as well as in Bihar therefore are known locally as Khowar Khoh or Cave of the (painted) marriage chamber.

Mela is a religious fair with establishments of profane entertainment.

1. Chakravarti, N.P., 1936 The Vikramkhol Rock Inscription; *Annual Report of the Archaeological Survey of India* 1930-34 Part 1, p 229. Fabri, C.L., 1934 Latest Attempt to read the Indus Script, *Indian Culture* Vol. I, pp. 51–6. Fabri, C.L., 1936 The Vikramkhol Inscription, (Editorial remark); *Annual Report of the Archaeological Survey of India* 1930-34; Part 1. p 230, Pl. CXIX a. Jayaswal, K.P.. 1933 The Vikramkhol Inscription, Sambalpur District, The Indian Anti*quary* Vol. LXII, pp 58-60.

2. Mohapatra, G.C., 1982 Notes on the Vikramkhol and Usakoti Rockshelters in Orissa; *Man and Environment*, Vol. VI, pp 97-100;

Pathy, D., 184 Rock Shelter Paintings of Orissa; Chitra, *An Annual on Arts and Aesthetics*, B.K. College of Arts & Crafts, Bhubanneshwar, pp 11-5;

3. Neumayer, E. 1993. Op. cit.

4. Ibid. Fig 268

5. Ibid

Neumayer E., 1988 Felsbilder In Orissa; Selbstverlag, Wien;

1060 Vienna Gumpendorferster
114/21 Austria.

ERWIN NEUMAYER

Kunal : A New Indus – Saraswati Site

The recently excavated site of Kunal (Lat. 29° 30' N and 75° 41' E Long) is in tehsil Ratia of Distt. Hissar in the State of Haryana. It can be approached from Bhuna, a town 12 km from the site. It is located on the banks of now dried-up course of the Vedic river Saraswati. The settlement is not more than three acres in extent; the hub is only half of it. The total occupational deposit is only around 3.10 m. The site has been under excavations by two comparatively young and very skilled excavators in the service of the Govt. of Haryana – J.S. Khatri and M. Acharya - for the last three years. Recently, K.N. Dikshit, G.L. Possehl and S. P Gupta visited the site and also examined the remains unearthed there but was under close study of R. S. Bisht, the excavator of Banawali, primarily because Banawali is also on the Saraswati and about 20 km away, as the crow flies. Of course, many other archaeologists have also visited the site and examined the material. The sites has left archaeological records of the process of change which led to the formation of the Harappan culture. The records are as under: Initially, the land was slightly undulated and also low hence the first settlers brought from nearby region huge quantities of red kankary soil and dumped that here to make the land even as well raise the general level of the ground by about 0.71 m. That the people started living on this artificially raised ground is clear enough from the construction of the dwellings.

A dwelling in the site has been found consisting of two units – one round and adjacent to it one refuse pit. What is, however, most significant to note is that the dwellings were semi-subterranean, sometimes erroneously called 'pit dwellings'. It is usually 2 m in diametre and 1.10 m in depth with rammed floor and smoothened walls. The pits are found cut through not only the artificially raised red clay platform of .71 m thickness but also the natural soil. The discovery of a few post–holes around the dwelling pits dug on the ground level plus the rather shallowness of the pits proves beyond doubt that a hut at least 2 m high wattle–and–daub structure was raised above the ground.

The pottery repertoire is equally very significant. It is dominated by the so–called Hakra Ware found in the lowest levels of Jalilpur and is devoid of several Kalibangan I fabrics. It has also a handmade near black–and–red ware. There is also a dull chocolate coloured burnished ware with parin marks, the like of which has not been reported from many sites. A dull red ware with wavy incised decorations on the outer surface found at several Early Harappan sites was a major component of the pottery repertoire. However, the most characteristic pottery of this period is the dull red (or red washed) pottery with painted decorations in two colours – black outline and white filling. It is in profusion; quantitatively more than those found at Banawali, Kalibangan and Kot Diji. Some designs are also monochrome, criss–cross diamond shaped geometric patterns done in black or sepia. The faunal and floral painted motifs are most noteworthy, the former includes bull head with highly curved and decorated horns and the latter a large variety of pipal leaf.

The cultural complex includes, besides a very rich and almost exclusive pottery repertoire, a large number of bone tools, micro beads of chalcedony and copper implements such as arrowheads and fish–hooks. It may be noted that a number of arrowheads resembled those found by R.C. Agrawal at Ganeshwar in Rajasthan – in them the two sides show marked curvature at the base. The other type is, of course, the usual inverted 'V' shaped, with sides absolutely straight. This is termed as 'Period IA'.

Period IB represents the expansion of the settlement and elaboration of the semi–subterranean houses of round pits. First, the size increased from 1/2 to 1 m; these huts now measured 2.64 m, 2.75 m, 2.92 m in diameter, Moreover, the pits were now lined with finely moulded mud bricks of very special sizes such as 11 × 24 × 39; 10 × 37 and 11 × 38 cm. The maximum number of courses found intact so far is five. Some of them have brought to light well designed as well constructed mud brick hearths.

The pottery repertoire of Pd. Id continues to occur in large numbers, mainly the bichrome red ware using black and white colours for paintings of faunal and floral designs, including the bull head, with highly curved horns marked with three parallel lines of white and black colours alternating in rhythmic fashion. The pipal leaf, beautifully hatched, or solidly filled, or else leaf–within–leaf pattern, using black, sepia and white colours, presents the most popular, and perhaps the most sacred motif.

More significantly, now we get practically all the six Kalibangan I fabrics in pottery, including the grey ware, internally incised red ware, pots with roughened surface at the bottom achieved by splashing wet clay, etc. These are also the potteries found in the lowest levels of Banawali, Siswal, and other sites on the Saraswati and Drishadvati rivers. The black–and–red ware also continues to occur in small quantities and so also the plain dull chocolate coloured burnished ware with paring marks on thick fabric.

But what is most significant from our point of view is the first occurrence of red sturdy ware pots of well levigated clay. Some of these pots have forms closer to the classical Harappan forms, such as beakers and jars. We have clearly observed the beginning of mature Harappan shapes, fabric, thickness, etc. but in dull red ware, grey ware and dull chocolate ware. We have from this level terracotta cakes also.

Period IC represents the real Transitional Phase between the Eary Harappan and Mature Harappan culture–complexes. the dwellings changed from the semi–subterranean huts to regular square rectangular houses built of standardised mud bricks on the ground level which was further raised at various points to provide height and stability to the living quarters. The brick size, it may be noted, are in two ratios 1:2:3 and 1:2:4 (9 × 18 × 36 cm; 11 × 44 cm; 13 × 26 × 39 cm; 11 × 22 × 33 cm), both used simultaneously while it is generally believed that the former ratio was adopted by the Sothi–Kot Diji people, i.e., the Early Harappan while the latter was adopted by the Harappans. It is common knowledge that 1:2:3 ratio bricks can not always produce the so–called 'English Bond' architecture in which the joints always fall in the middle of the bricks of the upper and the lower courses while the bricks of 1: 1f(1,2) :3 ratio do produce perfect 'English bond, a feature that produces greatest strength to the structure and saves it falling apart in blocks. It further establishes the fact that the Mature Harappan technologies started appearing in the Early Harappan times in the field of architecture also. Further, the houses, though extremely modest in dimension and elaboration when compared to those of the Mature Harappan period, developed drainage system also comparable to at least one of the most popular types used at Harappa, Mohenjodaro, Kalibangan, Banawali and Lothal – soakage jars fixed in the streets pits were made to do the same job. Both the devices were adopted to keep the streets neat and clean. discovery of refuse pits further helped the people not to choke the lanes streets with household rubbish.

It is sometimes believed that the Early Harappans did not develop devices to store grain but at Kunal, during this period we do find round silos or pits plastered with chunam and clay mixture.

Period Ic has been divided into three structural Phases Ic (i), Ic (ii) and Ic (iii). And significantly these structural phases also exhibit features which clearly demonstrate developing stages of culture. Each one is marked, it may be noted with the feature generally labelled 'change with continuity'. The houses, the drainage system, the street, etc. did not change much except for the fact that as the time passed, the dwellings became slightly larger and better built. And this is not too surprising because the site remained throughout its existence only a village.

Phase Ic (i) is the most significant phase. In one of the rectangular brick houses, the excavators found a virtual treasure of gold and silver ornaments placed in a silver sheet and buried in a plain simple dull red globular pot of early Harappan fabric. The silver objects include two tiaras, one small and one large, each with a large fully opened flower having petals topped with a decoration like the Greek letter alpha. Never before such magnificent objects were found at any Harappan or Indus–Saraswati site. And this is not all. Along with these two silver objects one large silver armlet with horizontal mouldings was also found. This too is a unique object. The three together, it seems quite likely, belonged to some *raja* or king, else a socially distinguished elite because not only the forms of the objects but also because the metal silver are foreign to the region. As a matter of fact, the objects themselves are exotic but since at no other place such ornaments of royal association have been found, it is difficult to make conjectures about the place of their orign.

From a different cache, found in another house of the same period, a large number of gold ornaments with disc beads, cup–shaped beads, round sheet beads with thread–channel, barrel–shaped tubular beads with facets all over the surface, etc. have also been found. Beads in terracotta but of shapes identical with the metal ones are found from several houses. Similarly, large hoards of lapis lazuli micro–beads and 92 beads of agate make the whole gamut of luxury items as 'richest' when seen in the context of the rural nature of the settlement and Sothi culture – complex. But this is not all. Most of the shapes were similar to those found at Harappa and Mohenjodaro. This too proves beyond doubt that Mature Harappan types of stone and metal beads were manufactured centuries before the emergence of Harappan cities. And this includes classical faience and carnelian beads too. Small chert blades are also not wanting.

Significantly, copper objects included of the so–called Mature Harappan types, e.g. coiled finger rings, coiled cones, inverted 'V' shaped arrowheads, flat axe and fish–hooks, spear heads, etc. There is at least one copper–smelting furnace found at the site. From here a classical example of terracotta crucible with molten metal still sticking to the inner surface has come to light. Undoubtedly, therefore, the copper ingots came from some other site but the objects were manufactured locally. Similarly, one pottery kiln has also come to light.

And above all, the discovery of as many as six steatite and one shell seals makes it absolutely clear that typical Mature Harappan square seals with knobbed back along with a hole were made centuries before the emergence of the urban centres in the Saraswati and the Indus basins. The seals, however, bear only geometric designs, all of which are found in the Mature Harappan context. Thus, neither writing, nor human and animal pictures of the Mature Harappan types have been found here. A part of this lacuna was filled up, at another Eartly Harappan site, Dholavira in Kutch, where stage III, also the Transitional Phase, has yielded four steatite square seals with pictures of typical Harappan human, animal and floral motifs, though still without association of a Mature Harappan writing.

Deptt. of Archaeology, Govt. of Haryana, Chandigarh

J. S. KHATRI AND M. ACHARYA

Scientific Studies of Kunal Site, Distt. Hissar, Haryana

A few scientific techniques have recently been used in archaeological investigations at Kunal (29° 30' N – lat. and 75° 41′ E long.) distt. Hissar, Haryana (India). Excavation at Kunal was initiated in 1986 and is still continuing. Preliminary archaeological studies indicated that findings are of Pre-Harappan age. With a tool of science in hand archaeologist can unfurl the mysteries of past. Such a work has begun in the Deptt. of Archaeology and Museums, Haryana where the author is doing scientific investigations. Brief details of the work done are as under :

1. Identification of a few Bones and Molluscas from the Holocene Beds of Kunal, Hissar Haryana

First visit for scientific studies was made during July 1987 when systematic sampling and processing of sediments were conducted. Preliminary investigation of bone was conducted and for identification help from the Centre of Advanced Studies in Geology, Punjab University, Chandigarh was taken. In addition to bones a few molluscas were also recovered and identified. Taphonomical analysis suggested distinct and separate modes of accumulation. The micro mammals probably secondarily concentrated from the faecal pallets of predatory animals while the boviods represent accumulation in fluvial flood plain environments. Small mammals comprised of rodents while in mega verteberates mainly referable to bovidae. Of the five molluscan genera found from the site four molluscas have been found to occur in shallow stagnant water. The only one gensus occurring in running water is *Parravsia, Vivapara bengalansis* a widely distributed species is known to conceal itself in mud in drought season.

The fresh water habitat and the modern form of the fossils suggests the existence of fresh water basin in which *Vivapara bengalensis. Gibbula, Dissortama* and *Lamellideus* flourished and *Parreysia* must have been brought by the influx of some nearby river.

2. Palaeo – Environmental Studies

Environment comprises climate (temperature, precepitation and humidity) prevailing in that particular region and part of its physiography, the nature and composition of soils and the presence of plants and animal life with their interaction upon them singly are jointly ultimately determines the climate of that area. The inference regarding past environment is usually drawn through geomorphological, pedological, archaeological, palaeontological and palaeobotanical studies. An attempt has been made here to study the palaeoenvironment of Kunal area in sub recent time based on palynological data. For this clay sample from jacket embedded in the top layer of the trench W/D 2 layer 1 was analysed and laboratory investigations were conducted in the CAS in Geology, Punjab University, Chandigarh. Preliminary studies of microflora indicated that the Kunal area was once covered with mesophytic vegetation seemingly belonging to various families of flowering plants such as Ranunculaceae, Crucifere, Polygonacea, Nympheacaceae, Amranthaceae, Compositae, Batulaceae, Mimosidcal, Labiate, etc. The fauna and flora suggests that the atmosphere was surcharged with excessive humidity. This climatic conditions do not tally with the present semi-desertic climate of the region. The climate of the region has witnessed a sharp shift from warm humid to semi arid nature. For conducting the carbon dating samples have already been collected and are being analysed to ascertain the exact age.

3. Non Destructive X-Ray Microanalysis of Artifacts and Jewellery from Kunal

(a) *Scanning Electron Microscope Energy Dispersive X–Ray (SEM–EDAX) Analysis*

Energy dispersive analysis of X-rays is the attachment of SEM, it gives about the constituents present in the sample. It is used for surface investigation.

SEM–EDAX is a most versatile tool for the examination of metal art objects. Polished surface analysis revealed about the fabrication history and present state of preservation of the antiquities. Elemental distribution map obtained using EDAX helps to see compositional change on the surface. Metal salt analysis is possible with this equipment and morphological structures of metal wrapped yarns with its elemental composition can be studied.

In order to undertake non-destructive microanalysis on the rare and precious metal made jewellery. EDAX was carried on three different sets of articles. Silver platelets contains 71.94% silver, 6.64% aluminium and 21.42% of chloride. Percentage of Gold in the disc shaped bowls is found to be 69.50% while it is 83.55% in pendant and 77.71% in gold tublar bead. Copper percentage varies from 30.32% to 42.80 in three copper arrow heads. In future this study may prove to be useful to know the source of ore for extraction of metal, as generally a particular type of impurity is found in metal extracted from the ore from a particular mine. Thus study of microanalysis of the metal will be a very useful tool that too without destroying the valuable archaeological findings.

(b)*Elemental Analysis Of Soil Samples – A Study Using Energy Dispersive X–Ray Flourescence* (EDXRF) *Technique.*

The elemental analysis by X-ray flourescence has proved to be a very good direct and sensitive non-destructive method for museum objects. The physical principles of the XRF techniques are based on the possibility of detecting the characteristic X–rays emitted by the sample during photon–induced atomic transition. The analysis of flourescence radiation in terms of energy which identifies the element, and in terms of intensity, which is related to its abundance, allows non-destructive qualitative and under certain condition quantitative elemental determinations.

The trace elemental concentration in minerals play an important role in studies of chemical processes. The elemental profile may give us information about the genesis of minerals and the relationships between different chemical/geological structures.

Elemental analysis of the soil samples was carried out using EDXRF spectrometer. In the soil samples sixteen elements are present namely K, Ca, Ti, Mn, Fe, Cu, Zn, Ga, Br, Rb, Sr, Y, Zr, Nb, Au and Pb have been quantified using both the excitation energies of 22.6 and 5.96 Kev.

Concentration of all the elements present varies. There are only two samples which show the presence of gold (Au) traces. One of the samples contains about Au 141.1871 ug/g and the second 14.36921 ug/g gold. The presence of gold traces are of much significance for the archaeological excavation site which reveals that goldsmith activity might be going on in that area. Further investigations are under-study for the presence of the Au in the soil sample which was recovered from the silver necklace container.

Acknowledgements

The author pays her gratitude to Mrs. Shakuntla Jakhu, IAS Director Archaeology and Museum, Government of Haryana, Chandigarh for constant encouragement to conduct scientific studies. The author shall be failing in her duty if she does not acknowledge Prof. Ashok Sahin, Chairman and Dr. R.Y. Singh, CAS in Geology, P.U. Chandigarh for allowing and helping her in practical/instrumentational work in their laboratories for SEM-EDAX and Palynological studies. The author is also thankful to Dr. Bakshish Chand Department of Physics, P.U. Chandigarh for XRF studies.

Deptt. of Archaeology, Govt. of Haryana, Chandigarh

SHUBH KIRAN SHARMA

Excavations at Bhorgarh

Bhorgarh (Lat 28' 5° N and Long 77' 5° E) is located at a distance of 30 km. from Delhi railway station towards north of Delhi. The mound is situated 500 m. west of Bhorgarh village and 2 km. north-west of Narela railway station. Bhorgarh is well connected with Delhi by road also.

Originally, the mound was spread over several acres of land but villagers converted almost all the mound into an agriculture land after levelling the area, thus leaving a very small portion of mound intact. The eastern side of the mound houses a modern grave-yard. Presently the mound is surrounded by cultivated field. The mound which remains intact measures 130 m. from east to west and 100 m. from north to south. The tootal occupational deposit of the mound is about 180 cm. Once upon a time, the river Yamuna used to flow near this mound but now it has changed its course and shifted about 10 km. towards south. Traces of the ancient mound may also be seen on the eastern side of the village behind the Govt. School near the bus stop which proves that part of the village is settled on the ancient site itself.

The Department of Archaeology, Govt. of Delhi, under the direction of Dr. B.S.R. Babu had taken up excavation at this ancient site for two successive seasons during the years 1992-93 and 1993-94. Excavations yielded a four-fold cultural sequence from the late Harappan period upto medieval time, covering a span of about 2500 years. The following cultural periods have been identified at Bhorgarh.

Period I: Late Harappan (Second millennium B.C.)

Period II: Painted Grey Ware Culture (First millennium B.C.)

Period III: Kushan (Second and Third centuries A.D.)

Period IV: Medieval (Sixteenth and Seventeenth Centuries A.D.)

Period I: Lowest level at Bhorgarh yielded late Harappan material particularly the thick red ware pots. Though the habitational area of this period couldn't be traced, the discovery of graves of this period suggests that the habitational area must have been well within the periphery of the mound which might have been damaged by the cultivators or it might be still buried. Two graves were exposed. Grave pits were dug out in the alluvium of river Yamuna and later filled by the same soil and as such, while exposing the graves it became difficult to identify the pit-line.

Grave No. 1 : It is an extended burial. The body was buried in almost north-south orientation. Three pots were placed behind the head as burial goods. Out of them one is a small bowl while other two are small globular vases of two different sizes. The skeleton has a long stretcher with calculated length of 176 cm. Both hands were folded from elbo and seems to have been placed on shoulders. The epithysis of the long bones are damaged. Bones of the leg portion (tarsel, metatarsel, phalanges) remained inside the section.

Grave No. 2 : This is also an extended burial with almost north-south orientation and almost parallel to grave No. 1. Interestingly, this grave does not contain any burial goods. Left hand of this skeleton was kept straight parallel to the vertebral column. The skeleton was in very fragile condition.

Period II: Painted Grey Ware culture succeeded the late Harappan at Bhorgarh. It has a rich deposit, measuring 45 cm. on average. Occurrence of PGW pottery in abundance at this site proves that this culture dominated Bhorgarh settlement once upon a time. The post-holes identified in one of the trenches suggest that people used to live in circular huts supported by wooden posts. In another trench, a hearth made of lump of clay was exposed.

As already pointed out, a huge quantity of PGW pottery was unearthed from the excavation at Bhorgarh. Important shapes are straight-sided bowls with flat base, deep bowls with sagger base and a miniature *hāndī*. Basin and vases of associated red ware fabric have also been noticed. PGW sherds were painted with black pigment either on inner or outer surface and sometimes on both sides. All designs were painted with free hand.

Circles, concentric circles, semicircles, flowers with three or nine petals, dotted designs, dots inside two parallel lines, strokes, wavy lines, intersecting loops, balloon design, hook design are only some of the common designs that decorated the earthenware. Most of the designs are similar to those designs found on the pottery of this period from Hastinapur, Ahichchatra, Attranijikheda.

Beads made of carnelian, clay beads of *ghaṭa*-shape, terracotta animal figurines, hop scotches and fragments of iron implements are some of the other important antiquities of this period.

Period III: This site was reinhabited during the Kushan period. Stuctural activity has been noticed in two phases. The first one used mud bricks. In one of the trenches deeply excavated, it clearly shows the presence of mud bricks and two occupational layers as evidenced by mud floors. The second phase of activity is witnessed by burnt brick structures.

STR-1 : this seems to be part of a house complex. Western part of the structure was destroyed and levelled by the farmers for cultivation purpose. There are seven courses of bricks.

STr 2 : Three courses of bricks of the same size as used in STR 1 forming into a wall seems to be part of a house complex. Against this wall, a mud floor has been noticed. The floor was rammed with small pot sherds, stone nodules, etc. However, at a later stage, huge pits were dug out for dumping garbage.

In one of the trenches, an oven of this period was beautifully exposed.

Terracotta animal figures, one female, probably of Mother-Goddess(?), copper coins, terracotta beads, iron implements and two terracotta sealings with the legend 'SU PA KA SA' in Brahmi letters are some of the important antiquities discovered at the site.

A variety of pottery has been collected from the deposits of this period. The main shapes include typical incurved bowls, dishes, basins, sprinklers, handis, lids (with knobs and ink-pot type), lamps and different sizes of vases. Pots were decorated sometime with black pigment and rarely with white pigment. Geometrical designs were made near the neck portion. A few stamped designs were also noticed of which Sun motif is quite important.

Period IV : The main concentration of the medieval period is noticed on the eastern side of the mound. Unfortunately, the entire portion was destroyed by the farmers. Hence considerable evidence of that period could not be gathered. A small wall made of lakhori bricks in four courses has been exposed. Many lakhori brick structures erected during this period may be noticed within 2 km. area which includes a huge tank constructured at Narela dating back to the Mughal period.

Sherds of procelain and celadon ware have been collected alongwith Hukka chelam made of red ware from this level at Bhorgarh.

B.S.R. Babu

Department of Archaeology,
Govt. of Delhi, Delhi-110006.

Plate I. Kuramathi : Buddhist Ruins.

Plate II. Toddu : A Stupa.

Plate III. Toddu : A Stupa Railing.

Plate IV. A Stupa.

Plate V. Landu : An Entrace of Stupa.

Plate VI. Gaddu : Buddha Figure in Bronze.

BOOK REVIEWS

Chakrabarti, Dilip K. *Archaeology of Eastern India, (Chhotanagpur Peateau and West Bengal)* Munshiram Manoharlal Pub. (New Delhi, 1993) pp. 225 + XVI, Price: Rs. 450/-

Like the elitist politicians, high-profile archaeologists also did not pay enough attention to the archaeology of Chhotanagpur Plateau and those parts of West Bengal which are close to the Plateau. However, from time to time efforts were made to explore the river valleys for locating sites of Stone Ages, the reviewer himself had joined Late V.D. Krishnaswami to explore the basin of Kansavati. In the pre-Partition days, the so-called Asura sites, monuments and 'megalithic' burials were located, explored and excavated. The pages of *Indian Archaeology-A Review* volumes give summary accounts of many attempts to explore this region consisting of districts like Palamau, Hazaribagh, Girdih, Ranchi, Singhbhum, Santhal Parganas, Purulia, Bankura, Burdwan, Midnapur and Birbhum. Dr. Chakrabarti also explored some parts of this region of Bihar and Bengal along with his students.

The presents work contains the details of his own work as well as the works done in this region during the last 100 years. The author has summarised and tabuted the data of all such works. He has also high-lighted the archaeological problems of this region. For example, the chalcolithic period represented by black-and-red ware which may be dated between 2000 B.C. and 1000 B.C. or 700 B.C. is still not fully known and documented. Beginning of iron may go back in some places to 1000 B.C. and in other places to 300 B.C. or even later. The Coper Hoards can hardly be dated in this region with any degree of precision.

The Palaeolithic, Mesolithic and Neolithic periods are also known only in parts, and largely through surface collections, the good geological, geomorphological and palaeoenvironmental studies are still to be undertaken.

The area was, however, always a paradise for anthropologists and linguists and as the author has admirably pointed out all kinds of speculations regarding migrations of peoples and their separateness from the rest of the country were made and projected as sound history, by and large the theories were motivated being the products of distorted perceptions.

Here is, therefore, a very welcome book by a senior author for all these archaeologists, anthropologists and linguists who would like to work in this region in future.

S.P. Gupta

Sinha, B.P. *Twilight of the Imperial Guptas*, National Centre for Oriental Studies, Delhi, 1993, pp. 340, Price Rs. 600/-

The history and culture of the Imperial Guptas have been widely studied subjects but the period A.D. 450-550 according to the author, actually represents the twilight-the period between the sun-set and dusk in Indian history. The work, which is divided into seven chapters with four Appendices, is an attempt to narrate the decline of Imperial Guptas and for this events, mainly political and dynastic, have been unfolded.

With a survey on the location of the Magadh Kingdom, the author has discussed the death of Kumargupta I and the accession of Purnagupta, whereas in the next chapter he narrates the story of ascendancy of Skandgupta and his successor Kumargupta-II. Other chapters deal with Budhagupta and his successors, including the break-up of the Gupta Empire.

The Gupta polity and cultural policy have been discussed in detail. According to the author these rulers followed the ideal of Cakravartin of Kautilya and Brahmanic sacrifices of the Asvamedha and Vajapeya. They also had a well organised administrative machinery. The identification of the capital of the Gupta empire is also discussed.

The author, who is the foremost scholar on the subject of later Guptas, has not confined himself to the twilight of the Imperial Guptas but has also discussed the dominant role of the Guptas in shaping the political history of the country. It is a welcome addition to our knowledge.

K.N. Dikshit

Lahiri, Nayanjot *Archaeology of Indian Trade Routes* (Oxford University Press, New Delhi, 1992) pp. 461 + XVI, 60 maps and charts, Price Rs. 495/-

Here is book on a subject dealing exclusively with ancient Indian geography and trade-routes, spanning a period of more than 6000 years - from the Neolithic, around 7000 B.C. to the Early Iron Age, around 200 B.C. but focussing mainly on Early Harappan (4000 B.C.) periods. The approach is archaeological and geological although historical sources, wherever required, have also been utilised. Thus, location of ancient sites in broad geographical regions and present-day political boundaries, such as Sind and Baluchistan, Maharashtra, Punjab and Haryana, location of sources of raw materials used in manufacturing material items, such as gold, silver, lapis and copper, have been painstakingly collected from old and new publications (19th and 20th centuries) and plotted on maps as well arranged in charts to allow the data to speak for themselves more than make them speak; the comments and conclusions are minimum and balanced. The suggested trade-routes are, of course, based upon author's own perception of the past.

We have here, therefore, for the first time, a book which has systematically arranged the available relevant data, made visually rich, on a subject which has produced scores of books but with much less of data at the command of the authors. Every serious student of the subject will, therefore, find it more informative than the best of the books ever written on the subject.

The subject of archaeology of trade-routes is, however, more complex than sometimes made-out in the book written under the guidance of one of the leading archaeologists, Dr. Dilip K. Chakrabarty, whose approach to the subject can be noticed on every second page of the book. For example, the kind of geographical model based upon regional approach and adopted in the book may not always reveal the past-as-it-was. The 'river-basin' model is also based on geographical approach and in many examples it is perhaps much more productive to use it than the regional model for one very simple reason - in the pre-Industrial periods, the navigable rivers like the Ganga, Saraswati and Indus provided more viable trade-routes than amorphous regions such as 'Southern Baluchistan' covering as diverse geomorphological formations as deserts, mountains, river valleys and seas, both deep and shallow. Even if we agree with the author's presumption that these diverse regions do get integrated through the compulsions of trade–demand and supply– it remains to be explained by the author as to what may have been the mechanism of trade which is more important for us to understand if we want to visualise the ancient trade-routes than anything else. The presumption of the author and her guide are that the production centres are nearest to the source materials and this the reviwer fails to appreciate in the context of the Indus-Saraswati urbanised society which engaged itself in long-distance internal and external trade. Production is based upon the availability of traditional craftsmen who may or may not live in the areas of raw materials. Even today the towns of Khurja, Ferozabad, Bhadohi do not produce even a single item which the craftsmen in these settlements use for manufacturing respectively glazed pottery, glass bangles and woollen carpets. The element of 'Routes for the Procurement of Raw Materials' is critical and important but absolutely secondary to the basic concept of 'trade' which is based on the decisive factor of 'market' or the element of 'buyer', i.e. consumption.

However, these are the larger questions which we hope the teacher and the taught will keep in mind when they individually or collectively produce a fresh book on the subject, because through the present book they have clearly established the fact they have full control over the relevant data, interpretation is an entirely different mattter.

S.P. Gupta

Agrawal, O.P., Misra A.K. and Jain Kamal K., *Removal of Plants and Trees from Historic Building*, Indian Conservation Institute, Lucknow, 1994, Price Rs. 100/-

The book is divided into five chapters and contains 3 Appedices. The growth of plants and trees on historical buildings is very harmful since in later stages and it poses serious problems in tropical countries, specially in South Asia. In this book, the authors have compiled the relevant information and have discussed the nature of higher plants and deterioration caused by them. The control measures for plants growing on monuments is known as Weed Science and the removal of these unwanted plants, trees, climbers and creepers have been termed as weed eradication and weed control. While dealing with 'control' it is suggested that the application of any herbicide on stone surface must be tested beforehand because its discriminate use may lead to permanent damage.

The use of different methods for injecting chemicals into the tree-trunks have also been suggested and recommendation have been given for the maintenance of buildings against the growth of plants and trees.

A list of common plants growing on Indian monuments with availability of herbicides in India and a glossary of technical terms have been given in the appendices, which is extremely useful for everyone engaged in archaeological conservation.

This publication is a good reference-book for Indian conservators.

K.N. Dikshit

Chaudhry, Sumita, *Beggars of Kaligaht*, Calcutta, Memoir No. 75, Anthropological Survey of India, Calcutta, pp. 110,

The books is an attempt for knowing the social norms and cultural patterns prevelent among the different groups of beggars of Kalighat mostly hailing from Darbhanga, Jainagar and Midnopore. In India giving alms to the beggars is considered a way of washing one's sin and a very act of religious merit which provides a major cultural prop to sustain the institution of beggary. The important begging centres are where pilgrims and devotees have to offer material objects to them, although in major towns beggars also flock while waiting at important traffic light where our thrusts a coin indifferently in his palm just to get rod of him.

Divided into eight chapters, the author reviews the problem of beggars and begging in India. She has provided a good survey of earlier works on this problem carried out in Greater Bombay, Delhi, Kanpur, Ranchi and Meerut. She has also made references to the works on the slums and pavement dwellers of Calcutta. She has observed a breakdown of traditional values and customs among the beggars specially at the level of family institutions.

In fact these was a need of such a work which gives a detailed treatment of the problem – nut at the sametime the work is equally silent on the action side on the issue of providing a better life to these underprivileged by the society and other social organisations. There are some people whose encounters with beggar children have transformed their lives. The voluntary organisations including government agencies under Ministry of Social Welfare deriving support from legislation are doing a lot but a proper national rehabilitation programme for mitigating the plight of beggars up to a certain extent is the need of the hour. However, we must also admit that as a nation we have never organised ourselves to make it issue of public awareness about the negative side of this problem which give rise to increase in violence, abuse of drugs, prostitution and renereal diseases.

Her works on the whole is informative and useful.

K.N. Dikshit

Pandey, Jai Narain, *Purattava Vimarsh*, Pramanik Publications, Allahabad, Allahabad, pp. 551. Price Rs 501/-

The present book by the author was a long felt need for the students of arachaeology in North Indian Universities. In fact very low attempt were made in the past in describing the specific problems of archaeology in Indian context from the point of view of the students studying through the Hindi medium. The author has tried to describe the development phases of archaeological studies in India with great patience and skill. It is an excellent text book on the subject.

The author has classified his work into twentythree chapters. The early part of the book deals with the definition, scope, development in archaeological techniques and a survey of archaeological discoveries in world context. Subsequently attempts were made to describe the progress of archaeological studies and methodology used in discovering the past in India.

As we go through the work, it becomes apparent that author has taken all precautions in presenting the uptodate account of development of different cultures in the Indian Sub-continent and has also freely used scientific data available by modern dating techniques. The description of Stone Age cultures are quite informative and have been dealt meticulously. A chapter has also been devoted to important excavated sites in India.

I hope that this very important work in chaste and flawless Hindi which is quite comprehensive and well presented will be widely read by students and scholars and author will keep in consideration to revise it further in the light of new material available from the forthcoming World Archaeological Congress in India.

K.N. Dikshit

Appendix

RAMA JANMABHUMI INSCRIPTIONS FROM AYODHYA

1. ओं नमः शिवाय... सुविक्रमतो रतारततादिता प्रांशुत्वेननिश चर्न्वर्पा ।।

2. ॐ शतगुद्देशां च धानरत्तनुं केचन्त प्रमदोद्भद्रः कुहागिरिग्रामाहारकणद्ब्रह्माण्डं करसंपुटेनविबुधान्वा...भभार्गव विभ्रवतावानवद्वंसोवतंसो भुवः। यस्मिन–

3. ---ल सक्षियि (नि ?)चिरस्थायिन्या देवदुजद्रावा(?)स्रोपचिते परार्थवेदनारंध्वानयंजज्ञिरे।। वे चण्डीपतिचंडराडवन चूडा---व्रह्माणोदकथालवधूसवषिप्रस्थायि--कीर्त्तियः। वी वीरास्तत्रकुलेजनिजगृहे–

4. य भार्गवीया भवत्क्षीष क्षत्रियशेषरक्षणविधौवद्धंनियोगग्रहः।। यंग्र्यवदेवकुलमाकुलतानिवृत्तिनिर्व्यूढनं प्रतिमाजन्मभूमिः। यत्रातिसाह ससह ग्रयनिद्वधामामामेजनितजगद्विष्नतमोत्त–

5. म श्रीः।। मामेदयास्तुवपुष्पितपषथुनृथानिष्णाति रसाधिरयासरसेद्रिगार्धो इत्युद्नृपन्नमुदिनंसक्षिर(शवासा)मामेप--- जगदेजगेक---युन्धकेलिदलिताखिलमेदनिल्लपल्लीसह ग्रवनितासुनिकुंजगासु। उत्कंटा

6. काचिटपिनोचिटविष्ठिताकोतंच्छस्तनेदुजकेनेपुगुहुर्लिखंतनीपुराकीर्त्त्याव्यस्तन्तदसुतनुनाद्यु। शितमनामनस्वीस्वर्लाकंर्पार्थति गुपेत---शयिनींससर्व्वसंक्षातंक---वर्भ्यसल्लक्षपपतेश्रियाशार्दूक्षहुतभुजितिवा–

6. शानिरमयः।। तद्वामनिः सीमनद्यमन्योरन्यौरसाकारनदानशक्तिः। अमानुषपंपौरुपमाविरासी सल्लक्षपे विश्वविलक्षपन्ततः।। युन्धःश्रीक-----करणवाहुर्महावाहिनीकीर्त्ति–पकारविधयेते---यदं

8. शलक्षज्यनापिविनातिजोपकरणन्येतानिनिःकंटकंयसांमाक्ष्यपरिक्षदं विदविलचितावितानोज्जितं।। समस्तजितराज्येास्यचिरं गिरित्रशपदरु---धृतोयूर्द्धायोजहारासुकृति। ---

9. वियर्तादिनीवधधे हिमगिरिगुहागेहद्वारेदरीविशेषधी। प्रथमलिखितासिद्धैर्यस्यप्रशस्तिपदावलींपठंतिनिपुपंस्त्रैपंगोवान्नभरत्तल चारिणां।। कैलासाचल---सानुमलक्ष--षुमेरोःशिरोतामर्मूर्द्धाधारिपीतटभुवि

10. स्थानेष्वतान्येष्ववृत्वातप्पर्णशिल्पजाप्रतिकृतिवृन्धोपदेशात्पतिप्राप्त्येग्रेचरकन्यकाभिरनिशंयद्वाहुरभ्यर्चते।। च ।। भवत्यद्धासः पेशलैरिपूसिद्धिरस्यहत्नवन्यजगद्भिः। गेहेयस्यश्रीविलासाभिरामेम्या।

11. नाद्वेतगीयतेक (वासयश्रीः)।।अमरपुरपुरंध्रीवंधुतामव्यलीकांभजतिसुकृतवासोत्रसल्लक्षपाख्ये। प्रति च पुरिवतस्यप्राप्य राधोनवद्यंशुभंमुदितविवेकंशोकमौ--लंतव।। अल्हण्णःप्रपयसलः रुतांगर्ज्जतांक्ररुव

12. कोटिरुववटः। आनिमा(या?)यनमनिद्धवेनयःप्रभूतांप्रकृतिचंचलाश्रियं।। लोकोत्तरः खलुकोपियदाभिमुख्येहंकाटकशिवगल संभृतोपि (हुंकारशिवगलच्चिरस्तंसृतोपि?)। संसारिपाशभिः-दृशैरमयम्यजाताशलप्वाः सुकृतद्वः कृतकंनृच्छ्राग्र।।

13. पौरुपप्रतिरंध्रीतिगुरंध्रीतिचविन्यतां। येनलोकानुरद्धापिप्रतिषिद्धानमोन्नरे।। (तस्यात्मजो)जगतिमेघसुतःश्रुतायःश्रीमानरुदनय चंद्रपदातिलप्यः। गोविन्दचन्द्रधरणीन्द्रगुरुप्रसादात्साकेतमंडलपतित्वम

(Continued)

14. लाभयेन।। राशचत्मयरदवानद्भितरिपुस्थंधेनयुद्धोद्धुरावीरास्तेननकेयलवलवतादोदुग्यादमोचिताः।। अप्युद्दामरमुपदान
निरतस्वाल्लेनैरैकान्ततोद्वरारूढवन्यतामदां---योकलाट्टकरस्त्याजितः।। ---त्स्वातवि

15. शालशैलशिखरश्रेपीशिलासंहति। व्यूहैर्विष्णुहरेहिरण्यकलशश्रीसुन्दरमन्दिरं। पूर्वैरप्यकृतंकृतंनृपतिभिर्यनेदमित्यद्भुतं।।
ससारार्णवरीघ्रलंघनलघुपादान्वियाद्यतिपयोधि(नृपेन्द्र)क्षितिपालराज्य

16. स्थेत्यनिरस्तंद्रभुजार्गलस्य। अथप्रपेदेस्यपदंकनीयानायुष्यचंद्रोल्लहणसूनुरेव।। नसाहसांकेननशूद्रकेपतस्योपमानंविनधुः
कवीन्द्रा। कृतांतियायस्यपुरोनकानव्यगवाक्षेधनुराततज्यं।।

17. उद्दामसौधविबधालयनीमयोध्यास्तेननयनिहुतवेशसेन। साकेतमंडलमशचण्डकारिकूपवापीप्रतिश्रयंतडागसहश्रमिश्रं।निजनिरो
धविध्रवेनिजवल्लभानांहेम-ल-शिलातलतला

18. लीनाः। करत्तूरिकपेतरुणीश्रवणोपभोम्स्मयोग्यंजगुःसरसमशभरसौयशोस्य।। अविमुक्तविशालाक्षीललितानन्दितासदायेसीवकस्स्य
देहश्रीःमतांनिर्वापकारणं।। अविपाचितरन्हिरण्यक

19. रिपुंसंयम्यवापंरपेकुर्व्वापोवलिराजवाहुदलनंकृत्वाभूव्विक्रमान। कुव्वन्दुष्टदशाननव्यप्तननकोपन्यःसदशाधिको---
प्रयोर्दता---। आ---

20. तोनिहन्तिपाशचात्यभीतिमपिभीषपबाहुदंडः। तेजःप्रभावजयतांगट्टसीहमेवपूर्वापरा---प्रजानां रिपामतद्रिध्वस्यातेक्षितौराज
---आयुष्य---

–T. P. Verma and A.K. Singh

Captions of Illustrations
Rock Paintings of Hazaribagh, Bihar

Sl. No.

1. Sarayia ; Mesolithis (?) ; Red ; Length : 8 cm
2. Sarayia : Mesolithic (?) ; height: 10 cm
3. Saraiyia : Mesolithic (?) ; Red ; Height : 5 cm
4. Sarayia : Mesolithic (?) ; Red ; Height : 7 cm
5. Sarayia : Mesolithic (?) Red ; Height : 6 cm
6. Sarayia : Mesolithic (?) Red ; height of central figure : 11 cm
7. Sarayia : Mesolithic (?) Red ; Height: 6 cm

7a. Sarayia: Mesolithic (?) Red ; Height: 6 cm

8. Sarayia: Mesolithic (?) Red ; Height : 15 cm
9. Sarayia : Mesolithic (?) Red ; Height : 25 cm
10. Isko; Mesolithic (?) ; white ; Length : 20 cm
11. Isko ; Mesolithic (?) ; Red and (stippled) white ; Length : 30cm

11a. Isko ; Mesolithic (?) ; Red and (stippled) white ; Length : 30cm

12. Isko ; Mesolithic (?); Red and (stippled) white ; Length : 30cm
13. Isko ; Mesolithic (?) ; Red and (stippled) white ; Length : 35cm
14. Isko; Mesolithic (?); Red and white ; Length : 40cm
15. Isko; Mesolithic (?); Red and (stippled) white ; Height: 20cm
16. Isko; Mesolithic (?); Red : Height : 100cm
17. Isko; Mesolithic (?); Red: Height : 20cm
18. Isko; Mesolithic; white over red foundation ; Length : 30 cm
19. Isko; Mesolithic (?); Red; Height: 30cm

19a. Isko; Mesolithic (?); White over red; Height : 40 cm

20. Isko; Mesolithic (?); Red and stippled white ; Height: 8 cm
21. Isko ; Mesolithic (?) ; Red broken line shown in natural cavity ; Height : 30 cm

21a. Isko ; Mesolithic (?) ; Red ; Height : 30 cm

22. Isko ; Mesolithic (?) ; Red over white foundation ; Height : 8 cm

22a. Isko ; Mesolithic (?) ; Red ; Height : 20 cm

23. Isko ; Mesolithic (?) ; Red; Height : 40 cm

23a. Isko ; Mesolithic (?) ; White, broken lines denote natural cavity

24. Isko ; Mesolithic (?) ; Red ; Height : 25 cm
25. Isko ; Mesolithic (?) ; White over red foundation ; Length : 30 cm
26. Isko ; Mesolithic (?) ; Red ; Height : 25 cm
27. Isko ; Mesolithic (?) ; White ; Height : 25 cm
28. Isko ; Mesolithic (?) ; Red ; Height : 40 cm
29. Isko; Mesolithic (?) Red and stippled white; Length : 20 cm
30. Isko; Mesolithic (?) Red and stippled white; Height : 30 cm
31. Isko; Mesolithic (?) Red and stippled white; Height : 30 cm
32. Isko; Mesolithic (?) Red and stippled white; Height : 40 cm

32a. Isko; Mesolithic (?) Red, broken line denotes natural exfoliation ; Length : 7 cm

33. Isko; Mesolithic (?) ; Red and stippled ; Height : 20cm
34. Isko; Mesolithic (?) Red ; Height : 20 cm
35. Isko; Mesolithic (?) Red ; Height : 20 cm
36. Isko; Mesolithic (?) Red ; Height : 20 cm
37. Isko; Mesolithic (?) Red ; Height : 7 cm

37a. Isko; Mesolithic (?) Red , Height : 7 cm

38. Isko; Historic (?); Engraving ; Height : 35 cm
39. Raham ; Mesolithic (?) ; Red ; Height : 32 cm

40. Raham ; Period (??) ; Red ; Length : 12 cm

41. Raham ; Mesolithic (?) ; square design red; underlying deer in yellow ; Height of square : 25 cm

42. Raham ; Mesolithic (?) ; Red ; Height : 8 cm

43. Raham ; Mesolithic (?) ; Red and yellow; Height of anthropomorph : 25 cm

44. Tirthangi; Mesolithic; Red and yellow ; Height of central figure : 10 cm

45. Tirthangi ; Mesolithic ; Red and stippled white ; Length ? cm

46. Tirthangi ; Mesolithic ; (?) Red ; Length of deer with antlers : 25 cm

47. Tirthangi ; Mesolithic ; (?) Red and stippled white ; Height: 20 cm

48. Tirthangi; Mesolithic; (?) Red ; White (stippled) and Red: Height (?) cm

49. Tirthangi ; Mesolithic ; (?) Red ; Length : 15 cm

49a. Tirthangi ; Mesolithic ; (?) Red and stippled white ; Height : 12 cm

50. Tirthangi ; Mesolithic ; (?) White over red foundation ; Length : 15 cm

50a. Tirthangi; Mesolithic; (?) Red over foundation; Length: cm

51. Tirthangi; Historic; (?) Red ; Height: 15 cm

52. Satpahar ; Mesolithic (?); Red; Length : 44 cm

53. Satpahar ; Mesolithic (?); Red amd white; Length : 48 cm

54. Satpahar ; Mesolithic (?); Animals white cross like design Red; Length of the left animal : 40cm

55a. Satpahar 2 ; Mesolithic (?) ; Animals in white ; square designs partly in red and white ; Length of second animal from right : 30 cm

55b. Satpar 2; Mesolithic (?); Animals in white; Length of second animal from right : 30 cm

Detail of 55

55c. Satpar 2 ; Mesolithic (?) Animals in white, square designs Red and white

55d. Satpahar 2 ; Mesolithic (?) Animals in white, square designs Red and white

56. Satpahar 2 ; Mesolithic (?) ; Red and stippled white ; Length : 15 cm

ILLUSTRATIONS

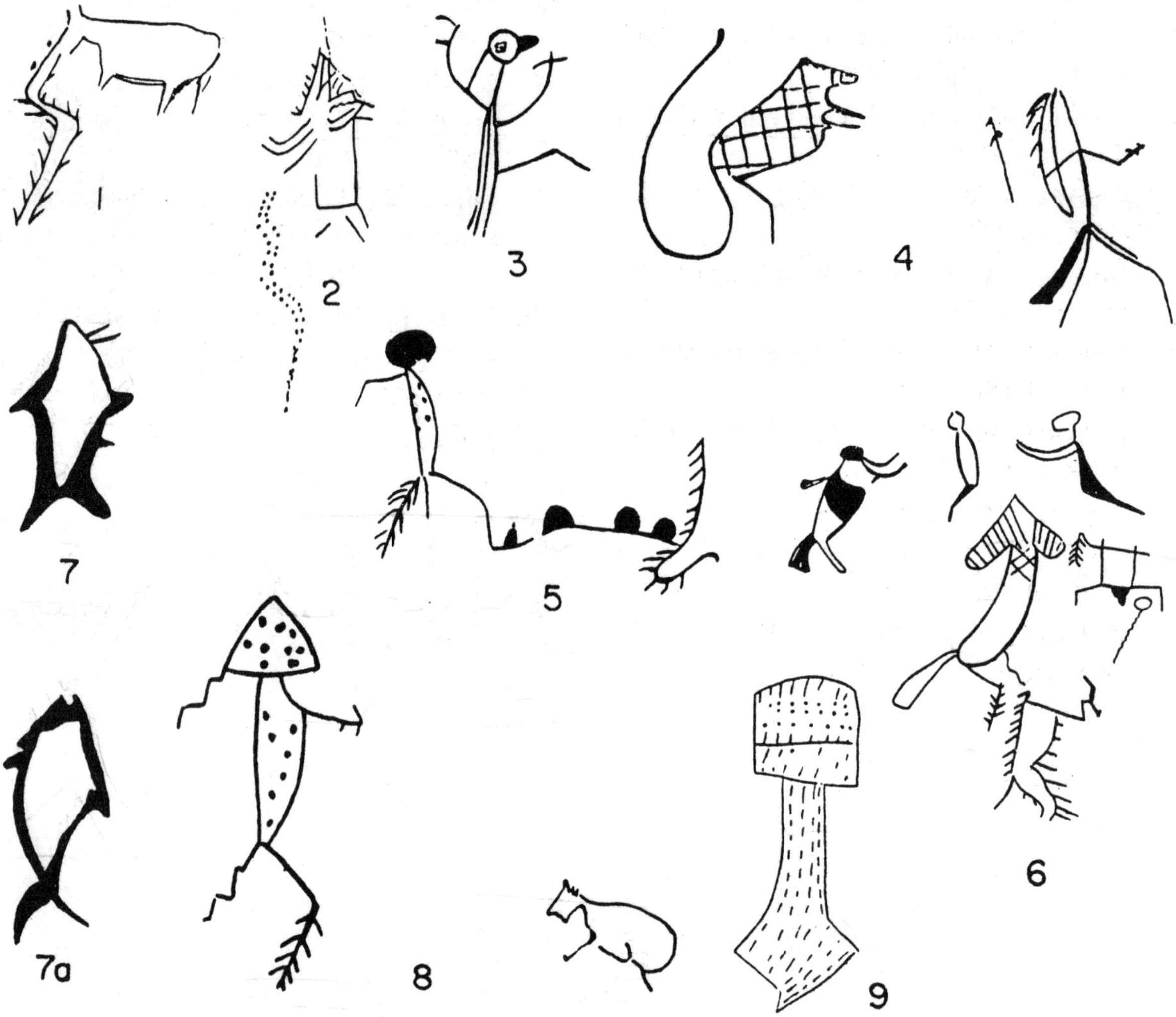

SARAYIA

10
11
11a
12
13
14
15
16
17
18
19
19a
20
20a
23
21
21a
22
22a
23 a.

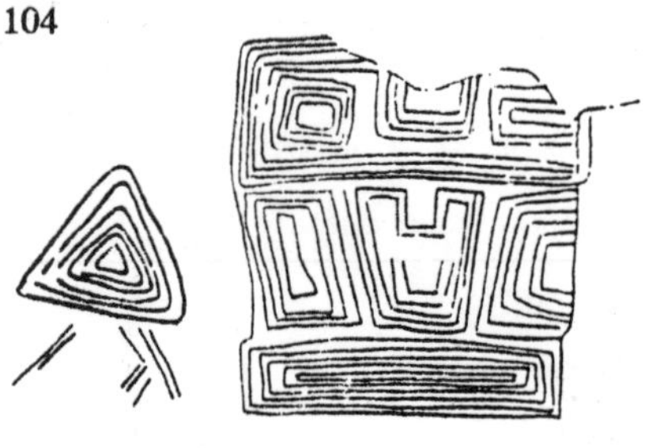

24

25

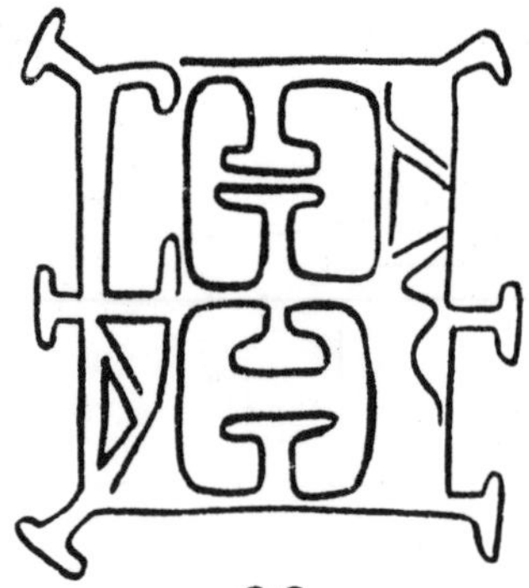

26

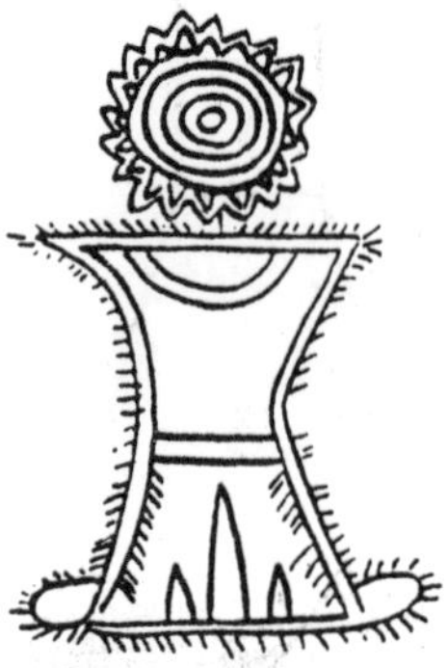

27

28

29

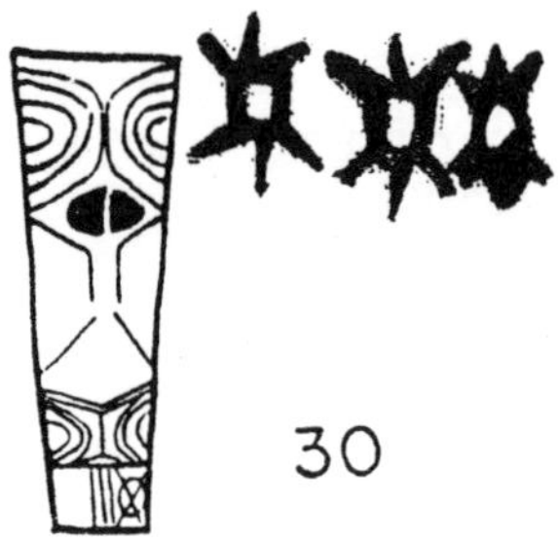

30

31

32

32a

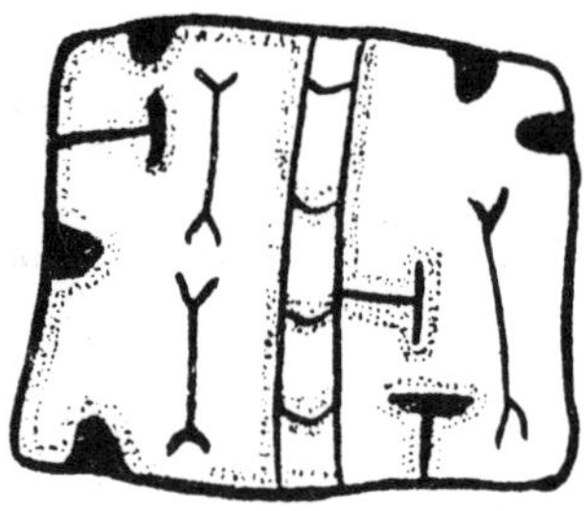

33

37

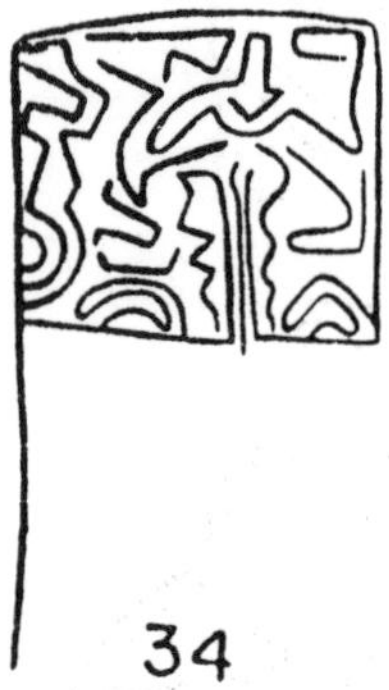

34

35

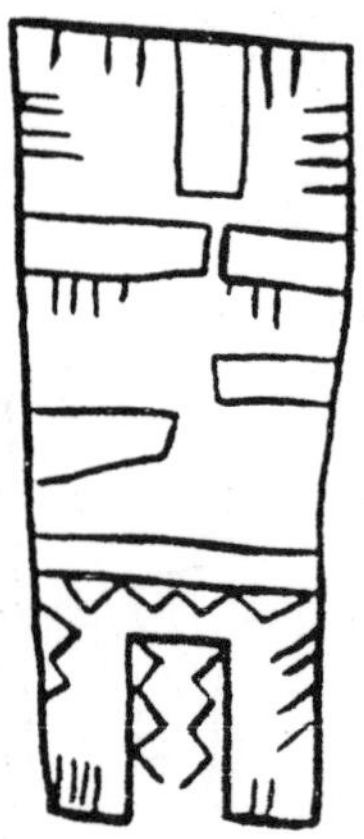

36

37a

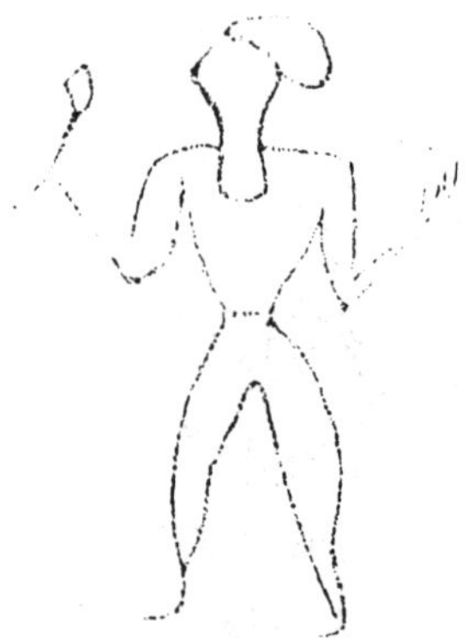

38

39

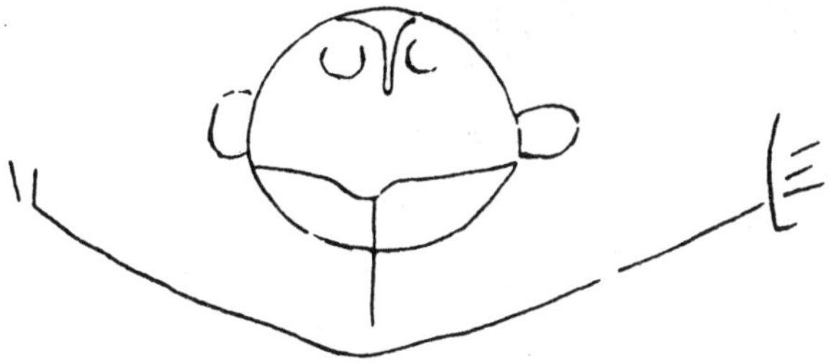

40

42

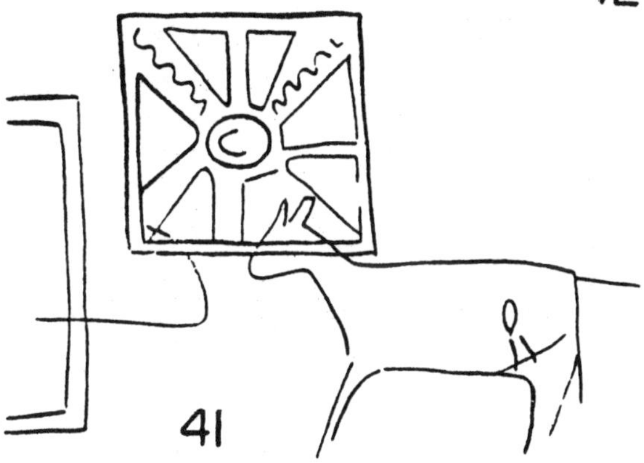

41

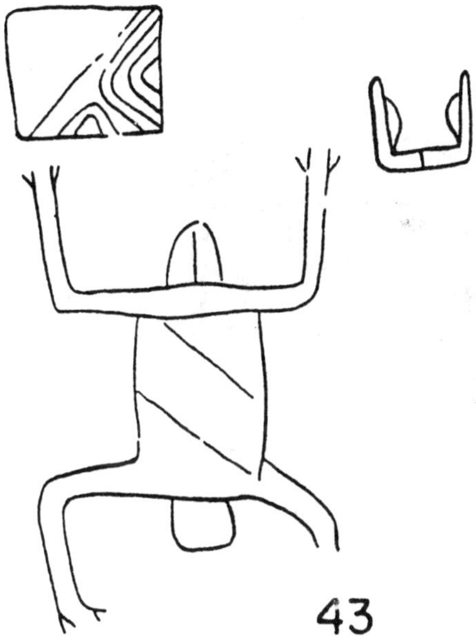

43

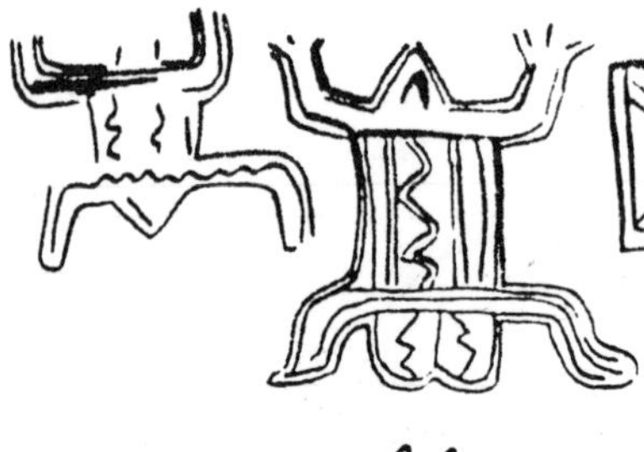

44

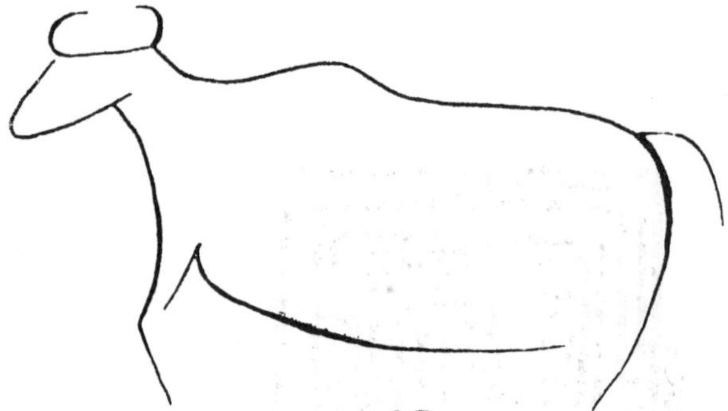

45

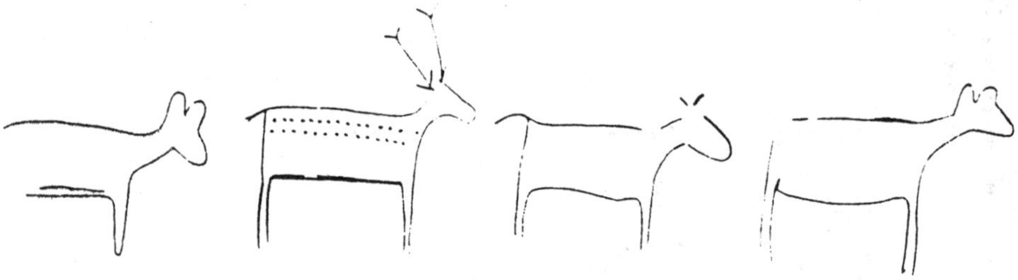

46

49

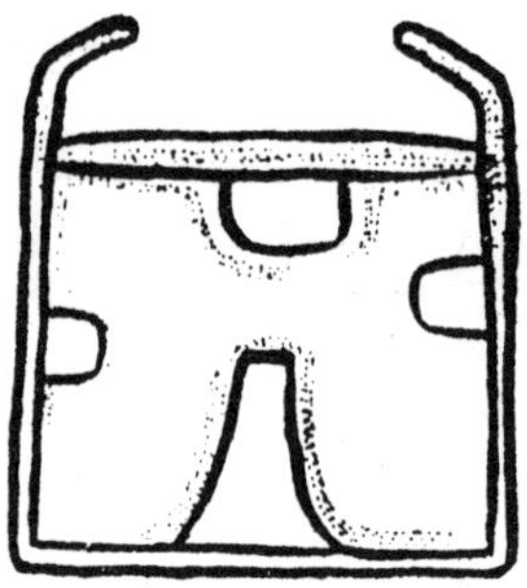

47

48

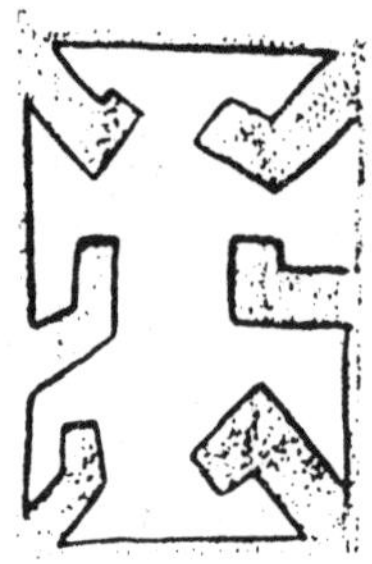

49a

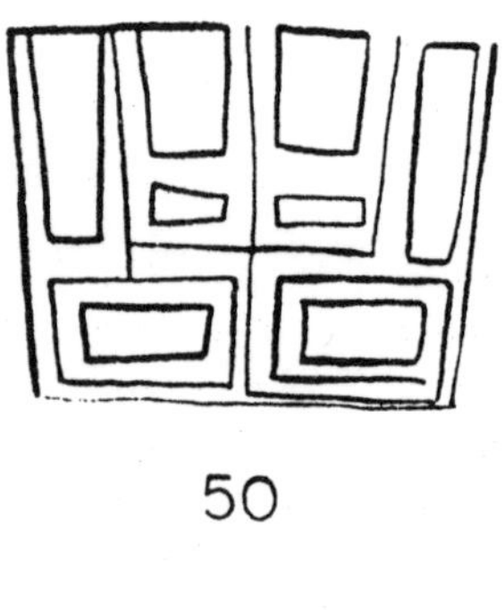

50

50a

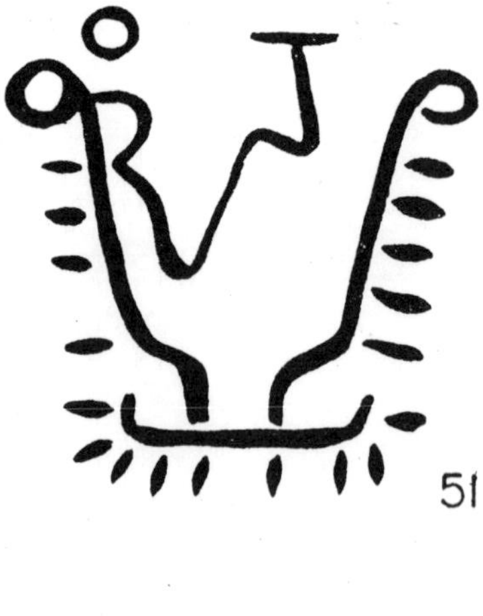

51

TIRTHANGI

52

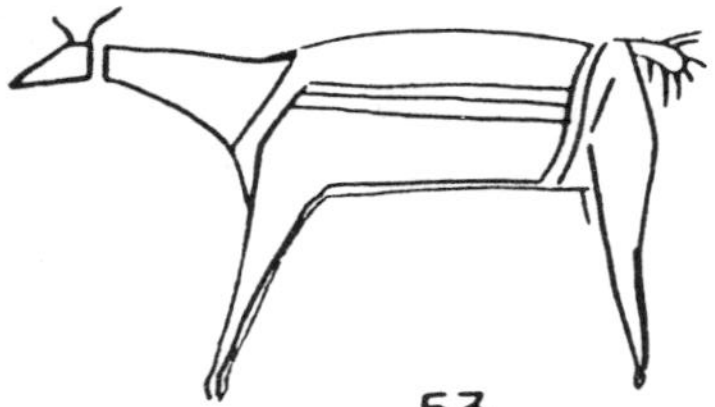
53

55

55a

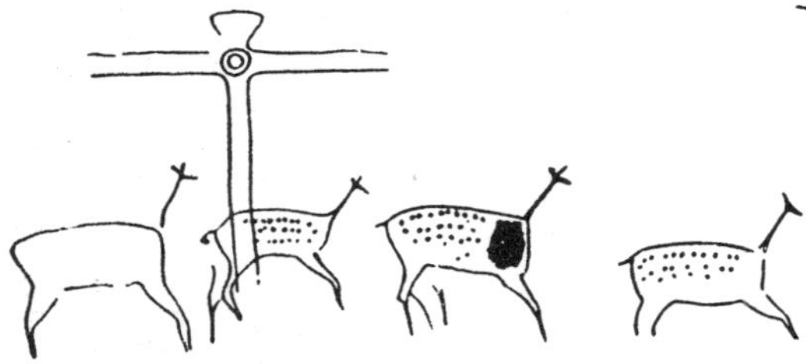
54

55c

55d

56

55b

INDIAN ARCHAEOLOGICAL SOCIETY, NEW DELHI

RECEIPT AND PAYMENT ACCOUNT FOR THE YEAR 1994-95

Receipt	Amount	Payment	Amount
By Opening Balances:—			
Cash in hand	148-09	To Honorarium	51,675-00
Balance with Bank	1,52,930-20	To Ground Rent to DDA	23,000-00
Fixed Deposit	15,00,000-00	To Travelling Exp.	3,088-00
By Bank Interest	1,02,714-00	To Electricity/Water Charges	3,357-00
		To Conveyance Expenses	14,592-10
By Donations	4,00,150-00		
By Grant-in-Aid received from		To Conference Expenses	8,900-00
ICHR	14,250-00	To Audit Fees 92-93, 1993-94	5,750-00
By Institutional Fees	2,500-00	To Printing & Sty.	11,423-15
		To Municipal Taxes	66,687-00
By Membership Fees	890-00	To World Archil. Conference	9,000-00
By Delegation Fees	3,900-00	To Awards	22,000-00
By Life Membership Fees	4,100-00	To Refreshment Charges	558-90
		To Freight & Cartage	120-00
By Sale of Publications	10,820-00	To Bank Charges	123-00
By Service Charges	2,500-00	To Postage	3,148-50
By Closing balance	4-30	To Misc. Expenses	2,386-00
S.B.I. A/C No: 35914		To Accounting Charges	300-00
		To Books & Periodicals	1341-80
		To Professional Charges	550-00
		To Office Equipment	5,180-00
		To Furniture & Fixture	680-00
		To Construction A/c	4,09,868-55
		To Advance to Contractors Ramji Das	12,000-00
		Dina Nath	33,500-00
		To Closing Balances	
		Cash in hand	50-59
		Cheques in hand	637-00
		S.B.I A/c No: 37915	4,990-00
		Fixed deposits	15,00,000-00
	21,94,906-59		2194,906-59

GENERAL SECRETARY — TREASURER

For Rajan Sharma & Co.,
Chartered Accountants.

OFFICE BEARERS OF THE INDIAN ARCHAEOLOGICAL SOCIETY

Headquarters:

INDIAN ARCHAEOLOGICAL SOCIETY
B-17, Institutional Area, Mehrauli, New Delhi - 110 016
Tel: S.P. Gupta/Shashi Asthana - 3388067
K.N. Diskhit - 6948971